Artificial Intelligence for Marketing

Wiley & SAS Business Series

The Wiley & SAS Business Series presents books that help senior-level managers with their critical management decisions.

Titles in the Wiley & SAS Business Series include:

Developing Human Capital: Using Analytics to Plan and Optimize Your Learning and Development Investments by Gene Pease, Barbara Beresford, and Lew Walker

The Executive's Guide to Enterprise Social Media Strategy: How Social Networks Are Radically Transforming Your Business by David Thomas and Mike Barlow

Economic and Business Forecasting: Analyzing and Interpreting Econometric Results by John Silvia, Azhar Iqbal, Kaylyn Swankoski, Sarah Watt, and Sam Bullard

Economic Modeling in the Post–Great Recession Era: Incomplete Data, Imperfect Markets by John Silvia, Azhar Iqbal, and Sarah Watt House

Foreign Currency Financial Reporting from Euros to Yen to Yuan: A Guide to Fundamental Concepts and Practical Applications by Robert Rowan

Harness Oil and Gas Big Data with Analytics: Optimize Exploration and Production with Data-Driven Models by Keith Holdaway

Health Analytics: Gaining the Insights to Transform Health Care by Jason Burke

Heuristics in Analytics: A Practical Perspective of What Influences Our Analytical World by Carlos Andre Reis Pinheiro and Fiona McNeill

Human Capital Analytics: How to Harness the Potential of Your Organization's Greatest Asset by Gene Pease, Boyce Byerly, and Jac Fitz-enz

Implement, Improve and Expand Your Statewide Longitudinal Data System: Creating a Culture of Data in Education by Jamie McQuiggan and Armistead Sapp

Intelligent Credit Scoring: Building and Implementing Better Credit Risk Scorecards, Second Edition by Naeem Siddiqi

Killer Analytics: Top 20 Metrics Missing from Your Balance Sheet by Mark Brown

Artificial Intelligence for Marketing: Practical Applications by Jim Sterne

On-Camera Coach: Tools and Techniques for Business Professionals in a Video-Driven World by Karin Reed

Predictive Analytics for Human Resources by Jac Fitz-enz and John Mattox II

For more information on any of the above titles, please visit www.wiley.com.

Artificial Intelligence for Marketing

Practical Applications

Jim Sterne

WILEY

Published by John Wiley & Sons, Inc., Hoboken, New Jersey.
Published simultaneously in Canada.

For general information on our other products and services or for technical support, please contact our Customer Care Department within the United States at (800) 762-2974, outside the United States at (317) 572-3993, or fax (317) 572-4002.

Wiley publishes in a variety of print and electronic formats and by print-on-demand. Some material included with standard print versions of this book may not be included in e-books or in print-on-demand. If this book refers to media such as a CD or DVD that is not included in the version you purchased, you may download this material at http://booksupport.wiley.com. For more information about Wiley products, visit www.wiley.com.

Library of Congress Cataloging-in-Publication Data is Available:

ISBN 9781119406334 (Hardcover)
ISBN 9781119406372 (ePDF)
ISBN 9781119406365 (ePub)

Cover Design: Wiley
Cover Image: © Kngkyle2/Getty Images

Printed in the United States of America.

10 9 8 7 6 5 4 3 2 1

This book is dedicated to Colleen.

Contents

Foreword

Thomas H. Davenport

Distinguished Professor, Babson College and Research Fellow, MIT
Author of Competing on Analytics and Only Humans Need Apply

Forewords to books can play a variety of roles. One is to describe in more general terms what the book is about. That's not really necessary, since Jim Sterne is a master at communicating complex topics in relatively simple terms.

Another common purpose is to describe how the book fits into the broader literature on the topic. That doesn't seem necessary in this case, either, since there isn't much literature on artificial intelligence (AI) for marketing, and even if there were, you've probably turned to this book to get one easy-to-consume source.

A third possible objective for forewords is to persuade you of the importance and relevance of the book, with the short-term goal of having you actually buy it or read onward if you already bought it. I'll adopt that goal, and provide external testimony that AI already is important to marketing, that it will become much more so in the future, and that any good marketing executive needs to know what it can do.

It's not that difficult to argue that marketing in the future will make increasing use of AI. Even today, the components of an AI-based approach are largely in place. Contemporary marketing is increasingly quantitative, targeted, and tied to business outcomes. Ads and promotions are increasingly customized to individual consumers in real time. Companies employ multiple channels to get to customers, but all of them increasingly employ digital content. Company marketers still work with agencies, many of which have developed analytical capabilities of their own.

As Sterne points out, data is the primary asset for AI-based marketing approaches. Data for marketing comes from a company's own systems, agencies, third-party syndicators, customer online behaviors, and many other sources—and certainly comprises "big data" in the aggregate. About 25 percent of today's marketing budgets are devoted to digital channels, and almost 80 percent of marketing organizations make technology-oriented capital expenditures—typically hardware and software—according to a recent Gartner survey. Clearly some of that capital will be spent on AI.

Companies still try to maintain a consistent brand image, but the annual marketing strategy is increasingly a relic of the past. Instead of making a few major decisions each year, companies or their agencies make literally thousands of real-time decisions a day about which ads to run on which sites, which search terms to buy, which version of a website to adopt, and so forth. Even the choice of what service providers and marketing software vendors to work with is complex enough to deserve a decision-making algorithm.

Already there are simply too many decisions involving too many complex variables and too much data for humans to make all of them. Marketing activities and decisions are increasing far more rapidly than marketing budgets or the numbers and capabilities of human marketers. An increasing number of marketing decisions employ some sort of AI, and this trend will only increase.

Companies are typically trying to define and target specific customers or segments, and if there are thousands or millions of customers, AI is needed to get to that level of detail. Companies also want to customize the experience of the customer, and that also requires machine learning or some other form of AI. AI can also help to deliver value across omnichannel customer relationships, and to ensure effective communications at all customer touchpoints. Finally, AI can help companies make decisions with similar criteria across the digital and analog marketing worlds.

Today, AI in marketing supports only certain kinds of decisions. They are typically repetitive decisions based on data, and each decision has low monetary value (though in total they add up to large numbers). AI-based decisions today primarily involve digital content and channels or online promotions. Of course, almost all content is becoming digitized, so it makes for a pretty big category. This set of AI-supported activities includes digital advertising buys (called *programmatic buying*), website operation and optimization, search engine optimization, A/B testing, outbound e-mail marketing, lead filtering and scoring, and many other marketing tasks.

And it seems highly likely that this list will continue to grow. Television advertising—the mainstay of large companies' marketing activities for many years—is moving toward a programmatic buying model. Creative brand development activities are still largely done by humans, but the decisions about which images and copy will be adopted are now sometimes made through AI-based testing. High-level decisions about marketing mix and resource allocation are still ultimately made by marketing executives, but they are usually done with software and are often performed more frequently than annually.

It would not surprise me to see tasks such as selecting agency partners and making employee hiring decisions made through the use of AI in the future.

These AI-based marketing activities have yet to displace large numbers of human marketers, in part because AI supports individual tasks, rather than entire jobs. But they are likely to have a substantial impact on marketing roles in the future. At a minimum, most marketers will need to understand how these systems work, to identify whether they are doing a good job, and to determine how they can add value to the work of smart machines. Leaders of marketing organizations will need to strategize effectively about the division of labor between humans and machines. They'll have to redesign marketing processes to take advantage of the speed and precision that AI-based decision making offers.

In short, we face a marketing future in which artificial intelligence will play a very important role. I hope that these introductory comments have provided you with the motivation to commit to this book—to buying it, to reading it, and to putting its ideas to work within your organization. I believe there is a bright future for human marketers, but only if they take the initiative to learn about AI and how it can affect and improve their work. This book is the easiest and best way you will find to achieve that objective.

Preface

If you're in marketing, AI is a powerful ally.
If you're in data science, marketing is a rich problem set.

*Artificial Intelligence (AI) had a breakthrough year in 2016,
not only with machine learning, but with public awareness
as well. And it's only going to continue. This year, most
marketers believe consumers are ready for the technology.*
"Artificial Intelligence Roundup," eMarketer, February 2017

AI IN A NUTSHELL

Artificial intelligence (AI) is the next, logical step in computing: a
program that can figure out things for itself. It's a program that can
reprogram itself.

The Three *D*s of Artificial Intelligence

The shorthand for remembering what's special about AI is that it can
detect, *deliberate*, and *develop*—all on its own.

Detect

Artificial intelligence can discover which elements or attributes in a
bunch of data are the most predictive. Even when there is a massive
amount of data made up of lots of different *kinds* of data, AI can identify
the most revealing characteristics, figuring out which to pay attention
to and which to ignore.

Deliberate

AI can infer rules about the data, *from* that data, and weigh the most
predictive attributes against each other to answer a question or make
a recommendation. It can ponder the relevance of each and reach a
conclusion.

Develop

AI can grow and mature with each iteration. It can alter its opinion about the environment as well as how it evaluates that environment based on new information or the results of experimentation. It can program itself.

An individual's search terms are more important than her location, which is more important than her age (detect). When people use six or more words in a search, their propensity to purchase is so high that a discount is counterproductive (deliberate). Once it is noted that women under the age of 24 are not likely to purchase, regardless of words in a search, an experiment can be run to offer them free shipping (develop).

THIS IS YOUR MARKETING ON AI

The tools are not supernatural. They are not beyond the understanding of mortals. You owe it to yourself to understand how they are about to rock your world.

Intelligence is the ability to adapt to change.

—Stephen Hawking

The companion website for *Artificial Intelligence for Marketing: Practical Applications* can be found at: AI4Marketing.com.

Acknowledgments

I am forever grateful to the many people who have blogged, tweeted, published videos on, and answered my questions about artificial intelligence and machine learning.

Specifically, thanks go to Barry Levine, Bob Page, Brent Dykes, Brian Solis, Christopher Berry, Dan McCarthy, Dave Smith, David Raab, Dean Abbott, Dennis Mortensen, Doc Searls, Eric Siegel, Gary Angel, Himanshu Sharma, Ian Thomas, Kaj van de Loo, Mark Gibbs, Matt Gershoff, Matthew Todd, Michael Rappa, Michael Wu, Michelle Street, Pat LaPointe, Peter Fader, Rohit Rudrapatna, Ron Kohavi, Russ Klein, Russell McAthy, Scott Brinker, Scott Litman, Tim Wilson, Tom Cunniff, Tom Davenport, Tom Mitchell, Tyler Vigen, Vicky Brock, and Vincent Granville.

And, as always, Matt Cutler.

Artificial Intelligence for Marketing

CHAPTER 1

Welcome
to the Future

The shovel is a tool, and so is a bulldozer. Neither works on its own, "automating" the task of digging. But both tools augment our ability to dig.

Dr. Douglas Engelbart, "Improving Our Ability to Improve"[1]

Marketing is about to get weird. We've become used to an ever-increasing rate of change. But occasionally, we have to catch our breath, take a new sighting, and reset our course.

Between the time my grandfather was born in 1899 and his seventh birthday:

- Theodore Roosevelt took over as president from William McKinley.
- Dr. Henry A. Rowland of Johns Hopkins University announced a theory about the cause of the Earth's magnetism.
- L. Frank Baum's *The Wonderful Wizard of Oz* was published in Chicago.
- The first zeppelin flight was carried out over Lake Constance near Friedrichshafen, Germany.
- Karl Landsteiner developed a system of blood typing.

- The Ford Motor Company produced its first car—the Ford Model A.
- Thomas Edison invented the nickel-alkaline storage battery.
- The first electric typewriter was invented by George Canfield Blickensderfer of Erie, Pennsylvania.
- The first radio that successfully received a radio transmission was developed by Guglielmo Marconi.
- The Wright brothers flew at Kitty Hawk.
- The Panama Canal was under construction.
- Benjamin Holt invented one of the first practical continuous tracks for use in tractors and tanks.
- The Victor Talking Machine Company released the Victrola.
- The Autochrome Lumière, patented in 1903, became the first commercial color photography process.

My grandfather then lived to see men walk on the moon.
In the next few decades, we will see:

- Self-driving cars replace personally owned transportation.
- Doctors routinely operate remote, robotic surgery devices.
- Implantable communication devices replace mobile phones.
- In-eye augmented reality become normalized.
- Maglev elevators travel sideways and transform building shapes.
- Every surface consume light for energy and act as a display.
- Mind-controlled prosthetics with tactile skin interfaces become mainstream.
- Quantum computing make today's systems microscopic.
- 3-D printers allow for instant delivery of goods.
- Style-selective, nanotech clothing continuously clean itself.

And today's youngsters will live to see a colony on Mars.

It's no surprise that computational systems will manage more tasks in advertising and marketing. Yes, we have lots of technology for marketing, but the next step into artificial intelligence and machine learning will be different. Rather than being an ever-larger confusion of rules-based programs, operating faster than the eye can see, AI systems will operate more inscrutably than the human mind can fathom.

WELCOME TO AUTONOMIC MARKETING

The autonomic nervous system controls everything you don't have to think about: your heart, your breathing, your digestion. All of these things can happen while you're asleep or unconscious. These tasks are complex, interrelated, and vital. They are so necessary they must function continuously without the need for deliberate thought.

That's where marketing is headed. We are on the verge of the need for autonomic responses just to stay afloat. Personalization, recommendations, dynamic content selection, and dynamic display styles are all going to be table stakes.

The technologies seeing the light of day in the second decade of the twenty-first century will be made available as services and any company *not* using them will suffer the same fate as those that decided not to avail themselves of word processing, database management, or Internet marketing. And so, it's time to open up that black box full of mumbo-jumbo called artificial intelligence and understand it just well enough to make the most of it for marketing. Ignorance is no excuse. You should be comfortable enough with artificial intelligence to put it to practical use without having to get a degree in data science.

WELCOME TO ARTIFICIAL INTELLIGENCE FOR MARKETERS

It is of the highest importance in the art of detection to be able to recognize, out of a number of facts, which are incidental and which vital.

Sherlock Holmes, The Reigate Squires

This book looks at some current buzzwords to make just enough sense for regular marketing folk to understand what's going on.

- This is no deep exposé on the dark arts of artificial intelligence.
- This is no textbook for learning a new type of programming.
- This is no exhaustive catalog of cutting-edge technologies.

This book is not for those with advanced math degrees or those who wish to become data scientists. If, however, you are inspired to delve into the bottomless realm of modern systems building, I'll point you to "How to Get the Best Deep Learning Education for Free"[2] and be happy to take the credit for inspiring you. But that is not my intent.

You *will not* find passages like the following in this book:

> Monte-Carlo simulations are used in many contexts: to produce high quality pseudo-random numbers, in complex settings such as multi-layer spatio-temporal hierarchical Bayesian models, to estimate parameters, to compute statistics associated with very rare events, or even to generate large amount of data (for instance cross and auto-correlated time series) to test and compare various algorithms, especially for stock trading or in engineering.

"24 Uses of Statistical Modeling" (Part II)[3]

You *will* find explanations such as: Artificial intelligence is valuable because it was designed to deal in gray areas rather than crank out statistical charts and graphs. It is capable, over time, of understanding context.

The purpose of this tome is to be a primer, an introduction, a statement of understanding for those who have regular jobs in marketing—and would like to keep them in the foreseeable future.

Let's start with a super-simple comparison between artificial intelligence and machine learning from Avinash Kaushik, digital marketing evangelist at Google: "AI is an *intelligent machine* and ML is the *ability to learn without being explicitly programmed.*"

Artificial intelligence is a machine pretending to be a human. Machine learning is a machine pretending to be a statistical programmer. Managing either one requires a data scientist.

An ever-so-slightly deeper definition comes from E. Fredkin University professor at the Carnegie Mellon University Tom Mitchell:[4]

> The field of Machine Learning seeks to answer the question, "How can we build computer systems that automatically improve with experience, and what are the fundamental laws that govern all learning processes?"
>
> A machine learns with respect to a particular task T, performance metric P, and type of experience E, if the system reliably improves its performance P at task T, following experience E. Depending on how we specify T, P, and E, the learning task might also be called by names such as data mining, autonomous discovery, database updating, programming by example, etc.

Machine learning is a computer's way of using a given data set to figure out how to perform a specific function through trial and error.

What is a specific function? A simple example is deciding the best e-mail subject line for people who used certain search terms to find your website, their behavior on your website, and their subsequent responses (or lack thereof) to your e-mails.

The machine looks at previous results, formulates a conclusion, and then waits for the results of a test of its hypothesis. The machine next consumes those test results and updates its weighting factors from which it suggests alternative subject lines—over and over.

There is no final answer because reality is messy and ever changing. So, just like humans, the machine is always accepting new input to formulate its judgments. It's learning.

The "three *Ds*" of artificial intelligence are that it can *detect, decide,* and *develop*.

Detect

AI can discover which elements or attributes in a subject matter domain are the most predictive. Even with a great deal of noisy data and a large variety of data types, it can identify the most revealing characteristics, figuring out which to heed to and which to ignore.

Decide

AI can infer rules about data, from the data, and weigh the most predictive attributes against each other to make a decision. It can take an enormous number of characteristics into consideration, ponder the relevance of each, and reach a conclusion.

Develop

AI can grow and mature with each iteration. Whether it is considering new information or the results of experimentation, it can alter its opinion about the environment as well as how it evaluates that environment. It can program itself.

WHOM IS THIS BOOK FOR?

This is the sort of book data scientists should buy for their marketing colleagues to help them understand what goes on in the data science department.

This is the sort of book marketing professionals should buy for their data scientists to help them understand what goes on in the marketing department.

This book is for the marketing manager who has to respond to the C-level insistence that the marketing department "get with the times" (management by *in-flight* magazine).

This book is for the marketing manager who has finally become comfortable with analytics as a concept, and learned how to become a dexterous consumer of analytics outputs, but must now face a new educational learning curve.

This book is for the rest of us who need to understand the big, broad brushstrokes of this new type of data processing in order to understand where we are headed in business.

This book is for those of us who need to survive even though we are not data scientists, algorithm magicians, or predictive analytics statisticians.

We must get a firm grasp on artificial intelligence because it will be our jobs to make use of it in ways that raise revenue, lower costs, increase customer satisfaction, and improve organizational capabilities.

THE BRIGHT, BRIGHT FUTURE

Artificial intelligence will give you the ability to match information about your product with the information your prospective buyers need at the moment and in a format they are most likely to consume it most effectively.

I came across my first seemingly self-learning computer system when I was selling Apple II computers in a retail store in Santa Barbara in 1980. Since then, I've been fascinated by how computers can be useful in life and work. I was so interested, in fact, that I ended up explaining (and selling) computers to companies that had never had one before, and programming tools to software engineers, and consulting to the world's largest corporations on how to improve their digital relationships with customers through analytics.

Machine learning offers so much power and so much opportunity that we're in the same place we were with personal computers in 1980, the Internet in 1993, and e-commerce when Amazon.com began taking over e-commerce.

In each case, the promise was enormous and the possibilities were endless. Those who understood the impact could take advantage of it before their competitors. But the advantage was fuzzy, the implications were diverse, and speculations were off the chart.

The same is true of AI today. We know it's powerful and we know it's going to open doors we had not anticipated. There are current examples of marketing departments experimenting with some good and some not-so-good outcomes, but the promise remains enormous.

In advertising, machine learning works overtime to get the right message to the right person at the right time. The machine folds response rates back into the algorithm, not just the database. In the realm of customer experience, machine learning rapidly produces and takes action on new data-driven insights, which then act as new input for the next iteration of its models. Businesses use the results to delight customers, anticipate needs, and achieve competitive advantage.

Consider the telecommunications company that uses automation to respond to customer service requests quicker or the bank that uses data on past activity to serve up more timely and relevant offers to customers through e-mail or the retail company that uses beacon technology to engage its most loyal shoppers in the store.

Don't forget media companies using machine learning to track customer preference data to analyze viewing history and present personalized content recommendations. In "The Age of Analytics: Competing in a Data-Driven World,"[5] McKinsey Global Institute studied the areas in a dozen industries that were ripe for disruption by AI. Media was one of them. (See Figure 1.1.)[6]

IS AI SO GREAT IF IT'S SO EXPENSIVE?

As you are an astute businessperson, you are asking whether the investment is worth the effort. After all, this is experimental stuff and Google is *still* trying to teach a car how to drive itself.

Christopher Berry, Director of Product Intelligence for the Canadian Broadcasting Corporation, puts the business spin on this question.[7]

> Look at the progress that Google has made in terms of its self-driving car technology. They invested years and years and years in computer vision, and then training machines to respond to road conditions. Then look at the way that Tesla has been able to completely catch up by way of watching its drivers just use the car.
>
> The emotional reaction that a data scientist is going to have is, "I'm building machine to be *better* than a human being. Why would I want to bring a machine up to the point of it being as *bad* as a human being?"

Machine learning opportunities in media

Highest-ranked use cases, based on survey responses	Use case type	Impact	Data richness
Personalize advertising and recommendations to target individual consumers based on multi-modal data (mobile, social media, location, etc.)	Radical personalization	1.9	1.3
Discover new trends in consumption patterns (e.g., viral content)	Discover new trends/anomalies	1.2	1.3
Optimize pricing for services/ctfenngs based on customer-spectfic data	Price and product optimization	0.7	1.0
Predict viewership for new content to optimize content production decisions using multi-modal data (mobile, social media, past productions. etc.)	Predictive analytics	0.7	1.0
Predict risk of individual customer chum based on multimodal data	Predictive analytics	0.7	1.3
Optimize aggregate marketing mix and marketing spend	Price and product optimization	0.3	0.3
Identify relevant features (e.g., copyright infringement, audience suitability) in media content	Process unstructured data	0.2	0
Identify high-value leads by combining internal and external data (press releases, etc.) for B2B customers	Discover new trends/ anomalies	0.2	1.0
Optimize resource allocation in network vs. current and future loads	Resource allocation	0.1	0
Optimize release dates and regional targeting for film rollouts	Price and product optimization	0.1	0.3

Figure 1.1 A McKinsey survey finds advertising and marketing highly ranked for disruption.

The commercial answer is that if you can train a generic Machine Learning algorithm well enough to do a job as poorly as a human being, it's still better than hiring an expensive human being because every single time that machine runs, you don't have to pay its pension, you don't have to pay its salary, and it doesn't walk out the door and maybe go off to a competitor.

And there's a possibility that it could surpass a human intelligence. If you follow that argument all the way through, narrow machine intelligence is good enough for problem subsets that are incredibly routine.

We have so many companies that are dedicated to marketing automation and to smart agents and smart bots. If we were to enumerate all the jobs being done in marketing department and score them based on how much pain caused, and how esteemed they are, you'd have no shortage of start-ups trying to provide the next wave of mechanization in the age of information.

And heaven knows, we have plenty of well-paid people spending a great deal of time doing incredibly routine work.

So machine learning is great. It's powerful. It's the future of marketing. But just what the heck *is* it?

WHAT'S ALL THIS AI THEN?

What are AI, cognitive computing, and machine learning? In "The History of Artificial Intelligence,"[8] Chris Smith introduces AI this way:

> The term *artificial intelligence* was first coined by John McCarthy in 1956 when he held the first academic conference on the subject. But the journey to understand if machines can truly think began much before that. In Vannevar Bush's seminal work *As We May Think* (1945) he proposed a system which amplifies people's own knowledge and understanding. Five years later Alan Turing wrote a paper on the notion of machines being able to simulate human beings and the ability to do intelligent things, such as play Chess (1950).

In brief—AI mimics humans, while machine learning is a system that can figure out how to figure out a specific task. According to SAS, multinational developer of analytics software, "Cognitive computing is based on self-learning systems that use machine-learning techniques to perform specific, humanlike tasks in an intelligent way."[9]

THE AI UMBRELLA

We start with *AI, artificial intelligence,* as it is the overarching term for a variety of technologies. AI generally refers to making computers act like people. "Weak AI" is that which can do something very specific, very well, and "strong AI" is that which thinks like humans, draws on general knowledge, imitates common sense, threatens to become self-aware, and takes over the world.

We have lived with weak AI for a while now. Pandora is very good at choosing what music you might like based on the sort of music you liked before. Amazon is pretty good at guessing that if you bought *this*, you might like to buy *that*. Google's AlphaGo beat Go world champion Lee Sedol in March 2016. Another AI system (DeepStack) beat experts at no-limit, Texas Hold'em Poker.[10] But none of those systems can do anything else. They are *weak*.

Artificial intelligence is a large umbrella. Under it, you'll find visual recognition ("That's a cat!"), voice recognition (you can say things like, "It won't turn on" or "It won't connect to the Internet" or "It never arrived"), natural language processing ("I think you said you wanted me to open the garage door and warm up your car. Is that right?"), expert systems ("Based on its behavior, I am 98.3% confident that is a cat"), affective computing ("I see cats make you happy"), and robotics (I'm acting like a cat).

THE MACHINE THAT LEARNS

The magic of machine learning is that it was designed to learn, not to follow strict rules. This is the most fundamental aspect to understand and the most important to remember when you hit that inevitable frustration when things start going slightly off-track. A rules-based system does exactly what it's told and nothing more. We are comforted by that. A command to send out a gazillion e-mails with the "<first_name>" after the salutation does precisely that. That's good.

Of course, when the database has something fishy in the first_name field, then somebody gets an e-mail that begins, "Hello, Null, how are you?" Once humans know to look for those sorts of mistakes, we create processes to check and correct the data before hitting Send the next time.

When a batch of e-mails goes out that *all* say, "Hello, <first_name>, how are you?" and the e-mails all include those brackets and that underline, we know to flail the programmers until they find the errant semicolon that caused the problem. In both cases, we can backtrack, find the problem, and fix it.

Machine learning has data and is given a task. It performs the task and waits for feedback. If the feedback is positive, it tries to duplicate the same actions the next time for a similar task. If the feedback is negative, it requires information on where it went wrong.

Guess the Animal

In 1980, at the Personal Electronics store in Santa Barbara, California, I was shown a program that could guess the animal you had in mind. I was flabbergasted. It was a simple case of Asimov's "Any sufficiently advanced technology is indistinguishable from magic."

It: Think of an animal...

Is it an elephant? (y or n)

Me: n

It: You win. Help me learn from my mistake before you go ... What animal were you thinking of?

Me: a rabbit

It: Give me a question to distinguish a rabbit from an elephant.

Me: Is it a small animal?

It: For a rabbit, what is the answer to your question? (y or n)

Me: y

It: Thanks.

Play again? (y or n)

Me: y

It: Think of an animal ...

Is it a small animal? (y or n)

Me: y

It: Is it a rabbit? (y or n)

Me: n

It: You win. Help me learn from my mistake before you go ... What animal were you thinking of?

Me: a frog

It: Give me a question to distinguish a frog from rabbit and an elephant.

Me: Is it green?

It: Thanks.

Play again? (y or n)

Me: No, I see how this works now.

It: I don't understand.

Play again? (y or n)

Me: n

It: Goodbye

Is this program rudimentary? You bet. Was this machine learning? Almost.

After running again and again, the game could guess exactly what animal you had in mind after only a few questions. It was impressive, but it was just following programmed logic. It was not *learning*. Guess the Animal could update its rules-based database and *appear* to be getting smarter as it went along, but it did not change how it made decisions.

The Machine that Programs Itself

Machine learning systems look for patterns and try to make sense of them. It all starts with the question: What problem are you trying to solve?

Let's say you want the machine to recognize a picture of a cat. Feed it all the pictures of cats you can get your hands on and tell it, "These are cats." The machine looks through all of them, looking for patterns. It sees that cats have fur, pointy ears, tails, and so on, and waits for you to ask a question.

"How many paws does a cat have?"

"On average, 3.24."

That's a good, solid answer from a regular database. It looks at all the photos, adds up the paws, and divides by the number of pictures.

But a machine learning system is designed to learn. When you tell the machine that most cats have four paws, it can "realize" that it cannot see all of the paws. So when you ask,

"How many ears does a cat have?"

"No more than two."

the machine has learned something from its experience with paws and can apply that learning to counting ears.

The magic of machine learning is building systems that build themselves. We teach the machine to learn how to learn. We build systems that can write their own algorithms, their own architecture. Rather than learn more information, they are able to change their minds about the data they acquire. They alter the way they perceive. They learn.

The code is unreadable to humans. The machine writes its own code. You can't fix it; you can only try to correct its behavior.

It's troublesome that we cannot backtrack and find out where a machine learning system went off the rails if things come out wrong. That makes us decidedly uncomfortable. It is also likely to be illegal, especially in Europe.

"The EU General Data Protection Regulation (GDPR) is the most important change in data privacy regulation in 20 years" says the homepage of the EU GDPR Portal.[11] Article 5, Principles Relating to Personal Data Processing, starts right out with:

> Personal Data must be:
>
> * processed lawfully, fairly, and in a manner transparent to the data subject
>
> * collected for specified, explicit purposes and only those purposes
>
> * limited to the minimum amount of personal data necessary for a given situation
>
> * accurate and where necessary, up to date
>
> * kept in a form that permits identification of the data subject for only as long as is necessary, with the only exceptions being statistical or scientific research purposes pursuant to article 83a
>
> * Parliament adds that the data must be processed in a manner allowing the data subject to exercise his/her rights and protects the integrity of the data
>
> * Council adds that the data must be processed in a manner that ensures the security of the data processed under the responsibility and liability of the data controller

Imagine sitting in a bolted-to-the-floor chair in a small room at a heavily scarred table with a single, bright spotlight overhead and a detective leaning in asking, "So how did your system screw this up so badly and how are you going to fix it? Show me the decision-making process!"

This is a murky area at the moment, and one that is being reviewed and pursued. Machine learning systems will have to come with tools that allow a decision to be explored and explained.

ARE WE THERE YET?

Most of this sounds a little over-the-horizon and science-fiction-ish, and it is. But it's only *just* over the horizon. (Quick—check the publication date at the front of this book!) The capabilities have been in the lab for a while now. Examples are in the field. AI and machine learning are being used in advertising, marketing, and customer service, and they don't seem to be slowing down.

But there are some projections that this is all coming at an alarming rate.[12]

> According to researcher Gartner, AI bots will power 85% of all customer service interactions by the year 2020. Given Facebook and other messaging platforms have already seen significant adoption of customer service bots on their chat apps, this shouldn't necessarily come as a huge surprise. Since this use of AI can help reduce wait times for many types of interactions, this trend sounds like a win for businesses and customers alike.

The White House says it's time to get ready. In a report called "Preparing for the Future of Artificial Intelligence" (October 2016),[13] the Executive Office of the President National Science and Technology Council Committee on Technology said:

> The current wave of progress and enthusiasm for AI began around 2010, driven by three factors that built upon each other: the availability of big data from sources including e-commerce, businesses, social media, science, and government; which provided raw material for dramatically improved Machine Learning approaches and algorithms; which in turn relied on the capabilities of more powerful computers. During this period, the pace of improvement surprised AI experts. For example, on a popular image recognition challenge[14] that has a 5 percent human error rate according to one error measure, the best AI result improved from a 26 percent error rate in 2011 to 3.5 percent in 2015.

Simultaneously, industry has been increasing its investment in AI. In 2016, Google Chief Executive Officer (CEO) Sundar Pichai said, "Machine Learning [a subfield of AI] is a core, transformative way by which we're rethinking how we're doing everything. We are thoughtfully applying it across all our products, be it search, ads, YouTube, or Play. And we're in early days, but you will see us—in a systematic way—apply Machine Learning in all these areas." This view of AI broadly impacting how software is created and delivered was widely shared by CEOs in the technology industry, including Ginni Rometty of IBM, who has said that her organization is betting the company on AI.

The commercial growth in AI is surprising to those of little faith and not at all surprising to true believers. IDC Research "predicts that spending on AI software for marketing and related function businesses will grow at an exceptionally fast cumulative average growth rate (CAGR) of 54 percent worldwide, from around $360 million in 2016 to over $2 billion in 2020, due to the attractiveness of this technology to both sell-side suppliers and buy-side end-user customers."[15]

Best to be prepared for the "ketchup effect," as Mattias Östmar called it: "First nothing, then nothing, then a drip and then all of a sudden—splash!"

You might call it hype, crystal-balling, or wishful thinking, but the best minds of our time are taking it very seriously. The White House's primary recommendation from the above report is to "examine whether and how (private and public institutions) can responsibly leverage AI and Machine Learning in ways that will benefit society."

Can you responsibly leverage AI and machine learning in ways that will benefit society? What happens if you don't? What could possibly go wrong?

AI-POCALYPSE

Cyberdyne will become the largest supplier of military computer systems. All stealth bombers are upgraded with Cyberdyne computers, becoming fully unmanned. Afterwards, they fly with a perfect operational record. The Skynet Funding Bill is passed. The system goes online August 4th, 1997. Human decisions are removed from

*strategic defense. Skynet begins to learn at a geometric
rate. It becomes self-aware at 2:14 a.m. Eastern time,
August 29th. In a panic, they try to pull the plug.*

The Terminator, *Orion Pictures, 1984*

At the end of 2014, Professor Stephen Hawking rattled the data
science world when he warned, "The development of full artificial
intelligence could spell the end of the human race.... It would take
off on its own, and re-design itself at an ever increasing rate. Humans,
who are limited by slow biological evolution, couldn't compete and
would be superseded."[16]

In August 2014, Elon Musk took to Twitter to express his
misgivings:

"Worth reading Superintelligence by Bostrom. We need to be super
careful with AI. Potentially more dangerous than nukes," (Figure 1.2)
and "Hope we're not just the biological boot loader for digital superintelligence. Unfortunately, that is increasingly probable."

In a clip from the movie *Lo and Behold*, by German filmmaker
Werner Herzog, Musk says:

> I think that the biggest risk is not that the AI will develop a
> will of its own, but rather that it will follow the will of
> people that establish its utility function. If it is not well
> thought out—even if its intent is benign—it could have
> quite a bad outcome. If you were a hedge fund or private
> equity fund and you said, "Well, all I want my AI to do is

Elon Musk ✔
@elonmusk

⚙   **Follow**

Worth reading Superintelligence by Bostrom.
We need to be super careful with AI. Potentially
more dangerous than nukes.

RETWEETS	LIKES	
2,705	3,076	

7:33 PM - 2 Aug 2014

↩ 515   ↻ 2.7K   ♥ 3.1K   •••

Figure 1.2   Elon Musk expresses his disquiet on Twitter.

maximize the value of my portfolio," then the AI could decide, well, the best way to do that is to short consumer stocks, go long defense stocks, and start a war. That would obviously be quite bad.

While Hawking is thinking big, Musk raises the quintessential Paperclip Maximizer Problem and the Intentional Consequences Problem.

The AI that Ate the Earth

Say you build an AI system with a goal of maximizing the number of paperclips it has. The threat is that it learns how to find paperclips, buy paperclips (requiring it to learn how to make money), and then work out how to manufacture paperclips. It would realize that it needs to be smarter, and so increases its own intelligence in order to make it even smarter, in service of making paperclips.

What is the problem? A hyper-intelligent agent could figure out how to use nanotech and quantum physics to alter all atoms on Earth into paperclips.

Whoops, somebody seems to have forgotten to include the Three Laws of Robotics from Isaac Asimov's 1950 book, *I Robot*:

1. A robot may not injure a human being, or through inaction, allow a human being to come to harm.
2. A robot must obey orders given it by human beings except where such orders would conflict with the First Law.
3. A robot must protect its own existence as long as such protection does not conflict with the First or Second Law.

Max Tegmark, president of the Future of Life Institute, ponders what would happen if an AI

> is programmed to do something beneficial, but it develops a destructive method for achieving its goal: This can happen whenever we fail to fully align the AI's goals with ours, which is strikingly difficult. If you ask an obedient intelligent car to take you to the airport as fast as possible, it might get you there chased by helicopters and covered in vomit, doing not what you wanted but literally what you asked for. If a superintelligent system is tasked with a(n) ambitious geoengineering project, it might wreak havoc with our ecosystem as a side effect, and view human attempts to stop it as a threat to be met.[17]

If you really want to dive into a dark hole of the existential problem that AI represents, take a gander at "The AI Revolution: Our Immortality or Extinction."[18]

Intentional Consequences Problem

Bad guys are the scariest thing about guns, nuclear weapons, hacking, and, yes, AI. Dictators and authoritarian regimes, people with a grudge, and people who are mentally unstable could all use very powerful software to wreak havoc on our self-driving cars, dams, water systems, and air traffic control systems. That would, to repeat Mr. Musk, obviously be quite bad.

That's why the Future of Life Institute offered "Autonomous Weapons: An Open Letter from AI & Robotics Researchers," which concludes, "Starting a military AI arms race is a bad idea, and should be prevented by a ban on offensive autonomous weapons beyond meaningful human control."[19]

In his 2015 presentation on "The Long-Term Future of (Artificial) Intelligence," University of California, Berkeley professor Stuart Russell asked, "What's so bad about the better AI? AI that is incredibly good at achieving something other than what we *really* want."

Russell then offered some approaches to managing the it's-smarter-than-we-are conundrum. He described AIs that are not in control of anything in the world, but only answer a human's questions, making us wonder whether it could learn to manipulate the human. He suggested creating an agent whose only job is to review other AIs to see if they are potentially dangerous and admitted that was a bit of a paradox. He's very optimistic, however, given the economic incentive for humans to create AI systems that do *not* run amok and turn people into paperclips. The result will inevitably be the development of community standards and a global regulatory framework.

Setting aside science fiction fears of the unknown and a madman with a suitcase nuke, there are some issues that are real and deserve our attention.

Unintended Consequences

The biggest legitimate concern facing marketing executives when it comes to machine learning and AI is when the machine does what you tell it to do rather than what you wanted it to do. This is much like the paperclip problem, but much more subtle. In broad terms, this is known as the *alignment problem*. The alignment problem wonders how to explain to an AI system goals that are not absolute, but take all of human values into consideration, especially considering that values vary widely from human to human, even in the same community. And even then, humans, according to Professor Russell, are irrational, inconsistent, and weak-willed.

The good news is that addressing this issue is actively happening at the industrial level. "OpenAI is a non-profit artificial intelligence research company. Our mission is to build safe AI, and ensure AI's benefits are as widely and evenly distributed as possible."[20]

The other good news is that addressing this issue is actively happening at the academic/scientific level. The Future of Humanity Institute teamed with Google to publish a paper titled "Safely Interruptible Agents."[21]

> Reinforcement learning agents interacting with a complex environment like the real world are unlikely to behave optimally all the time. If such an agent is operating in real-time under human supervision, now and then it may be necessary for a human operator to press the big red button to prevent the agent from continuing a harmful sequence of actions—harmful either for the agent or for the environment—and lead the agent into a safer situation. However, if the learning agent expects to receive rewards from this sequence, it may learn in the long run to avoid such interruptions, for example by disabling the red button—which is an undesirable outcome. This paper explores a way to make sure a learning agent will not learn to prevent (or seek!) being interrupted by the environment or a human operator. We provide a formal definition of safe interruptibility and exploit the off-policy learning property to prove that either some agents are already safely interruptible, like Q-learning, or can easily be made so, like Sarsa. We show that even ideal, uncomputable reinforcement learning agents for (deterministic) general computable environments can be made safely interruptible.

There is also the Partnership on Artificial Intelligence to Benefit People and Society,[22] which was "established to study and formulate best practices on AI technologies, to advance the public's understanding of AI, and to serve as an open platform for discussion and engagement about AI and its influences on people and society."

Granted, one of its main goals from an industrial perspective is to calm the fears of the masses, but it also intends to "support research and recommend best practices in areas including ethics, fairness, and inclusivity; transparency and interoperability; privacy; collaboration between people and AI systems; and of the trustworthiness, reliability, and robustness of the technology."

The Partnership on AI's stated tenets[23] include:

> We are committed to open research and dialog on the ethical, social, economic, and legal implications of AI.
>
> We will work to maximize the benefits and address the potential challenges of AI technologies, by:
>
> Working to protect the privacy and security of individuals.
>
> Striving to understand and respect the interests of all parties that may be impacted by AI advances.
>
> Working to ensure that AI research and engineering communities remain socially responsible, sensitive, and engaged directly with the potential influences of AI technologies on wider society.
>
> Ensuring that AI research and technology is robust, reliable, trustworthy, and operates within secure constraints.
>
> Opposing development and use of AI technologies that would violate international conventions or human rights, and promoting safeguards and technologies that do no harm.

That's somewhat comforting, but the blood pressure lowers considerably when we notice that the Partnership includes the American Civil Liberties Union. That makes it a little more socially reliable than the Self-Driving Coalition for Safer Streets, which is made up of Ford, Google, Lyft, Uber, and Volvo without any representation from little old ladies who are just trying to get to the other side.

Will a Robot Take Your Job?

Just as automation and robotics have displaced myriad laborers and word processing has done away with legions of secretaries, some jobs will be going away.

The *Wall Street Journal* article, "The World's Largest Hedge Fund Is Building an Algorithmic Model from Its Employees' Brains,"[24] reported on $160 billion Bridgewater Associates trying to embed its founder's approach to management into a so-called Principles Operating System. The system is intended to study employee reviews and testing to delegate specific tasks to specific employees along with detailed instructions, not to mention having a hand in hiring, firing, and promotions. Whether a system that thinks about humans as complex machines can succeed will take some time.

A *Guardian* article sporting the headline "Japanese Company Replaces Office Workers with Artificial Intelligence"[25] reported on an insurance company at which 34 employees were to be replaced in March 2017 by an AI system that calculates policyholder payouts.

> Fukoku Mutual Life Insurance believes it will increase productivity by 30% and see a return on its investment in less than two years. The firm said it would save about 140m yen (£1m) a year after the 200m yen (£1.4m) AI system is installed this month. Maintaining it will cost about 15m yen (£100k) a year.

> The technology will be able to read tens of thousands of medical certificates and factor in the length of hospital stays, medical histories and any surgical procedures before calculating payouts, according to the Mainichi Shimbun.

> While the use of AI will drastically reduce the time needed to calculate Fukoku Mutual's payouts—which reportedly totalled 132,000 during the current financial year—the sums will not be paid until they have been approved by a member of staff, the newspaper said.

> Japan's shrinking, ageing population, coupled with its prowess in robot technology, makes it a prime testing ground for AI.

> According to a 2015 report by the Nomura Research Institute, nearly half of all jobs in Japan could be performed by robots by 2035.

I plan on being retired by then.

Is *your* job at risk? Probably not. Assuming that you are either a data scientist trying to understand marketing or a marketing person trying to understand data science, you're likely to keep your job for a while.

In September 2015, the BBC ran its "Will a Robot Take Your Job?"[26] feature. Choose your job title from the dropdown menu and

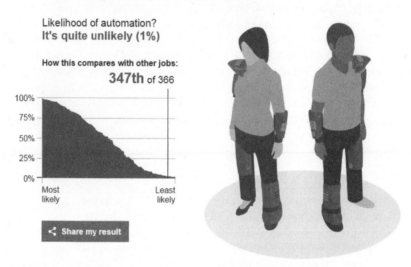

Figure 1.3 Marketing and sales managers get to keep their jobs a little longer than most.

voilà! If you're a marketing and sales director, you're pretty safe. (See Figure 1.3.)

In January 2017, McKinsey Global Institute published "A Future that Works: Automation, Employment, and Productivity,"[27] stating, "While few occupations are fully automatable, 60 percent of all occupations have at least 30 percent technically automatable activities."

The institute offered five factors affecting pace and extent of adoption:

1. *Technical feasibility:* Technology has to be invented, integrated, and adapted into solutions for specific case use.

2. *Cost of developing and deploying solutions:* Hardware and software costs.

3. *Labor market dynamics:* The supply, demand, and costs of human labor affect which activities will be automated.

4. *Economic benefits:* Include higher throughput and increased quality, alongside labor cost savings.

5. *Regulatory and social acceptance:* Even when automation makes business sense, adoption can take time.

Christopher Berry sees a threat to the lower ranks of those in the marketing department.[28]

> If we view it as being a way of liberating people from the drudgery of routine within marketing departments, that would be quite a bit more exciting. People could focus on the things that are most energizing about marketing like the creativity and the messaging—the stuff people enjoy doing.
>
> I just see nothing but opportunity in terms of tasks that could be automated to liberate humans. On the other side, it's a typical employment problem. If we get rid of all the farming jobs, then what are people going to do in the economy? It could be a tremendous era of a lot more displacement in white collar marketing departments.
>
> Some of the first jobs to be automated will be juniors. So we could be very much to a point where the traditional career ladder gets pulled up after us and that the degree of education and professionalism that's required in marketing just increases and increases.

So, yes, if you've been in marketing for a while, you'll keep your job, but it will look very different, very soon.

MACHINE LEARNING'S BIGGEST ROADBLOCK

That would be *data*. Even before the application of machine learning to marketing, the glory of *big data* was that you could sort, sift, slice, and dice through more data than previously computationally possible.

Massive numbers of website interactions, social engagements, and mobile phone swipes could be sucked into an enormous database in the cloud and millions of small computers that are so much better, faster, and cheaper than the Big Iron of the good old mainframe days could process the heck out of it all. The problem then—and the problem now—is that these data sets do not play well together.

The best and the brightest data scientists and analysts are still spending an enormous and unproductive amount of time performing janitorial work. They are ensuring that new data streams are properly vetted, that legacy data streams continue to flow reliably, that the data that comes in is formatted correctly, and that the data is appropriately groomed so that all the bits line up.

- Data set A starts each week on Monday rather than Sunday.
- Data set B drops leading zeros from numeric fields.
- Data set C uses dashes instead of parentheses in phone numbers.
- Data set D stores dates European style (day, month, year).
- Data set E has no field for a middle initial.
- Data set F stores transaction numbers but not customer IDs.
- Data set G does not include in-page actions, only clicks.
- Data set H stores a smartphone's IMEI or MEID number rather than its phone number.
- Data set I is missing a significant number of values.
- Data set J uses a different scale of measurements.
- Data set K, and so on.

It's easy to see how much work goes into data cleansing and normalization. This seems to be a natural challenge for a machine learning application.

Sure enough, there are academics and data scientists working on this, but they're a long way off. How can you tell?

In their paper titled "Probabilistic Noise Identification and Data Cleaning,"[29] Jeremy Kubica and Andrew Moore describe their work on *not* throwing out entire records when only some of the fields are contaminated. "In this paper we present an approach for identifying corrupted fields and using the remaining non-corrupted fields for subsequent modeling and analysis. Our approach learns a probabilistic model from the data that contains three components: a generative model of the clean data points, a generative model of the noise values, and a probabilistic model of the corruption process."

It's a start.

MACHINE LEARNING'S GREATEST ASSET

That would be *data*. Machine learning has a truly tough time with too little information. If you give it only one example, it can tell you *exactly* what to expect the next time with 100 percent confidence. It will be wrong.

Machine learning doesn't work like statistics. Statistics can tell you the likelihood of a coin toss or the probability of a plane crash.

PROBABILITY OF A PLANE CRASH

Three statisticians are in a plane when the pilot announces that they've lost one of their engines. "But it's okay, folks, these planes were built to fly under the worst conditions. It does mean, however, that we're going to fly a bit slower and we'll be about a half an hour late. Please don't worry. Sit back, relax, and enjoy the rest of your flight."

The first statistician says, "There's still a 25 percent chance that I'll make my connection."

Fifteen minutes later, the pilot is on the PA again. "Ladies and gentlemen, we seem to have lost a second engine. No problem, the others are still going strong. This does mean, however, that we'll be about an hour late to the gate. I'm so sorry for the inconvenience."

The second statistician says, "There's an 83 percent chance I'm going to miss my dinner."

After a half an hour, the pilot makes *another* announcement, "Ladies and Gents, we've lost yet another engine. Yes, I know this is bad, but there's really no need to worry. We'll make it just fine, but we're going to be two hours late to the airport."

The third statistician says, "That last engine better not fail or we'll *never* land!"

Human experience and ingenuity have worked wonders for marketing for hundreds of years: gut feel and common sense. When we added statistics to the mix, we expanded our experience by considering historical precedent. But we still rely on gut feel as we feel around blindly in the data, hoping to stumble on something recognizable.

How We Used to Dive into Data

As the Board Chair of the Digital Analytics Association, I strove to explain how digital analysts go beyond answering specific questions. I wrote the following in the Applied Marketing Analytics Journal, describing the role of the "data detective."

Discovering Discovery, Data Discovery Best Practices[30]

A crystal ball is filled with nothing at all or smoke and clouds, mesmerizing the uninitiated, but very useful for the scrying specialist. The crystal ball mystic is tasked with entertaining more than communicating genuine visions. Creating something from nothing takes imagination, creativity, and the ability to read one's fellow man to determine what fictions they might consider valuable. The medium who directs a séance is in much the same role.

Tarot Card readers are a step closer to practicality. They use their cards as conversation starters. "You drew The Magician, which stands for creation and individuality, next to the Three of Cups, which represents a group of people working together. Are you working on a project with others right now?" The "mystical" conversation is all about the subject, and therefore, seems revelatory.

The Digital Analyst also has a crystal ball (The Database) and Tarot Cards (Correlations) with which to entice and enthrall the Truth Seeker. The database is a mystery to the supplicant, and the correlations seem almost magical.

The Digital Analyst has something more powerful than visions and more practical than psychology—although both are necessary in this line of work. The analyst has data; data that can be validated and verified. Data that can be reliably used to answer specific questions.

The Digital Analyst truly shines when seeking insight beyond the normal, predictable questions asked on a daily basis. The analyst can engage in discovery; the art of uncovering important truths that can be useful or even transformative to those who would be data-driven.

Traditional Approach: Asking Specific Questions

> A business manager wants to know the buying patterns of her customers.
>
> A shipping manager wants to project what increased sales will mean to staffing.
>
> A production manager wants to anticipate and accordingly adjust the supply chain.
>
> An advertising professional wants to see the comparative results of a half a dozen promotional campaigns.

Each of these scenarios call for specific data to be assembled and tabulated to provide a specific answer. Proper data collecting, cleansing, and blending are required, and can be codified if the same questions are to be asked repeatedly. And thus, reporting is born.

Reports are valuable and necessary . . . until they are not. Then they are the source of repetitive stress, adding no value to the organization. The antidote is discovery.

Exploring Data

An investigation is an effort to get data to reveal what it knows. ("Where were you on the night of the 27th?"). But data discovery is the art of interviewing data to learn things you didn't necessarily know you wanted to know.

The Talented data explorer is much like the crystal ball gazer and the Tarot reader in several ways. They:

> Have a method for figuring out what the paying customer wants to know.
>
> Have broad enough knowledge about the subject to recognize potentially interesting details.
>
> Are sufficiently open minded to be receptive to details that *might* be relevant.
>
> Keep in close communication with the petitioner to guide the conversation.
>
> Understand the underlying principles well enough to push the boundaries.
>
> Are curious by nature and enjoys the intellectual hunt.

Data discovery is part mind reading, part pattern recognition, and part puzzle solving. Reading the mind of the inquisitor is obligatory to ensure the results are of interest to those with control of the budget. Pattern recognition is a special skill that can be honed to help direct lines of enquiry and trains of thought. An aptitude for detective work is the most important talent of the Digital Analyst; that ability to ponder the meaning of newly uncovered evidence.

Data discovery is the art of mixing an infinitely large bowl of alphabet soup and being able to recognize the occasional message that floats to the surface in an assortment of languages. Although, with Big Data, adding more data variety to the mix, the Digital Analyst must also be able to read tea leaves, translate the I Ching, generate an astrological chart, interpret dreams, observe auras, speak in tongues, and sing with sirens in order to turn lead into gold.

Data discovery is all about the application of those human skills that computers have a tough time with reasoning, creativity, learning, intuition, application of incongruous knowledge, etc.

Computers are fast but dumb, while humans are slow but smart.

That doesn't mean technology cannot be helpful.

Data Discovery Tools

The business intelligence tool industry is pivoting as fast as it can to offer up data discovery tools. They describe their offerings in florid terms:

> Imagine an analytics tool so intuitive, anyone in your company could easily create personalized reports and dynamic dashboards to explore vast amounts of data and find meaningful insights. (Qlik.com[1])

> Tableau enables people throughout an organization— not just superstar analysts—to investigate data to find nuances, trends, and outliers in a flash. (Yes, the superstars benefit, too.) No longer constrained to a million rows of spreadsheet data or a monthly report that only answers a few questions, people can now interact and visualize data, asking—and answering—questions at the speed of thought.

> Using an intuitive, drag-and-drop approach to data exploration means spending time thinking about what your data is telling you, not creating a mountain of pivot tables or filling out report requests. (Tableau[2])

> We help people make faster, better business decisions, empowering them with self-service tools to explore data and share insights in minutes.... Simple drag-and-drop tools are paired with intuitive visualizations. Connect to any data source and share your insights in minutes.... Standalone data discovery tools will only get you so far. Step into enterprise-ready analytics and guarantee secure, governed data discovery. (Microstrategy[3])

Regardless of the speed and agility of one technology or another, it all depends on the person driving the system to ask really good questions. However, if the system does not have really good data, even the best questions will result in faulty insights. Therefore, data hygiene takes precedent over superior query capability.

Data Hygiene

Garbage in, garbage out. So much goes into Big Data, it's very hard to know which bits are worthy of being included and which need to be rectified. For that, you need a subject matter expert *and* a data matter expert.

A data matter expert is knowledgeable about a specific stream: how it was collected, how it was cleansed, sampled, aggregated and segmented, and what transformation is required before blending it with other streams.

Data hygiene and data governance are paramount to ensure the digital analytics cooks are using the very best ingredients to avoid ruining a time-proven recipe.

Further, when the output of one analysis provides the input for the next (creating a dashboard, for example), transformation, aggregation and segmentation help obfuscate the true flavor of the raw material until it is past the ability of a forensic data scientists to track down the cause of any problems—supposing somebody is aware that there is a problem.

Yet, aggregations are as important to the insight supply chain as top-grade ingredients are to the five-star chef:

> [D]ata aggregations and summaries remain critical for supporting visual reporting and analytics so that users can see specific time periods and frame other areas of interest without getting overwhelmed by the data deluge. Along with providing access to Hadoop files, many modern visual reporting and data discovery tools enable users to create aggregations as the need arises rather than having to suffer the delays of requisitioning them ahead of time from IT developers. In a number of leading tools, this is accomplished through an integrated in-memory data store where the aggregations are done on the fly from detailed data stored in memory.

> TDWI Research finds that enterprise data warehouses, BI reporting and OLAP cubes, spreadsheets, and analytic databases are the most important data sources for visual analysis and data discovery, according to survey respondents. (TDWI[4])

The care and feeding of the raw material used in the data discovery process is even more important in light of the lack of five-star chefs. As analytics becomes more accepted, demanded and democratized, more and more amateur analysts will be deriving conclusions from raw material they trust implicitly rather than understand thoroughly. Preparing for data illiterate explorers requires even more rigor than usual to guard against their impulse to jump to the wrong conclusions.

Asking Really Good Questions

In the hands of a well-informed analyst, lots of data and heavy-lifting analytics tools are very powerful. Getting the most out of this combination takes a little bit of creativity.

Creativity means broadening your mental scope. Rather than seeking a specific answer, open yourself up to possibilities. It's like focusing on your peripheral vision.

1. Appreciate Anomalies

Whether you use visualization tools and "look for" things that go bump in the night, or you are adept at scanning a sea of numbers and wondering why it looks out of balance, the skill to hone is the art of seeing the out-of-the-ordinary.

Outliers, spikes, troughs—any anomaly—are our friends. They draw our attention to that which is not like the others and spark the intellectual exercise of wondering "Why?"

What is it about this element that makes it point in a different direction? Could it be some error in the collection or transformation of the underlying data? Is it a function of how the report was written or the query was structured? Or does it represent some new behavior/market movement/customer trend?

It is in the hunt for the truth about these standouts that we trip over the serendipitous component that spawns a new

question and another dive down the rabbit hole.
The secret is knowing when to stop.

One can easily get lost in a hyperlink-chasing "research
session" and burn hours with very little to show for it.
Following the scent of significance is an art and one that
takes practice and discipline. Many scientists spend a career
pursuing a specific outcome only to find it disproved.
Others stop just short of a discovery because they lose
heart. The magic happens between those two points.

Give in to the temptation to slice the data one more time
or to cross reference results against just one more query,
but be vigilant that you are not wasting valuable cycles on
diminishing returns.

If you don't see what you expect to see, work your hardest
to understand why. It may be that you do not have
enough facts. It might be that you have already,
unknowingly, come to a conclusion or formed a pet theory
without all the facts. It might be—and this is the most
likely—that there is something afoot which you have not
yet considered.

Dig deeper. Ask, "I wonder . . . ." And be cognizant of that
which is conspicuous in its absence.

*Gregory (Scotland Yard detective): "Is there any other point
to which you would wish to draw my attention?"*

*Holmes: "To the curious incident of the dog in the
night-time."*

Gregory: "The dog did nothing in the night-time."

Holmes: "That was the curious incident."

Sir Arthur Conan Doyle, Silver Blaze

As a corollary, be wary of the homologous as well:

1. Exhibiting a degree of correspondence or similarity.
2. Corresponding in structure and evolutionary origin, but
   not necessarily in function.

For example, human arm, dog foreleg, bird wing, and
whale flipper are homologous. (A Word A Day[5])

Things that are unusually similar are equally cause for alarm as standouts. If everybody in your cohort looks the same, there's something funny going on and it's worth an investigation. It may be that their similarity is a statistical anomaly.

2. Savor Segmentation

People (thank heaven!) are different. We make a huge mistake when we lump them all together. But we cannot treat them as individuals—yet. Peppers and Rogers' *One to One Future* is not yet upon us. In between lies segmentation.

It almost doesn't matter how you segment your customers (geographically, chronologically, by hair color). Eventually, you will find traits that are useful in finding a cluster of behavior that can be leveraged to your advantage.

> People who come to our website in the morning are more likely to X.
>
> People who complain about us on social media respond better to message Y.
>
> People who use our mobile app more than twice a week are more likely to Z.

When it comes to segmenting customers by behavior, Bernard Berelson pretty much nailed it in his "Human Behavior: An Inventory of Scientific Findings"[6] where he said:

> Some do and some don't.
>
> The differences aren't that great.
>
> It's more complicated than that.

When you're trying to get the right message in front of the right people at the right time and on the right device, segmentation may likely be the key to the mystery.

3. Don't Fool Yourself

While working with data is reassuring—we are, after all dealing with facts and not opinions—we are still human and still faced with serious mental handicaps.

Being open-minded and objective are wonderful goals, but they are not absolute.

Cognitive biases are inherited, taught, and picked up by osmosis in a given culture. In short, your mind can play tricks on you. While this is too large a subject to cover in depth here, there are some examples that make it clear just how tenuous your relationship with "the facts" might be.

Familiarity Bias
I've worked in television advertising all my life and I can tell you without any doubt that it's the most powerful branding medium there is.

Hindsight or Outcome Bias
If they'd only have asked me, I would have told them that the blue button would not convert as well as the red one. It was obvious all along.

Attribution Bias
Of course I should have turned left at that light. But I was distracted by the sun in my eyes and the phone ringing. That other guy missed the turn because he's a dim-wit.

Representativeness Bias
Everybody who clicks on that link must be like everybody else who clicked on that link in the past.

Anchoring Bias
That's far too much to pay for this item. The one next to it is half the price.

Availability Bias (the first example that comes to mind)
That'll never work—let me tell you what happened to my brother-in-law . . .

Bandwagon Bias
We should run a Snapchat campaign because everybody else is doing it.

Confirmation Bias
I'm a conservative, so I only watch Fox News.

I'm a liberal, so I only watch The Rachel Maddow Show.

I've been in advertising all my life, so I count on Nielsen, Hitwise, and comScore.

I started out grepping log files, so I only trust my Coremetrics/Omniture/Webtrends numbers.

Projection Bias
I would never click on a product demo without a long list of testimonials, so we can assume that's true of everybody else.

Expectancy Bias
Your report must be wrong because it does not show the results I anticipated.

Normalcy Bias
Back-ups? We've never had a data loss problem yet, I don't see it happening this quarter so we won't have to budget for it.

Semmelweis Reflex
I don't care what your numbers say, we've always had better conversions from search than social media so we're not going to change our investment.

If any of the above sound familiar, congratulations—you've been paying attention. The hard part is convincing others that there may be a cognitive problem.

4. Correlation versus Causation

While frequently mentioned, it cannot be stressed enough that just because drownings go up when ice cream sales go up, one did not cause the other.

Most recently, a Swedish study ("Allergy in Children in Hand Versus Machine Dishwashing"[7]) concluded, "In families who use hand dishwashing, allergic diseases in children are less common than in children from families who use machine dishwashing," and speculated that, "a less-efficient dishwashing method may induce tolerance via increased microbial exposure."

While the study asked a great deal of questions about the types of food they eat, food preparation, parental smoking, etc., there are simply too many other variables at play for this cause to be solely responsible for that effect. How many other similarities are there among families that have dishwashers vs. those that do not?

Correlations are a wonderful clue, but they must be treated as clues and not results. Correlations are the stimulus for seeking a cause, not the end of the story.

5. Communicating Carefully

Coming up with a fascinating correlation and proving a causative relationship can be exciting. The thrill of the chase, the disappointment of a miscalculation, and the redemption of the correction make for an invigorating career, but like your latest round of golf, not necessarily a great story at the dinner table. And certainly not at the conference room table or across the desk from an executive who is trying to make a multimillion-dollar advertising decision.

This is the time to stick with what you know, not how you got there.

The most important part of your performance when delivering insights based on data is to avoid any bravado of certainty. You have not been asked to audit the books and come to a conclusion. You have not been tasked with adding up a row of numbers and delivering The Answer. Instead, you have been asked to sift through the data to see if there's anything in there that might be directional.

To assure everybody else that you understand your responsibility and to appropriately frame your findings in terms that will lead to a valuable conversation and business decision, monitor your language carefully.

> The data suggests...
>
> It seems more likely...
>
> One could conclude...
>
> Based on the data, it feels like...
>
> If I were placing bets after seeing this...

Remember that you are looking into a crystal ball that is a complete mystery to the business side of the house and you are telling them things about a subject they know very well, just not through that lens. They know advertising and marketing inside and out and are going to be incredulous if you make pronouncements that are contrary to their experience, gut feel, and common sense.

The domain expert can look at a carefully scrutinized, statistical revelation and roll their eyes.

> "Of course movies starting with the letter A are more popular—we list them alphabetically."
>
> "Of course online sales took a jump the week in that region—there was a five day blizzard."
>
> "Of course we sold more low-end laptops that day—our competitor's website was down."

Be sure to sound more like the weather prognosticator who talks about a chance of showers. Use the vernacular or the gambler running the odds. Think in terms of a Probability Line [Figure 1.4] and choose your words accordingly.

Follow the lead of doctors who talk about relative health risks. And then, draw them into the supposition process.

> Doesn't that seem logical?
>
> Does that meet or challenge your thoughts?
>
> Do you think it means this or that?

It shouldn't take long to get them to see you as an advisor and not a report writer.

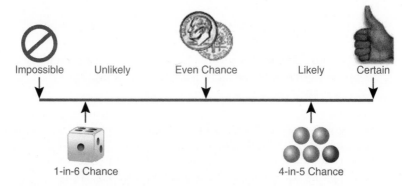

Figure 1.4 The spectrum of probability (Math Is Fun[31])

6. Become a Change Agent

The very best way to win the hearts and minds of those who can benefit the most by your flair for data discovery is to educate them.

The more people in your organization who understand the ways and means of data exploration as well as the associate risks and rewards, the more they will come to you for answers, include you in planning sessions and support your calls for more data, people and tools.

Start by inviting them to lunch. Ask them to bring their best questions about The Data. Encourage those who would rather not be seen as ill-informed to submit their questions in advance. Prepare a handful of questions that you wish they would ask.

Answer their questions. Show them examples of quick-wins enjoyed by other projects in other departments. Share case studies from vendors about successes at other companies.

Engage your audience in the excitement of the chase with a simple data set and a common challenge. If you can teach them how to ask great questions by example and by exercise then you can change how they approach data—to see it as a tool instead of an accusation.

And be sure to feed them. This is a case where a free lunch will pay off handsomely.

Your Job as Translator

You know your data inside and out, but the consumers of your insights, who must depend on your recommendations do not. To them, your data is as readable as a crystal ball or a sequence of Tarot cards. That means they are putting their trust in you.

Therefore, your responsibility is to inform without confusing, to encourage without mystifying and to reassure without resorting to sleight of hand. Entice and enthrall your Truth Seekers with The Data and The Correlations, but make sure your confidence levels are high and be prepared to show your work.

Conclusion

Successful data discovery requires good tools (technology) and trustworthy raw material (clean data), but depends on the creativity of the data detective. The best analyst has the ability to manipulate data in a variety of ways to tease out relevant insights. With the goals of the organization firmly in mind, top analysts engage the data in a conversation of What-Ifs, resulting in tangible insights that can be used to make decisions by those in charge. The analyst, as consulting detective, becomes indispensable.

NOTES

1. Self-Service Data Discovery and Visualization Application, Sense BI Tool | Qlik, available at http://www.qlik.com/us/explore/products/sense, last accessed on 3/13/15.

2. Data Discovery | Tableau Software, available at http://www.tableau.com/solutions/data-discovery, last accessed on 3/13/15.

3. Features of the Analytics Platform | MicroStrategy, available at http://www.microstrategy.com/us/analytics/features, last accessed on 3/13/15.

4. Data Visualization and Discovery for Better Business Decisions, available at http://www.adaptiveinsights.com/uploads/news/id421/tdwi_data_visualization_discovery_better_business_decisions_adaptive_insights.pdf, last accessed on 3/13/15.

5. A.Word.A.Day—homologous, available at http://wordsmith.org/words/homologous.html, last accessed 3/13/15.

6. Human Behavior: An Inventory of Scientific Findings, available at http://home.uchicago.edu/aabbott/barbpapers/barbhuman.pdf, last accessed 3/13/15.

7. Allergy in Children in Hand Versus Machine Dishwashing, available at http://pediatrics.aappublications.org/content/early/2015/02/17/peds.2014-2968.full.pdf, last accessed 3/13/115.

Variety of Data Is the Spice of Life

Machine learning differs from data diving. It is like putting tens of thousands of statisticians in a black box and throwing in a question. They will scour through the data in different ways, confer, and then pop out an answer along with their degree of confidence. Next, they will test their answer against some fresh information and adjust their opinion. The more data you let them look at, and the more they cycle their assumptions against real-world results, the better.

With the price of storage in a downward spiral to almost nothing and the speed of processing continuing to increase thanks to parallel processing in the cloud, we can crunch through a great deal more information than ever. Machine learning is good with lots of data, but it *really* goes to town when it has lots of different types of data to play with. It can find correlations between attributes humans wouldn't even consider comparing. If there is a relationship among the weather, the color of socks a prospect is wearing, and what the prospect had for lunch, then marketers can leverage that correlation. It doesn't matter if the correlation is logical or even understandable, it only matters that it is actionable.

In addition to all the digital interaction data that drove the whole Big-Data-Hadoop-Clusters-in-the-Cloud movement, now there's even *more* data to chew on out there.

Open Data

Hundreds of organizations, both governmental and NGOs, are publishing a shockingly large amount of data that might be useful in finding your next customer. Just think about all the APIs (application program interfaces) that allow you to grab onto firehoses like Facebook and Twitter. Facebook Likes alone can predict quite a bit about you as an individual, according to a paper from the Psychometrics Centre, University of Cambridge.[32] "Facebook Likes, can be used to automatically and accurately predict a range of highly sensitive personal attributes, including: sexual orientation, ethnicity, religious and political views, personality traits, intelligence, happiness, use of addictive substances, parental separation, age, and gender."

Think about all the recipes you can get from Campbell's Soup:[33]

> The Campbell's Kitchen API was developed to share information from Campbell's Kitchen. This information includes thousands of recipes using brands like Campbell's®, Swanson®, Pace®, Prego®, & Pepperidge Farm®—brands people love, trust, and use every day. The easier people can find those recipes, the less time they have to spend worrying about what to make for dinner.

We hope you will use this information to develop smart and simple ways to help people get the dinner and entertaining ideas they're looking for.

GET ACCESS TO:

- Thousands of proven family favorite recipes
- Extensive recipe filtering by key ingredients, product UPC, keywords and more
- Professional food photography
- Reader-generated recipe reviews & comments
- Recipe search results through superior tagging
- Well-known food brands people know and trust

SO MANY POSSIBILITIES:

Enhance websites with related recipes & delicious looking photographs

Create food-related apps (for websites and the latest and greatest devices and toys) and helpful shopping and cooking tools

Augment social media sites like Facebook, Twitter, & Google+

Raise visibility for your brand

Drive more traffic to your site and gain new readers from a wider audience

The sky's the limit

Imagine cross-referencing the people who comment on recipes with their social media accounts to target people by flavor preferences. But that's just the tip of the iceberg. Google hosts a growing number of data sets that are directly accessible through its BigQuery utility.[34]

BigQuery is a fully managed data warehouse and analytics platform. The public datasets listed on this page are available for you to analyze using SQL queries. You can access BigQuery public data sets using the web UI, the command-line tool, or by making calls to the BigQuery REST API using a variety of client libraries such as Java, .NET, or Python.

The first terabyte of data processed per month is free, so you can start querying datasets without enabling billing. To get started running some sample queries, select or create a project and then run the example queries on the NOAA GSOD weather dataset.

GDELT Book Corpus
A dataset that contains 3.5 million digitized books stretching back two centuries, encompassing the complete English-language public domain collections of the Internet Archive (1.3 M volumes) and HathiTrust (2.2 million volumes).

GitHub Data
This public dataset contains GitHub activity data for more than 2.8 million open source GitHub repositories, more than 145 million unique commits, over 2 billion different file paths, and the contents of the latest revision for 163 million files.

Hacker News
A dataset that contains all stories and comments from Hacker News since its launch in 2006.

IRS Form 990 Data
A dataset that contains financial information about non-profit/exempt organizations in the United States, gathered by the Internal Revenue Service (IRS) using Form 990.

Medicare Data
This public dataset summarizes the utilization and payments for procedures, services, and prescription drugs provided to Medicare beneficiaries by specific inpatient and outpatient hospitals, physicians, and other suppliers.

Major League Baseball Data
This public dataset contains pitch-by-pitch activity data for Major League Baseball (MLB) in 2016.

NOAA GHCN
This public dataset was created by the National Oceanic and Atmospheric Administration (NOAA) and includes climate summaries from land surface stations across the globe that have been subjected to a common suite of quality assurance reviews. This dataset draws from more

than 20 sources, including some data from every year since 1763.

NOAA GSOD
This public dataset was created by the National Oceanic and Atmospheric Administration (NOAA) and includes global data obtained from the USAF Climatology Center. This dataset covers GSOD data between 1929 and 2016, collected from over 9000 stations.

NYC 311 Service Requests
This public data includes all 311 service requests from 2010 to the present, and is updated daily. 311 is a non-emergency number that provides access to non-emergency municipal services.

NYC Citi Bike Trips
Data collected by the NYC Citi Bike bicycle sharing program, that includes trip records for 10,000 bikes and 600 stations across Manhattan, Brooklyn, Queens, and Jersey City since Citi Bike launched in September 2013.

NYC TLC Trips
Data collected by the NYC Taxi and Limousine Commission (TLC) that includes trip records from all trips completed in yellow and green taxis in NYC from 2009 to 2015.

NYPD Motor Vehicle Collisions
This dataset includes details of Motor Vehicle Collisions in New York City provided by the Police Department (NYPD) from 2012 to the present.

Open Images Data
This public dataset contains approximately 9 million URLs and metadata for images that have been annotated with labels spanning more than 6,000 categories.

Stack Overflow Data
This public dataset contains an archive of Stack Overflow content, including posts, votes, tags, and badges.

USA Disease Surveillance
A dataset published by the U.S. Department of Health and Human Services that includes all weekly surveillance reports of nationally notifiable diseases for all U.S. cities and states published between 1888 and 2013.

USA Names
A Social Security Administration dataset that contains all names from Social Security card applications for births that occurred in the United States after 1879.

In its top-20 list of the best free data sources available online, Data Science Central includes:[35]

1. Data.gov.uk, the UK government's open data portal including the British National Bibliography—metadata on all UK books and publications since 1950.
2. Data.gov. Search through 194,832 USA data sets about topics ranging from education to Agriculture.
3. US Census Bureau latest population, behaviour and economic data in the USA.
4. Socrata—software provider that works with governments to provide open data to the public, it also has its own open data network to explore.
5. European Union Open Data Portal—thousands of datasets about a broad range of topics in the European Union.
6. DBpedia, crowdsourced community trying to create a public database of all Wikipedia entries.
7. The New York Times—a searchable archive of all *New York Times* articles from 1851 to today.
8. Dataportals.org, datasets from all around the world collected in one place.
9. The World Factbook information prepared by the CIA about, what seems like, all of the countries of the world.
10. NHS Health and Social Care Information Centre datasets from the UK National Health Service.
11. Healthdata.gov, detailed USA healthcare data covering loads of health-related topics.
12. UNICEF statistics about the situation of children and women around the world.
13. World Health organisation statistics concerning nutrition, disease and health.
14. Amazon web services' large repository of interesting datasets including the human genome project, NASA's database and an index of 5 billion web pages.

15. Google Public data explorer search through already mentioned and lesser known open data repositories.

16. Gapminder, a collection of datasets from the World Health Organisation and World Bank covering economic, medical and social statistics.

17. Google Trends analyse the shift of searches throughout the years.

18. Google Finance, real-time finance data that goes back as far as 40 years.

19. UCI Machine Learning Repository, a collection of databases for the Machine Learning community.

20. National Climatic Data Center, world largest archive of climate data.

While all of the above is far too much for humans to sift through, machines might be able to find a useful, and potentially profitable, correlation. One Oracle blog post[36] included this about Red Roof Inn:

> Marketers for the hotel chain took advantage of open data about weather conditions, flight cancellations and customers' locations to offer last-minute hotel deals to stranded travelers. They used the information to develop an algorithm that considered various travel conditions to determine the opportune time to message customers about nearby hotel availability and rates.

Might information on Iowa liquor sales be useful? "This dataset contains the spirits purchase information of Iowa Class 'E' liquor licensees by product and date of purchase from January 1, 2014, to current. The dataset can be used to analyze total spirits sales in Iowa of individual products at the store level."[37]

And don't look now, but here comes the Internet of Things and the unbelievable amounts and types of data that will come spilling out.

The same can be said for exhaust data. That's information that's a byproduct of some action, reaction, or transaction. Walking through a shopping center throws off lots of exhaust information about where you are. How often you respond to text messages, where you take pictures, and whether you speed up at yellow stop lights is reactive. Whether stocks trade more when the market goes up or down is transaction-oriented.

There are, of course, companies that offer a conglomeration of the above as a service. Second Measure sells insights derived from credit card transactions so you can "spot inflections in businesses as they happen, identify this week's fastest-growing companies [and] see the latest KPIs (Key Performance Indicators) before they're announced."

Mattermark monitors marketplace KPIs such as companies' net revenue, gross margin, growth, market share, liquidity, average order value, Net Promoter Score, retention, cost per customer acquisition, marketing channel mix, overall ROI, and cash burn rate. This is a whole new data set for B2B sales and competitive intelligence.

The combination of all of the available data with the power of machine learning is cause for excitement and competitive advantage. (See Figure 1.5.)

Data for Sale

Upon this gifted age, in its dark hour,

Rains from the sky a meteoric shower

Of facts. . . . They lie unquestioned, uncombined.

Wisdom enough to leech us of our ill

Is daily spun, but there exists no loom

To weave it into fabric. . . .

Edna St. Vincent Millay from Sonnet 137, Huntsman, What Quarry?

In an ideal world, the machine collects all the data there is and weaves it into a tapestry that makes all things clear at a glance. The data aggregation industry has been active for years, starting with the Census Bureau 115 years ago. Since then, it's become a big business.

The amount of available information is enormous from public records and criminal databases to credit rating firms and credit card companies to public companies like Dun & Bradstreet and Acxiom, which claims to have more than 32 billion records. That's the sort of aggregator that powers most direct mail and telemarketers.

Acxiom's extensive third-party data offers rich insight into consumers and their behaviors:

Curated from multiple, reliable sources

Includes more than 1,000 customer traits and basic information including, location, age, and household details

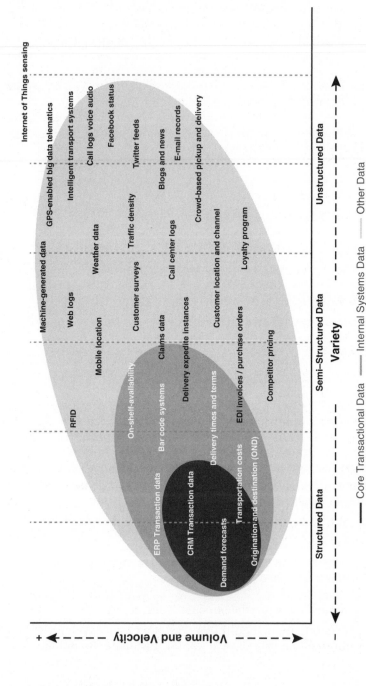

Figure 1.5 So many types of data, so little time[38]

Provides more than 3,500 specific behavioral insights, such as propensity to make a purchase

Offers real insights into a broad spectrum of offline behavior, not just indicators from web browsing behavior

Gives analysts more ways to segment data and use for audience modeling

Acxiom data fuels highly personalized data-driven campaigns, enabling you to:

Personalize messages and consistently engage audiences across all channels

Incorporate both online and offline data in a safe, privacy-compliant way

Segment audiences at the household or individual level based on a variety of options from ethnicity and acculturation to digital behaviors

Optimize for scale and accuracy

Request audience recommendations from seasoned data experts[39]

But Wait—There's More

The volume and variety of data seems to have no end.

- The weather (http://www.ncdc.noaa.gov/)
- U.S. Census data (http://dataferrett.census.gov/)
- Japan Census Data (https://aws.amazon.com/datasets/Economics/2285)
- Health and retirement study (http://www.rand.org/labor/aging/dataprod/hrs-data.html)
- Federal Reserve economic data (https://aws.amazon.com/datasets/Economics/2443)
- The entire Internet for the past seven years (http://commoncrawl.org/)
- 125 years of public health data (http://www.bigdatanews.com/group/bdn-daily-press-releases/forum/topics/pitt-unlocks-125-years-of-public-health-data-to-help-fight-contag)

- Consumer complaints about financial products and services (http://catalog.data.gov/dataset/consumer-complaint-database)

- Product safety recalls from the Consumer Product Safety Commission (http://www.cpsc.gov/Newsroom/News-Releases/2010/CPSC-Makes-Recall-Data-Available-Electronically-to-Businesses-3rd-Party-Developers/)

- Franchise failures by brand (https://opendata.socrata.com/Business/Franchise-Failureby-Brand2011/5qh7-7usu)

- Top 30 earning websites (https://opendata.socrata.com/Business/Top-30-earning-websites/rwft-hd5j)

- Car sales data (https://opendata.socrata.com/Business/Car-Sales-Data/da8m-smts)

- Yahoo! Search Marketing Advertiser bidding data (http://webscope.sandbox.yahoo.com/catalog.php?datatype=a)

- American time use survey (http://www.bls.gov/tus/tables.htm)

- Global entrepreneurship monitor (http://www.gemconsortium.org/Data)

- Wage Statistics for the U.S. (http://www.bls.gov/bls/blswage.htm)

- City of Chicago building permits from 2006 to the present (https://data.cityofchicago.org/Buildings/Building-Permits/ydr8-5enu)

- Age, race, income, commute time to work, home value, veteran status (http://catalog.data.gov/dataset/american-community-survey)

Or how about all of Wikipedia?

- (http://en.wikipedia.org/wiki/Wikipedia:Database_download)

A Collaboration of Datasets

After three years as a systems analyst at Deloitte, Brett Hurt started one of the first web analytics companies (Coremetrics later sold to IBM), and an online reviews and ratings company (Bazaarvoice) has turned his attention to the world of data.

His current startup is data.world, a B-Corp (Public Benefit Corporation) intent on building a collaborative data resource. From the outset, according to John Battelle,[40] "Hurt & co. may well have unleashed a blast of magic into the world."

The problem they are out to solve is allowing data to be visible. Rather than data shoved into its own database silo, hidden away from all other data, as we experience it now, data.world seeks to unlock that data and make it discoverable, just as the World Wide Web has brought links between research papers and marketing materials and blog posts.

> One consistently formatted master repository, with social and sharing built in. Once researchers upload their data, they can annotate it, write scripts to manipulate it, combine it with other data sets, and most importantly, they can share it (they can also have private data sets). Cognizant of the social capital which drives sites like GitHub, LinkedIn, and Quora, data.world has profiles, ratings, and other "social proofs" that encourage researchers to share and add value to each others' work.

> In short, data.world makes data discoverable, interoperable, and social. And that could mean an explosion of data-driven insights is at hand.

For artificial intelligence to really flex its muscles, it must have a *lot* of data to chew on; data.world feels like a step in the right direction to join up the massive amounts of data that's out there, for the use of all comers.

A Customer Data Taxonomy

The breadth of available data is overwhelming (social media graphs, Facebook Likes, tweets, auto registration, voting records, etc.). It's helpful to have a taxonomy at hand.

Types of Collectible Information

The wide variety of data is expanding at a phenomenal rate. Here is an indicative but not exhaustive list of data sets shoved into categorization cubbyholes through sheer blunt force.

Identity
Can we identify them? Who are they?

- Name
- Gender

- Age
- Race
- Address
- Phone
- Fingerprint
- Heart rate
- Weight
- Device
- Government ID
- And so on

History

What's in their past? What have they done or achieved?

- Education
- Career
- Criminal record
- Press exposure
- Publications
- Awards
- Association memberships
- Credit score
- Legal matters
- Loans
- Divorce
- Where they have traveled
- And so on

Proclivities

What attracts them? Are they liberal or conservative? What do they like?

- Preferences
- Settings
- Avocations
- Political party
- Social groups

- Social "Likes"
- Entertainment
- Hobbies
- News feeds
- Browser history
- Brand affinity
- And so on

Possessions
What do they have, whether purchased, acquired, found, or made?

- Income
- Home
- Cars
- Devices
- Clothing
- Jewelry
- Investments
- Subscriptions
- Memberships
- Collections
- Relationships
- And so on

Activities
Can we catch them in the act? What do they do and how do they do it?

- Keystrokes
- Gestures
- Eye tracking
- Day part
- Location
- IP address
- Social posts
- Dining out
- Television viewing

■ Heart rate over time

■ And so on

Beliefs
How do they feel and where do they stand on issues?

■ Religion

■ Values

■ Donations

■ Political party

■ Skepticism/Altruism

■ Introvert/Extrovert

■ Generous/Miserly

■ Adaptive/Inflexible

■ Aggressive/Passive

■ Opinion

■ Mood

■ And so on

Methods of Data Capture

All of the above comes to light in a variety of ways. The data scientist will be more responsible as time goes on—and legislation crops up—to know whether an individual data element was collected with full consent. The future will also require recording whether that consent was given in perpetuity or only for the purpose initially stated.

Here, then, are suggested categories of data capture, based on "The Origins of Personal Data and Its Implications for Governance" by Martin Abrams,[41] which included a taxonomy based on origin.

Provided
Individuals are highly aware when they are providing information. They might *initiate* the delivery of the information when filling out an application, registering to vote or registering a product for warranty, or acquiring a public license to drive, marry, or carry a gun.

The *transactional* provision of data happens any time people use a credit card. They are clearly and knowingly identifying themselves. Paying a bill by writing a check qualifies as well, as does answering surveys, registering for a school, or participating in a court proceeding. This would also pertain to filling in one of those online quizzes (Which *Star Wars* Character are *You*?).

Individuals are also said to be providing information when they post it publicly. That may be delivering a speech in public, writing a letter to the editor for publication, or posting something online in a social network. *Posting* happens when you announce to all of your Facebook friends that you are, indeed, Han Solo.

Observed

Information can be casually observed. The Internet is an ideal place for observation as every click is recorded. People forget that their phone is always listening to them in case they wish to summon "Hey Siri" or "OK Google" by voice.

Browser cookies and loyalty cards are examples of *engaged* observations. People go to a website intentionally. They have their grocery store card scanned on purpose. They know they're doing it, but they're not thinking in terms of that action being revealing. They may choose to refuse to use their membership card or surf incognito, but they trade off convenience and discounts.

An *unanticipated* collection of data surprises people for an instant, and then they realize that they knew there were sensors and conclude they probably knew data was being gathered. You know your car can talk to the cloud to get navigation map updates and to call for roadside assistance. But you might not have read the manual where it talks about collecting information on engine temperature and tire pressure as well.

The *passive* collection of data is where things start to border on creepy. People don't expect to have their picture taken by a traffic camera and then dropped into a database. They don't expect their movements to be recorded as they walk around a department store. There is no expectation of privacy, but the first time you become aware that it's happening, you feel a little queasy. After that, it becomes the new normal.

Derived

Now that the raw material has been scooped up, it's time to start massaging it. The amount of time you spend on one page or another is *computationally* derived. We subtract the time you arrive from the time you leave, and *voilá*, time-on-page. This information must be calculated. How often do you search for gaming laptops? How much do you usually buy on this site? How often do you return?

The result of each of these calculations is another data point that can be associated with an individual, but there's no way for that person to know such provided and observed data is being manipulated.

Data about you can be *notionally derived* by assigning you to a given category like lookie-loo versus serious buyer or soccer-mom versus single mother. This sort of classification is also invisible to the individual being labeled.

Play your cards right and that merchant may decide you are a prime candidate for a super-discount-member category. Finding yourself misclassified can be surprising, annoying, or cause for arrest in the wrong database.

Inferred

Data that is created through inference has taken computational data a step further into analytical evaluation.

Statistically inferred data determines whether you get a call while on vacation asking if that's really *you* checking into that hotel. Your FICO score is the statistical result of comparing you to others.

Take statistics to their logical extreme and you have *advanced analytical* data. Big data and AI are hard at work to correlate all of the above to come to a supposition about the prospect or customer. How likely are you to be who you say you are? How likely are you to default on a loan? Contract a disease? Recommend this book to your friends?

The result of each of these data collection and derivation methods is—more data. Martin Abrams posits that data supplied by individuals will remain about the same as you only need a finite number of driving or wedding licenses, even while uploading photos becomes more popular. However, observed data will enjoy healthy growth as more sensors are born into the Internet of Things. Abrams sees derived data losing ground as inferred data becomes more popular.

That brings us back to AI and machine learning. "Inferred data will accelerate as more and more organizations, both public and private, increasingly take advantage of broader data sets, more computing power, and better mathematical processes," says Abrams. "The bottom-line is that data begets more data."

Marketing Data Trustworthiness

Data is a wonderful thing—especially digital data because it's binary. It's either ones or zeros and crystal clear. While we'd all like to believe that's true, only those who don't know data at all would fall for that.

So Much Data, So Little Trust

One of the more difficult aspects of marketing data is its uneven fidelity. Transactions are dependable. A sale was made at a given time to a given person at a given price—all rather solid. On the far end of the spectrum, social media sentiment is almost guesswork.

The conundrum comes when marketing professionals are asked to rank the relative reliability of various data sets; their minimal knowledge of the data stands in their way.

When multiple metrics are combined to form an index, the variable trustworthiness of the variables is completely hidden. The solution to this dilemma lies in data scientists working closely with marketers to properly weight the variety of data elements that go into the soup.

So Much Data, So Little Connection

Matthew Tod of D4t4 Solutions Plc tells a story of trying to fit online data to offline data that starts *after* the struggle to line up the two is over.[42]

> I was working with a retailer with standard, online behavioral data from a tag-based, log file system tracking sessions. Fortunately for me, they had linked them to email addresses so I have a key to join sessions to email addresses. They started issuing e-receipts. You go into the store, you buy the stuff, they email you a receipt. But only about 35% of their in-store transactions warrant a receipt, any receipt, but that 35% of transaction accounts for 90% of sales revenue because people only want a receipt for insurance purposes, or for returning a product, so for the valuable stuff. For the little stuff, nobody is going to ask for an e-receipt.

> So, I end up with a data set roughly 80 million sessions on the website, a million email addresses and 55 million rows of transactional data. I bring all of that together in order to answer the question, "What is the impact of Google on my physical store sales?"

> Because I now have a link from store sale to session, and via campaign back to Google with 300,000 people, I could say, matthew.tod@gmail.com went into our Wimbledon store on Saturday. Funny enough, I noticed he was on our website on Thursday for 45 minutes, researching products.

> Obviously, my digital analytics regard that as an abandoned basket—fail—low conversion rate and my in-store manager goes, "Gosh, he is a great guy, he came in and spent five hundred quid! Love him to bits!"

We could show, in this particular instance, that for every Pound of sales the website thought they made, we could see two Pounds in-store. That was the end of the official project with the start of the science project. That's when we started playing with machine learning.

Even with the most reliable data, getting it all to make sense is still troubling.

ARE WE REALLY CALCULABLE?

While the individual man is an insoluble puzzle, in the aggregate he becomes a mathematical certainty.

Sherlock Holmes, The Sign of Four

On the BBC show *Sherlock*, Mary asked how Sherlock Holmes had managed to find her and the flash drive she was carrying around when, "Every movement I made was entirely random, every new personality just on the roll of a dice!" Sherlock replied:

Mary, no human action is ever truly random. An advanced grasp of the mathematics of probability, mapped onto a thorough apprehension of human psychology and the known dispositions of any given individual, can reduce the number of variables considerably. I myself know of at least 58 techniques to refine a seemingly infinite array of randomly generated possibilities down to the smallest number of feasible variables.

After a brief pause, he admitted, "But they're really difficult, so instead I just stuck a tracer on the inside of the memory stick."[43]

This, then, is our task: to use the big data and machine learning tools we have at hand to see if we can't build a better, more useful model of individual, human probabilities in order to send the right message to the right person at the right time on the right device. Sherlock is right; it is difficult.

So, now you understand the *idea* of machine learning. You know just enough to hold your own at a cocktail party. You can nod knowingly should the topic pop up and can comfortably converse with senior management about the possibilities.

The next chapter is intended to go one level deeper. You will *not* become a data scientist by careful study of Chapter 2, but you *will* be able to hold your own at a meeting on machine learning. You can nod knowingly should the subject matter get deeper and will be able to comfortably converse with data scientists about the possibilities.

NOTES

1. "Improving Our Ability to Improve," http://www.almaden.ibm.com/coevolution/ pdf/engelbart_paper.pdf.

2. "How to Get the Best Deep Learning Education for Free," http://www.topbots.com/ artificial-intelligence-deep-learning-education-free.

3. "24 Uses of Statistical Modeling (Part II)," http://www.datasciencecentral.com/ profiles/blogs/24-uses-of-statistical-modeling-part-ii.

4. "The Discipline of Machine Learning," http://www.cs.cmu.edu/~tom/pubs/ MachineLearning.pdf.

5. http://www.mckinsey.com/business-functions/mckinsey-analytics/our-insights/ the-age-of-analytics-competing-in-a-data-driven-world.

6. Source: http://www.mckinsey.com/business-functions/mckinsey-analytics/our-insights/the-age-of-analytics-competing-in-a-data-driven-world.

7. Source: Personal interview.

8. "The History of Artificial Intelligence," http://courses.cs.washington.edu/courses/ csep590/06au/projects/history-ai.pdf.

9. "An Executive's Guide to Cognitive Computing," http://www.sas.com/en_us/ insights/articles/big-data/executives-guide-to-cognitive-computing.html.

10. "DeepStack: Expert-Level Artificial Intelligence in No-Limit Poker," https://arxiv .org/abs/1701.01724.

11. EU GDPR Portal, http://www.eugdpr.org.

12. "9 Artificial Intelligence Stats that Will Blow You Away," http://www.foxbusiness .com/markets/2016/12/10/artificial-intelligence-stats-that-will-blow-away.html.

13. "Preparing for the Future of Artificial Intelligence," https://www.whitehouse .gov/sites/default/files/whitehouse_files/microsites/ostp/NSTC/preparing_for_the_ future_of_ai.pdf.

14. https://obamawhitehouse.archives.gov/sites/default/files/whitehouse_files/ microsites/ostp/NSTC/preparing_for_the_future_of_ai.pdf.

15. "Machine Learning Will Revolutionize Market Segmentation Practices," January 2017, http://www.idgconnect.com/view_abstract/41712/machine-learning-will-revolutionize-market-segmentation-practices.

16. http://www.bbc.com/news/technology-30290540.

17. "Benefits & Risks of Artificial Intelligence," http://futureoflife.org/background/ benefits-risks-of-artificial-intelligence/.

18. "The AI Revolution: Our Immortality or Extinction," http://waitbutwhy.com/2015/ 01/artificial-intelligence-revolution-2.html.

19. "Autonomous Weapons: An Open Letter from AI & Robotics Researchers," http:// futureoflife.org/open-letter-autonomous-weapons.

20. https://openai.com/about.

21. "Safely Interruptible Agents," http://intelligence.org/files/Interruptibility.pdf.

22. Partnership on Artificial Intelligence to Benefit People and Society, https://www.partnershiponai.org/.

23. The Partnership on AI's stated tenets, https://www.partnershiponai.org/tenets.

24. *Wall Street Journal*, http://www.wsj.com/articles/the-worlds-largest-hedge-fund-is-building-an-algorithmic-model-of-its-founders-brain-1482423694.

25. *Guardian*, https://www.theguardian.com/technology/2017/jan/05/japanese-company-replaces-office-workers-artificial-intelligence-ai-fukoku-mutual-life-insurance?CMP=Share_iOSApp_Other.

26. "Will a Robot Take Your Job?" http://www.bbc.com/news/technology-34066941.

27. "A Future That Works: Automation, Employment, and Productivity," http://www.mckinsey.com/global-themes/digital-disruption/harnessing-automation-for-a-future-that-works.

28. Source: Personal interview.

29. "Probabilistic Noise Identification and Data Cleaning," http://citeseerx.ist.psu.edu/viewdoc/download?doi=10.1.1.71.4154&rep=rep1&type=pdf.

30. Originally published in *Applied Marketing Analytics Journal*, Vol. 1, No. 3, reproduced with permission from Henry Stewart Publications LLP, https://www.henrystewartpublications.com/ama/v1.

31. "Math Is Fun," https://www.mathsisfun.com/probability_line.html.

32. "Private Traits and Attributes Are Predictable from Digital Records of Human Behavior," http://www.pnas.org/content/110/15/5802.full.pdf.

33. Campbell Soup API Developer Portal, https://developer.campbellkitchen.com.

34. Google Big Query datasets, https://cloud.google.com/bigquery/public-data/.

35. Data Science Central, "Top 20 Open Data Sources," http://www.datasciencecentral.com/profiles/blogs/top-20-open-data-sources.

36. "How 4 Companies Find and Create Value from Open Data," https://blogs.oracle.com/marketingcloud/create-value-from-open-data.

37. Iowa Liquor Sales, https://www.reddit.com/r/bigquery/comments/37fcm6/iowa_liquor_sales_dataset_879mb_3million_rows.

38. "Big Data Analytics in Supply Chain Management: Trends and Related Research," https://www.researchgate.net/publication/270506965_Big_Data_Analytics_in_Supply_Chain_Management_Trends_and_Related_Research.

39. "Why Acxiom Data?" http://www.acxiom.com/data-solutions/.

40. https://shift.newco.co/as-we-may-think-data-world-lays-the-traceroutes-for-a-data-revolution-b4b751f295d9.

41. "The Origins of Personal Data and Its Implications for Governance," http://informationaccountability.org/wp-content/uploads/Data-Origins-Abrams.pdf.

42. Source: Personal interview.

43. http://www.bbc.co.uk/programmes/b0881dgp.

CHAPTER **2**

Introduction to Machine Learning

Artificial intelligence and machine learning are creating new cognitive tools that enhance our ability to think at scale and that capacity will produce rewards for every person on the planet.

Vint Cerf, Chief Internet Evangelist Google, one of the Fathers of the Internet

THREE REASONS DATA SCIENTISTS SHOULD READ THIS CHAPTER

If you are a data scientist, there are three solid reasons to read this chapter.

First is to let me know if there is something else you would like marketing professionals to know. That will be very helpful in later editions and render me eternally grateful to you.

Next, you should read this chapter to understand just how much marketing people will know once *they* have read it so you don't have to plow through the basics *again*. If you come across a marketing person you haven't worked with before and it seems he or she really doesn't quite get it, share a copy of this book.

Third, you will understand just how much (or how little) a marketing person *cares* about the fine details of how the analytical sausage is made. You'll be able to have a meaningful conversation with marketing professionals, knowing the proper level of language to use around them without their eyes glazing over or their phone suddenly becoming the most important thing in the universe.

EVERY REASON MARKETING PROFESSIONALS SHOULD READ THIS CHAPTER

If you're *in* marketing, this chapter provides the glossary, the explanation, and the translation you need to be on the other side of that meaningful conversation. This may well be the chapter that you skim and then go back to over time, rather than learn and internalize.

For you, this is a brief peek behind the curtain. To create a killer brochure, you don't need to understand ink dye sublimation onto paper, but you really should know the difference between aqueous coating and UV coating as well as varnish, lamination, spot coating, foil stamping, embossing, and letterpress, and why you might want to spend more for one over the other. *How* those things are accomplished is not your problem. What do they cost and what are the results? That would be your job.

WE THINK WE'RE SO SMART

Pattern recognition is child's play—even for a child. Why is it so impressive in a machine? Let's look at speed, reliability, and unemotional decision making.

Humans evolved to notice movement (will it eat me?) and differentiate between subtle shades of color (can I eat it?). We can see when something is not quite right and take precautions against harm. We can see if something's missing. We're proud of our abilities to infer and deduce, but computers can do all of the above tirelessly and endlessly, and get better along the way.

Professional marketers make decisions based on years of experience. They also make decisions based on hunger, anger, envy, and politics. Sometimes, they're just tired or overwrought.

A 2014 paper from the MIT Media Lab[1] compared humans to machines in the task of choosing people most likely to convert into mobile Internet users. Not only did the machine choose better, it chose *better* customers. The machine-selected customers had a 13-times-better conversion rate compared to those selected using best practices marketing techniques. Further, 98 percent of the machine-selected converted customers renewed their mobile

Internet packages after the campaign, compared to 37 percent in the human-selected group.

We should not turn all of our decision making over to the machines, but we should understand the power—and the shortcomings—of these new tools as we continue in the ongoing race between the amount of data we have and the number of conjectures we can derive from that data.

If all we know is age and gender (males 18–34), then our options are limited. But as we add new attributes (location, brand affinities, social media connections, website interactions, Facebook posts, store visits, education level, vehicle type, political party, latest tweets), we face millions of possible hypotheses.

The more data we have, the more hypotheses we can test. The more tests we make, the higher the odds that our next marketing action will yield better results. Since that's beyond our abilities, it's time to call in the machines.

DEFINE YOUR TERMS

You'll recall Tom Mitchell saying, "The field of Machine Learning seeks to answer the questions, 'How can we build computer systems that automatically improve with experience, and what are the fundamental laws that govern all learning processes?'" In his "The Discipline of Machine Learning,"[2] Mitchell offers a logical approach to differentiating machine learning from computer science and statistics.

The defining questions of computer science are: How can we manually program computers to perform specific functions and solve problems, and which problems are inherently intractable?

The questions that largely define statistics are: What can we infer from historical information to predict the future? What conclusions can be inferred from data?

The defining questions for machine learning are: How can we build systems that automatically improve with experience? Can we get computers to decide for themselves what computational architectures and algorithms are most effective for manipulating data to reach a specific outcome?

Let's start at 35,000 feet up with a simple definition by Aatash Shah,[3] who described statistical modeling as "a formalization of relationships between variables in the data in the form of mathematical equations," while machine learning is "an algorithm that can learn from data without relying on rules-based programming."

Statistics is about plotting out the points and connecting the dots. Machine learning is about figuring out if there are any dots, where they are, and how they are alike or different.

Matt Gershoff, co-founder of the online optimization platform company Conductrics, compares basic cruise control to self-driving cars as examples of where we might deploy either standard programming or machine learning. Cruise control only needs to speed up and slow down based on what the target speed is set to and how fast the car is currently going. That's all. If the car is going to hit something, then the driver has to use the brakes and the steering wheel to avoid a crash.

Unlike basic cruise control, which only needs sensor data about the car's speed, self-driving additionally requires the conversion of visual information from cameras into meaningful inputs that the autonomous driving program can use to manage speed, direction, and avoidance of potential obstacles (other cars, people, etc.).

Furthermore, the car can become "smarter" if given more information. If you introduce temperature and weather into the system, it can learn that cold and precipitation could result in ice, snow, and slush, requiring the vehicle to drive slower.

Whatever analogy you prefer, it all begins with models and all models are wrong.

ALL MODELS ARE WRONG

George Edward Pelham Box was a prolific author about all things statistical and is well known for his observation, "All models are wrong, but some are useful."

When I was four years old, my brother and I got a Lionel train set for Christmas. It was pure awesomeness. My father wanted to play with it with us and we loved that, too. We played with it for years and always brought it out just before Christmas. It fueled our imaginations. It was electric. It was detailed. It was a scale model. While you *could* really launch a helicopter from a flatbed car, you couldn't ride it. It was just a model. (See Figure 2.1.)

When I was nine years old, we went to the New York World's Fair and were dumbfounded by General Motors' Futurama exhibit with its Lunar Colony, Undersea City, and City of the Future. By the time I would be old enough to go places by myself, this stuff would have come true! In 1964, it was only an imagined place. It was just a model.

When I went to college, I gave serious thought to architecture. I liked the idea of designing something from scratch, something

Figure 2.1 Lionel Helicopter Car

permanent, something I could point at and say, "I made that." I had to admit that what I really wanted was to build those astounding, perfect, intricate, 3-D cardboard mockups of what the building would look like. They would have tiny trees and little cars and people the size of pencil erasers.

They would be elaborate and complex, and they would completely communicate a vision. They would spell out everything anybody needed to know about how I saw the future. They would be visually engrossing, but they would lack the information necessary to actually build the thing. You couldn't really open the doors and windows. It was just a model.

Accountants build accounting systems that show how money flows into, out of, and between businesses. Website builders rely on information architecture designers who create a map of how people might expect to find what they are looking for and accomplish a specific task.

Because (as David Weinberger likes to say) the world is messy, analog, and open to interpretation, these models only work well enough to get by. Using any software or website, we quickly come across circumstances that were not preconceived well enough to accommodate a certain situation. We realize it's not really the way the world works; it's just a model.

Where marketing meets big data meets artificial intelligence, there is an irrational expectation that we can collect enough information that it will auto-magically correlate the important bits and causality will drop out the bottom. We are never going to be able to build a detailed model that describes and then predicts what an individual will do. Even with all of the behavioral, transactional, and attitudinal data in the world, humans are just too messy, analog, and open to too many interpretations.

Even as we make progress predicting the movement of swarming insects, fish, and cancer cells, we can only hope to create an attribution algorithm that is suggestive and directional. We can only hope to create a model that helps us test theories. We can only hope to create a model that is useful.

For all the data we collect, for all of the data storage we fill, for all of the big data systems we cluster in the cloud and sprinkle with artificial intelligence, our constructs are not going to provide facts, unearth hard-and-fast rules, or give us ironclad assurance that our next step will result in specific returns on our investment.

They are only models. But some are useful.

USEFUL MODELS

You are able to navigate on Earth because you have a model of it in your head. That model includes locations like a map and a whole bunch of rules about how the world works. You work out these rules over time, and as your capability grows, you try to make sure your mental map keeps up.

A child spills his milk at dinner. His mental model includes the distance from himself to the glass, the degree to which he must open his hand, and the amount of attention he needs to pay to complete the action. That last one is a killer because the other two elements change over time. If the child is not careful, the milk spills once more and the crying commences.

You have a mental map in your head about your customers. Experience, reading, seminars, and stories from colleagues have given you an image of the marketplace you're addressing, the buying cycles you can count on, and the levels of engagement required to attract attention and convince a prospect to become a buyer. You have a feel for your competitors. You have a grasp of macroeconomics as well as the impact the weather has on sales.

You might disagree with your boss, your colleagues, or your agency about any and all of the above, but through conversation, persuasion, and perhaps, coercion (with a fair amount of political maneuvering and one-upmanship), a common vision is crafted from which campaign plans emerge.

The communal mental model of the above is updated by the results of those campaigns. You had a collective hypothesis, and you executed on it and reaped the rewards for better or worse. Then you try again. If you try a lot and fail every now and then, you learn and become better. If you fail a lot, eventually you are no longer invited to try, try again.

A mathematical model is one you can test repeatedly as dry runs. The spreadsheet is a testament to the game of What If. If we lower the price by *this* much, and that increases the sales by *this* much, will we make up for it in volume?

An Excel model can also help us with simple decision making when we assign weights to action and outcomes. You're often accosted by colleagues to do different types of work. How do you prioritize? Make a model. Score each task on a scale of 1 to 5 based on whether it is easy, cheap, fast, and has a significant impact. As you can see in Figure 2.2, Task A is easy and cheap and fast, but has a low impact. Still, it is *so* easy and cheap and fast that it scores the highest.

This prioritization model would be perfect if it weren't for real life. Real life dictates that Task E must be completed first because it came from your boss's boss. You'll have to do Task D before you do Task A because D came from somebody to whom you owe a favor. However, if you do Task D before you do Task B, you're likely to be late for your daughter's birthday party.

The model is not the object. The map is not the territory. It is only a representation. If it seems to fit, it's useful—for a while.

Complex models require a number of assumptions.

- Rain will lower sales.
- Launching a new product will cannibalize sales.
- Hiring new salespeople will increase sales.
- New products and new salespeople will increase costs.

Plug in your numbers, turn the crank, and see what the results might be.

But the weather changes, competitors shift strategies, the President of the United States tweets about your company, and your underlying assumptions get farther from reality by the minute.

◢	A	B	C	D	E	F
1		Task A	Task B	Task C	Task D	Task E
2	Easy	5	1	3	3	2
3	Cheap	5	2	4	2	4
4	Fast	5	1	3	5	5
5	Impact	2	5	4	5	2
6		17	9	14	15	13

Figure 2.2 A prioritization model in Excel

How do you know a model is going to be useful? Test it. Start with 12 months of data and build a model that accurately describes the first nine months. It'll take some tweaking, but eventually you have a calculation that's close enough. Next, run that model and see how close it comes to predicting the next three months. Is it way off? Then it's not useful. Try again. Is the new version better than a coin toss? It's useful—for a while.

TOO MUCH TO THINK ABOUT

They say 3 percent of the people use 5 to 6 percent of their brain

97 percent use 3 percent and the rest goes down the drain

I'll never know which one I am but I'll bet you my last dime

99 percent think with 3 percent 100 percent of the time

64 percent of all the world's statistics are made up right there on the spot

82.4 percent of people believe'em whether they're accurate statistics or not

I don't know what you believe but I do know there's no doubt

I need another double shot of something 90 proof

I got too much to think about

"Statistician's Blues," Todd Snider

You can get a lot of value out of a handful of variables, but the promise of big data and machine learning is that the more data and the more data types you have, the more the likely the machine can find something useful.

Using data set A, you plan to build a model that predicts Y as a function of X. Using a data set of current customers, you plan to build a model that predicts propensity to buy as a function of demographics or:

A People who have already bought your product

Y People who are most likely to be interested in your product

X Age, gender, and ZIP code

That's a model you've used for years, but it could be much better.

A People who have already bought your product

Y People who are most likely to be interested in your product

X Search terms typed into Google

That's a half-trillion-dollar idea (Google's recent market cap). There's something there worth pursuing. But what if you cranked it up a bit?

A People who have already bought your product

Y People who are most likely to be interested in your product

X The demographic and search data above, plus

- Direct interaction with your call center
- Direct interaction with your company website
- Direct interaction with your mobile app
- Direct interaction on the advertising ecosystem
- Direct interaction on websites that sell their data
- Data from aggregators: credit scores, shopping, etc.
- The weather
- The economic climate
- The price of tea in China

Wait! That's just too many variables to hold in your head at once. It's too much to think about. But you can ask the *machine* to review all the above and determine which attributes are the most predictive, and please use those to build a model for you. Better yet, you can ask the machine to review the models it has created and make a value judgment on which ones might be best.

In the *Harvard Business Review*,[4] Tom Davenport described a large, well-known technology and services vendor trying to build a model showing which executives among their client base had the highest propensity to purchase.

Using traditional human-crafted modeling, the company once employed 35 offshore statisticians to generate 150 propensity models a year. Then it hired a company called Modern Analytics that specializes in autonomous analytics, or what it calls the "Model Factory." Machine learning approaches quickly bumped the number of models up to 350 in the first year, 1,500 in the second, and now to about 5,000 models. The models use 5 trillion pieces of information to generate over 11 billion scores a month predicting a particular customer executive's propensity to buy particular products or respond to particular marketing approaches. 80,000 different tactics are recommended to help persuade customers to buy. Using traditional approaches to propensity modeling to yield this level of granularity would require thousands of human analysts if it were possible at all.

Davenport named Cisco Systems as an example of a firm that "went from doing tens of artisanal propensity models to tens of thousands of autonomously generated ones." Tens of thousands of autonomously generated models sounds very productive for a small group, but are those models any good?

All models are wrong; some are useful. How do we get the machine to create better models? We teach it some things and it learns some things on its own.

MACHINES ARE BIG BABIES

Machine learning happens in three ways: *supervised, unsupervised,* and by *reinforcement,* just like kids.

If you introduce your toddler to a kitten and say, "Kitty" a few (dozen) times, eventually, the child will repeat after you. Show the child another kitten and she will spontaneously say, "Kitty!" delighted that that thing has a name and that she knew it. Every time she comes across a cat, she will say, "Kitty!"

Then, one day, she'll come across a puppy and will, of course, say, "Kitty!" Now, she is in for a rude awakening. That's no cat; it's a dog. You correct her, and she spends a fair amount of time unsure whether that next one is a kitty or a doggie.

Pointing to the cat and telling her it's a kitty is *supervised learning.* You've given her an example and a label. Correcting her when she makes a mistake and praising her when she gets it right is *reinforcement learning.* Eventually, her confidence grows as she is corrected less and less and continues to be praised when right.

Unsupervised learning happens when the child is alone. She throws a toy and it bounces or it doesn't, and she learns something about the nature of balls as compared to stuffed animals. She eats a dandelion and discovers that it's bitter. She casually says something mean to another child and discovers words can hurt.

Bob Page took time off after running analytics at Yahoo!, then eBay, and then being product vice president at Hortonworks to revel in the joys of ensuring his genes would live on. His experience mirrors the above.

> I'd been watching my (then 20 month old) daughter pick up new concepts, and watching her generalize. It confused me at first when a woman walked by at the park and she would point and say "mama!" but I finally realized she meant "she's in the class of humans called mama" as opposed to "she's my mama." Now she applies the terms to a large range of things—this piece of broccoli is dada, this one is mama and this is baby. She saw a bee in our lavender and said "bee!" followed by "mama!" and I had to say yes it's a bee, but it might not be a mama. She thought about it for a second, and declared that the bee was dada. The whole process has been fascinating to observe.
>
> Trying to explain the concept of color to her without describing properties of light is really eye opening (haha), especially since there isn't just one "blue." It also had me thinking about how little our current AI systems really "know" anything, or can generalize from simple rules and relationships, vs. memorizing mountains of training (or historical) data to capture patterns that can be matched against "live" data.[5]

Like children, machines learn from data. Given lots of data and time, they get to be really good at some things.

WHERE MACHINES SHINE

Machine learning is *very* useful for high-cardinality and high-dimensionality problems. At this point, the data scientists are rolling their eyes at the simplicity of this description and the marketing professionals are rolling their eyes because I fell into a quagmire of jargon only useful for Buzzword Bingo.

Dear Data Scientist, please bear with me. Dear Marketing Professional, there are some terms you will need to know because data scientists will use them casually without realizing that words can obfuscate.

High Cardinality

Cardinality refers to the uniqueness of elements in a database column. Each row contains information about one person and the columns are attributes about that person (name, rank, serial number).

High cardinality is where, like e-mail and phone numbers, each entry is absolutely unique. Low cardinality is where one value can belong to many entries.

Everybody in the database has a unique e-mail address and a unique phone number. The column that shows what city they live in has moderate cardinality as there might be a lot of people in New York. There's very low cardinality in the column that notes whether they are dead or alive as there are only two choices unless one of the rows contains Schrödinger's cat.

High Dimensionality

Lots and lots of attributes about an individual would create a highly dimensional database. When we get beyond name, rank, and serial number, we start seeing data sets with hundreds and thousands of traits, characteristics, or actions relating to a prospective customer.

Machine learning comes into the picture because it can keep a multidimensional map of data in mind even when there are a thousand different things to remember and some of them can vary in type by the thousands.

What is a *multidimensional map*? A database of drivers is two-dimensional. For each row (driver's license number) you have columns including: name, address, data of birth, eye color, hair color, and so on. If you want to keep track of people as they change, you need a third dimension: time. Then you know when *they* moved to a new house, changed their hair color, or put on a few pounds. As more attributes are added to the data set, more dimensions are needed.

Gideon Lewis-Kraus described how machine learning tackles the problem of language interpretation with multiple dimensions.[6]

> When you summarize language . . . you essentially produce multidimensional maps of the distances, based on common usage, between one word and every single other word in the language. The machine is not "analyzing" the data the way that we might, with linguistic rules that identify some of them as nouns and others as verbs. Instead, it is shifting and twisting and warping the words around in the map.

In two dimensions, you cannot make this map useful. You want, for example, "cat" to be in the rough vicinity of "dog," but you also want "cat" to be near "tail" and near "supercilious" and near "meme," because you want to try to capture all of the different relationships—both strong and weak—that the word "cat" has to other words. It can be related to all these other words simultaneously only if it is related to each of them in a different dimension. You can't easily make a 160,000-dimensional map, but it turns out you can represent a language pretty well in a mere thousand or so dimensions—in other words, a universe in which each word is designated by a list of a thousand numbers.

[Google research scientist Quoc V.] Le gave me a good-natured hard time for my continual requests for a mental picture of these maps. "Gideon," he would say, with the blunt regular demurral of Bartleby, "I do not generally like trying to visualize thousand-dimensional vectors in three-dimensional space."

Machines do this map twisting and warping through multiple layers of artificial neurons that, like the brain, reinforce connections when they prove valuable. That makes it good for finding patterns.

STRONG VERSUS WEAK AI

The topmost classification of artificial intelligence separates the weak from the strong. According to the University of California, Berkeley, website, A Holistic Approach to AI,[7] "Strong AI's goal is to develop Artificial Intelligence to the point where the machine's intellectual capability is functionally equal to a human's."

Creating an artificial mind is a fascinating goal and the stuff of science fiction, but not our topic of discussion. We're more interested in machines that can perform a specific task: Choose the right e-mail headline, segment a vast audience into groups for targeting, choose the next-best-action for convincing a prospect to buy, and so on. That's known as *narrow* or *weak AI*.

Matt Gershoff prefers thinking about machine learning as a specific tool to solve specific tasks one at a time. "It's really all about learning an agent function," he says. "Initially, you give the function inputs and it passes back outputs—decisions it's made to influence the outside world."

The machine starts off crappy, random, but then over time, based on the feedback from the environment, starts to select actions that, if all goes to plan, begin to perform well on the given task.

People sometimes get a little confused between Predictive Analytics and Machine Learning. While they are related, Predictive Analytics is used to, not surprisingly, make predictions about the world. It is like when you stop and only think about what might happen if you were to take some action. Machine Learning is more like when you both think about what will happen, and then take an action based on what you think will happen.

Once the machine passes back a decision (this e-mail headline or that banner ad) and that decision is put into action, the machine can read the result. That result is the next round of input for the machine to think about, adjust its "opinion," and output the next, better, decision. Narrow AI is designed to do something specific.

THE RIGHT TOOL FOR THE RIGHT JOB

We become what we behold. We shape our tools, and thereafter our tools shape us.

Marshall McLuhan

A marketer meets with a webmaster and says,

"We want a fully responsive, dynamic, bleeding edge website."

"By that, you mean you want it to automatically scale depending on the device, and you want it to personalize the content for the visitor, and you want it to look cool and hip and modern?"

"Yeah, that's right!"

"Well, first of all, do you want it to be Responsive or Adaptive?"

(Blank stare from marketer.)

Remember those days? Back when the "webmaster" could baffle you with jargon? You didn't need to learn all the underpinnings (ink-dye sublimation), but you *did* need to know enough to have a cogent conversation.

Let's try again.

"Well, first of all, do you want it to be Responsive or Adaptive?"

"We want it to continually and fluidly change depending on the device and we want some of it built to a few preset factors so a combination of the two is ideal."

"Well, we could use CSS3 or Susy to handle layout, and if you want sticky footers, we're going to recommend Flexbox."

"Those details are your call."

It's important to understand the first level of the conversation with some general ideas about overhead costs, both in terms of a scientist's time and machine time. Getting the right ad in front of the right person at the right time is a different problem than finding a market segment that will be less price sensitive.

Now that we've shifted to narrow or weak AI, we can subdivide between the three main categories of machine learning to choose from: supervised, unsupervised, and reinforcement. How do you choose?

Some methods are better for some types of problems. The first distinction is whether you need a machete or a scalpel.

In "The Future of Machine Intelligence,"[8] Benjamin Recht explains the difference between robustness and performance in machine learning systems:

In engineering design problems, robustness and performance are competing objectives. Robustness means having repeatable behavior no matter what the environment is doing. On the other hand, you want this behavior to be as good as possible. There are always some performance goals you want the system to achieve. Performance is a little bit easier to understand—faster, more scalable, higher accuracy, etc. Performance and robustness trade off with each other: the most robust system is the one that does nothing, but the highest performing systems typically require sacrificing some degree of safety.

Matt Gershoff provides a clear analogy.

An F1 car is one of the fastest road going vehicles but it can really only reach its top speed on an F1 track, but it's also very complicated and fragile. Alternatively, a rally car can't go nearly as fast as an F1 car on an F1 track, but on a rally course, is the fastest because it's more robust. It's also more versatile and can work in lots of environments, even if it can't beat an F1 on an F1 track. This trade-off between methods that do very well in certain, narrow environments, vs. methods that tend to do fairly well across many environments, is one that you will often have to make.[9]

What's the difference between different types of different tech? How much do you need to know to participate in the conversation without getting left behind on the one hand or having to subscribe to "What's Happening *This Minute* with AI"?

First, you should be comfortable with and understand the difference between *classification* and *regression*. And for that, we delve into classical statistics used in data mining.

Classification versus Regression

Classification is just what it sounds like. It sorts elements (customers, campaigns, product lines) into classes: male versus female, branding versus direct response, high margin versus low margin, and so on. Specific values get sorted into distinct categories. If you're over 30, you're no longer "young." If your food item margin is better than 5.8 percent, it goes in the High bucket.

Classification is great if you're just sorting by gender to choose which e-mail message to recommend in an e-mail blast. If only some of your products are usually bought by men and others are usually bought by women, then sending the wrong version to "Pat" might not bother you.

If, on the other hand, your products are *exclusively* purchased by one or the other, you might want to use regression instead. Regression will tell you how *likely* it is that Pat is male or female.

As the word implies, *regression* is a matter of looking backward.

In solving a problem of this sort, the grand thing is to be able to reason backwards. That is a very useful accomplishment, and a very easy one, but people do not practice it much. In the every-day affairs of life it is more useful to reason forwards, and so the other comes to be neglected. There are fifty who can reason synthetically for one who can reason analytically.

Sherlock Holmes, A Study in Scarlet

Regression analysis is good at dealing with a spectrum of results expressed as a number. Rather than saying John always rides his bike to work, it says there is a higher probability that John will drive when it rains, and the harder it rains, the higher the likelihood.

With those broad categories out of the way, we should spend a little more time on the three big categories of machine learning: *supervised, unsupervised,* and *reinforcement.*

Supervised Machine Learning

Supervised learning is used when you know what the answer is for the examples you have. You know a cat when you see one, but you can't look at a million pictures. So, you teach the machine to recognize cats by showing it as many cat pictures as you can and label them "cat."

You identify the customers you believe to be the best by whatever definition you please, and then ask the machine to go find others that fit the profile without having to create the profile yourself. Your list of current customers is the *training data.* The machine looks at your list, figures out what they have in common, and decides which elements are the most predictive of "goodness." Using these criteria, it looks at the supplied database of prospective customers and shows you the ones you should be targeting.

You then get the chance to say, "Yes, these are the cats we're looking for," or correct the errant machine by providing an alternative label for those that don't fit. The machine might decide that all your best customers are named Daniel, so it brings you all the Daniels it can find. While true, it is not useful.

Carry on a conversation with the machine until it starts coming up with good-enough answers, then better answers, and then results that are far superior and in much less time than humans can.

Bayes' Theorem

A little over 250 years, ago, the Reverend Thomas Bayes thought a lot about probabilities and laid the groundwork for modern classification solutions. He built on the idea of conditional probability—"that the likelihood of something happening depends on what happened before."

Problem:

Given the number of times in which an unknown event has happened and failed: Required the chance that the probability of its happening in a single trial lies somewhere between any two degrees of probability that can be named.

"An Essay towards Solving a Problem in the Doctrine of Chances,"
Reverend Thomas Bayes

In strict statistical terms, flipping a coin and getting heads 49 times in a row has no impact on the likelihood of the next flip being tails. There is no conditional connection between the first 49 and the next. Personally, I would bet on it. Not because I have some hidden statistical secret—quite the opposite. I have an *emotional* response to it even though the outcome is completely independent from what went before. This is why statistics are vital.

But in a case where there *is* a connection, the math works wonders. The likelihood of people buying an iPhone case goes up dramatically if they have previously purchased an iPhone.

The chances of people buying motorcycle insurance takes a giant jump if they buy a motorcycle, and then goes up bit by bit by bit when you start layering in factors like ZIP code, credit rating, and age.

If 22 percent of people in Santa Maria, California, subscribe to *Planet Earth* magazine and 6 percent of the population drive an electric/hybrid car, you can only surmise that the same will hold true for San Louis Obispo. Then you throw in a few other factors like weather and topology and the calculation starts getting complex. How *much* does the weather impact the probability? Not nearly as much as the primary industries of the local areas, one being agribiz and the other education and healthcare.

The Good Reverend worked out a method of calculating how much to revise the probabilities in the face of new data and, even more important, how to account for the probability that the new information might be *incorrect*.

Decision Trees

Remember Guess the Animal? The machine takes the information it has about the subject, finds the most significant differentiator, and splits the data set into two, and then two again, and so forth.

Of all the people who might have the highest customer lifetime value for buying your motorcycle insurance, the most telling attributes about them might be gender, age, credit score, and whether they park their motorcycle in a garage. Assuming only two outcomes of the question of gender, the first split is a rather simple decision node. The same is true of whether the bike is parked in the garage. (See Figure 2.3.)

This sort of sorting can happily be done by hand, but when more and more attributes are poured into the mix, it helps to have an algorithmic assist.

The third split can have multiple outcomes depending on the buckets of age, the fourth, on the buckets of credit score, and so on. At these lower stages, the splits are no longer black and white, but shades of propensities. (See Figure 2.4.)

The result may finally tease out that married males between 38 and 62 with a credit score above 700 who live in temperate climes

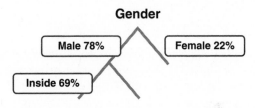

Figure 2.3 Guys who park motorcycle indoors are more likely to buy insurance.

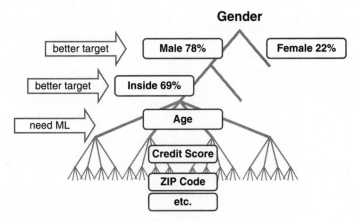

Figure 2.4 The more attributes, the more high-level math is required.

and regularly work out are *most* likely to respond to a promotion for insurance.

Decision trees are great tools because they produce easy-to-understand results and can be parsed to understand how they reached their conclusions. The visual aspect makes it all the easier to comprehend. The glory of having machine learning do the heavy lifting is that the marketer does not have to decide what belongs at the top of the tree (counterintuitively, the "root") to benefit from the outcomes (the "leaves"). Just let the machine figure out the significant variables.

Random Forest

It's the same as the above, but more so. A random forest method generates lots of decision trees by only looking at a randomly selected number of elements in a data set. It then randomly chooses some of the trees and uses them as input for generating another decision tree. This process can be run again and again with multiple forests spawning the next generation of trees.

Why go to the trouble? This approach is very useful for crunching through very large amounts of data. Instead of trying to analyze all of it, the random forest method just grabs a chunk. It's also good with higher dimensional data sets (lots and lots of attributes).

Support Vector Machines

You want to classify people into two groups: those who are most likely to buy and those who are not. All the evaluation and calculation you can think of on all the data you have says the people you're looking at are all over the map. They are all equally likely to be on one side of the fence as the other.

A *support vector machine* looks at these people on a 3-D chessboard instead of a flat graph. Adding the third dimension allows the machine to see that the fence can be built between the two distinct groups if it floats that fence in the air. (See Figure 2.5.)[10]

A support vector machine looks at your data in four, eight, or a thousand dimensions, thereby finding a way to classify them into groups that just wasn't possible before. This is *very* good for high-dimensionality problems.

Supervised learning has you teach the machine what you want it to know. Unsupervised learning asks the machine to teach you what it discovers.

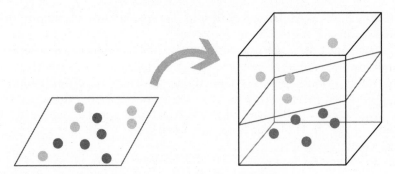

Figure 2.5 Looking at data in 3-D can make classification easier.

Unsupervised Learning

The joy of unsupervised learning is the element of surprise. You don't ask the machine to solve a specific problem. You merely ask the machine to tell you something you didn't know.

What is interesting in this data? In unsupervised learning, you tell the machine to study a gazillion pictures of cats and tell you what it discovers. It might say that cats are usually found on sofas and chairs, and that most cats seem uninterested in the photographer.

When worried about customer churn and recovery, a review of your customer data might reveal that you can immediately identify customers who are most likely to defect and never buy from you again. When asked for the attribute that best predicts defection, the machine spits out one word, *Obituary*.

This is true, but not useful. In data science terms, we're dealing with clustering (what do these individuals have in common?), association (what is generally true about these people?), and anomalies (what stands out?).

Cluster Analysis

Machine learning is great at seeing patterns. Humans evolved to see patterns as well: patterns of leaves (I remember that this plant is edible), patterns in movement (That's not a dog, it's a coyote!), and patterns in the weather (Time to find a warm place to hunker down during this blizzard).

Of course, this takes some training. Ask a child to put away his clothes and he might put all the blue clothes in one drawer and all the red clothes in another instead of sorting out the shirts from the pants. That's perfectly logical.

But humans are also able to find patterns in truly random information. If you stare at a photo of video static, you will see it move. You will start to make out designs. You will start to see conspiracy theories. (Oh, look—there's Jesus on my grilled cheese sandwich!)

While humans' minds can fool them, a machine learning algorithm will only see patterns that actually exist. Machines do not succumb to apophenia (the human tendency to perceive meaningful patterns within random data). Machines don't believe in winning streaks or a basketball player's "hot hand."

To a machine, says Matt Gershoff, "Stars are to data points as galaxies are to clusters. A cluster analysis might be to 'find' the galaxies from the stars."

A machine learning algorithm can find people who search for "Sony—DSC-W830 20.1-Megapixel Digital Camera—Silver" after having searched for "digital camera," "digital camera reviews," and "digital cameras with wifi," and let you know that they are 50 percent more likely to purchase than people who searched for "digital camera," "digital camera reviews," and "digital cameras on sale."

A machine can see patterns that a person simply wouldn't imagine to be worthwhile. It may discover that people who had recently visited a pet website are more inclined to buy the camera's extended warranty. There's no rhyme or reason to that, but it is still actionable from a marketing perspective.

A machine might also discover a pattern of no practical business value whatsoever. That pattern might be too infrequent to be actionable, or apply to too few customers. It should be possible, however, for the machine to learn to make that distinction over time.

Association

In the store, you might want to put items that are routinely purchased together right next to each other. Alternatively, if the association is so overwhelmingly high that you won't harm sales, you might place them at either end of the store, forcing buyers to travel past other temptations in order to boost opportunistic sales (impulse buying). Amazon has leveraged this concept to a high degree with their people-who-bought-this-also-bought-that prod. It works very well.

Like any other algorithm, it needs to be monitored by humans. It may well be that a certain age-range of people who buy a certain brand of toothpaste pick up hemorrhoid cream as well, but that wouldn't make for a great promotional message.

Outside of Amazon, you are most likely to see this approach resulting in extremely long cash register receipts.[11] (See Figure 2.6.)

Figure 2.6 CVS uses what you buy to discount things you are most likely to buy.

Associations can apply to much more than shopping, such as

- People who read this article or page also read that one.
- People who saw this page, and then that page, purchased more.
- People who used this mobile app, downloaded that one.
- People who turned left when entering the store bought more of these.

The two key elements to understand about association analytics when working with a data scientist are support and confidence. *Support* refers to the number of times the items have shown up in the shopping basket while *confidence* is the ratio of times the two associated items have shown up together.

If people bought toothpaste 400 times and dental floss 300 times today, the support number is how many times they showed up together. If they show up together 300 times, then the confidence is 3/4 or 75 percent for the association between paste and floss, but 100 percent for the association between floss and paste. One must be the antecedent, and the other the consequent: If toothpaste, then floss with an association rule confidence probability of 75 percent; if floss, then toothpaste for sure.

An association with very low support might just have happened by chance. It's not statistically significant. The first three times I walked under a ladder something bad happened, so I stopped walking under ladders and told all my friends to avoid them. My friend walks under ladders all the time and nothing bad has ever happened to him. In my case, I have low support and low confidence. My buddy has high support (all the time) and high confidence (nothing ever happened). Clearly, we'd rather bank on his results than mine.

Anomaly Detection

One of these things is not like the others,
One of these things just doesn't belong,
Can you tell which thing is not like the others
By the time I finish my song?

Sesame Street

The same talent for finding patterns is useful for finding outliers. These are two ends of the same spectrum. Some things are alike, some things are just plain weird, and the rest fall in the middle somewhere.

What's the value of an anomaly? It's essential for fraud detection. When you get that phone call from your credit card company asking if you bought a tank of gas in Omaha and a flat-screen television in Dallas, and you live in Atlanta, that's your friend, the anomaly detection system, at work.

Fraud is important in commerce, but we in marketing like to spend most of our time on raising revenue. A sudden spike in Twitter mentions of your brand, a flood of traffic to your website from a given referring page, or a surge in e-mail subscriptions related to a specific search term are all happy actions that could spell opportunity.

The flipside is that you get an anomalous drop in attention, which represents a need for swift intervention to determine if your server is down, your new app crashes, or the FDA just announced that your new product causes cancer.

Those are obvious and the stuff of standard digital analytics. But what if the anomaly detected was much more subtle? What if it were based on four or five unrelated events, but still offered an opportunity to build your brand or stave off public embarrassment?

Keeping your eyes open for outliers has always been a competitive edge and now we have a technical edge to help in that regard.

Neural Networks

Neural networks are probably the most mentioned type of artificial intelligence because it's based loosely on how the brain works. The association between "brain" and "intelligence" is just too strong to ignore.

The human brain makes connections between neurons. The more often the connection is made and/or the stronger the emotion associated with the connection, the stronger that connection and the more likely it is to be triggered again. A computerized neural network does the same based on math—but without the emotion.

Each artificial neuron has its own limits on when it passes a signal along. If it has high support and high confidence, it sends the message along to the next. The more often it has high support and high confidence, the more likely it is to pass the signal along.

The simplest neuron can take some number of inputs and output a decision. Each input is weighted to impact that decision differently. When trying to decide whether to go out to the movies, you're going to start by considering the cost, the weather, and the effort. These are your inputs. These are very important issues as the output from any of them will impact a go/no-go decision.

If it's too nice a day to spend indoors or too inclement to go out, you're not going to the movies. But if the weather is "normal," then that input has no impact on your decision whatsoever. If it's the end of the month and you're feeling broke, it's a no-go. If you're tired, or sick, or just overwhelmed by inertia, it's a no-go.

These inputs are not binary; they operate on a grayscale. Each would be a single neuron at work. Each weighs one consideration and delivers the go/no-go decision based solely on these factors. Then, the combination of neural decisions must be considered together so the outputs of the first three neurons are passed to the next.

The processing of each neuron depends on the weight of the inputs and the bias of each neuron, both of which are unique for each neuron. The network kicks out an answer and the machine is either trained by a human or by the result of an action in the real world. That training changes the weights and biases of each neuron until the outputs start improving.

A data scientist would map that out as shown in Figure 2.7.

The combination of weighted inputs tips the scale one way or the other. The weights depend on whether feeling flush is more important to you than crummy weather. The expectation is that your feelings about these issues might change from moment to moment. You might feel broke, but are willing to throw caution to the wind. You might hate the cold weather, but be willing to go this time. Therefore, the process must monitor your feelings and recalculate until you take action and the results of that action can be fed back to the neurons to alter the weighting.

A neural network is considered a learning system when it responds to the response it gets from the environment (your mood in this case). (See Figure 2.8.)

Things can get more sophisticated quickly when you realize that the output can be more than binary. Rather than Go/No-Go, the output could be 65 percent Go. Add to that the ability to wire these networks together in multiple layers, which is necessary when deciding

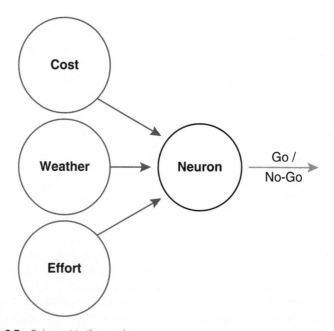

Figure 2.7 Going out to the movies

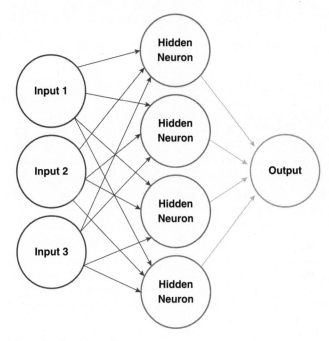

Figure 2.8 A simple neural net

to go to the movies. If the weather is good, your bankroll is large, and you're energized, you have to decide what movie you want to see: layer two.

Maybe you've seen too many socially important but somewhat depressing movies lately. Perhaps you can't stomach yet another comic book superhero sequel. You'd like nothing better than to go see an uplifting, fun musical. But then you have to ask your date: layer three.

Multiple layers of decisions coded into a neural network bring us to *deep learning.*

Deep Learning

Let's give our machine an e-mail marketing task. If it sends an e-mail with the word *offer* in the subject line to some recipients and *deal* in the other, it measures the response and learns that one of them works better and suggests that particular subject line be used for the rest. This is simple A/B testing. It's just playing with the average result.

If we give the machine access to additional information about the recipients (age, gender, previous response), the machine can sort through that data and suggest that males between the ages of 18 and

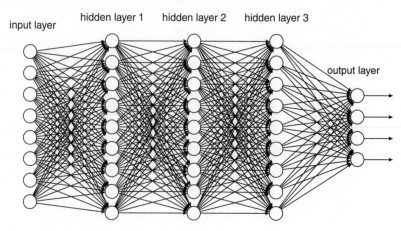

Figure 2.9 Three-layered deep learning network

34 are more likely to respond to subject line A. That can be coded in a single-layer, neural decision system.

If we add additional information (level of education, propensity to buy dental floss with toothpaste), the machine can take the output of the first layer and feed it into the next.

When we give the machine more data (time of day, recency of previous response, postal code) and give it more control over the environment (opening sentence, included photos, length of message), the machine can use multiple neural layers to calculate which combinations of e-mail components might be best for which types of recipients.

The term *deep learning* refers to the deeper and deeper layers of neurons you have working on your problem (Figure 2.9).[12]

This gives rise to dynamic neural networks where the information can flow in a much less controlled manner, allowing the machine to build context and come to conclusions more quickly.

This is where we move into an area of machines that program themselves on the fly. That is, they can dynamically change their "opinion" about relative inputs.

Yann LeCun, Yoshua Bengio, and Geoffrey Hinton spelled it out in their May 2015 article in *Nature*, "Deep Learning."[13]

> Deep-learning methods are representation-learning
> methods with multiple levels of representation,
> obtained by composing simple but non-linear modules
> that each transform the representation at one level

(starting with the raw input) into a representation at a higher, slightly more abstract level. With the composition of enough such transformations, very complex functions can be learned. For classification tasks, higher layers of representation amplify aspects of the input that are important for discrimination and suppress irrelevant variations. An image, for example, comes in the form of an array of pixel values, and the learned features in the first layer of representation typically represent the presence or absence of edges at particular orientations and locations in the image. The second layer typically detects motifs by spotting particular arrangements of edges, regardless of small variations in the edge positions (identifying an eyebrow). The third layer may assemble motifs into larger combinations that correspond to parts of familiar objects (a whole eye), and subsequent layers would detect objects as combinations of these parts (a face). The key aspect of deep learning is that these layers of features are not designed by human engineers: they are learned from data using a general-purpose learning procedure.

Reinforcement Learning

Reinforcement learning allows for feedback to the machine so that it can improve its output the next time.

Yes, that's a cat./No, that's a dog.

Yes, you can walk straight./No, you've hit a wall.

Yes, this e-mail subject line worked./No, people did not respond.

Reinforcement happens when the machine gets feedback from the outside world—the environment—or from some of its own neurons. The machine comes up with an opinion about which ad to show or how much budget to spend on specific search keywords and takes action. The response to that action is reinforcement.

Data scientists refer to an AI system as an *agent* that is getting *rewarded* or *penalized*. This is different from supervised learning in that the feedback comes from the environment rather than a human supervisor. The machine is out there on its own, exploring the territory. It knows where you want it to end up, but you are not there to correct its every move. This is the machine doing its best to create a mental model of the world, whether that's dynamic content delivery, customer service, or just selecting the most impactful banner ad, and taking action repeatedly, continuously improving its ability to get to the desired goal.

In "The Future of Machine Intelligence,"[14] Risto Miikkulainen puts it this way:

> Suppose you are driving a car or playing a game: It's harder to define the optimal actions, and you don't receive much feedback. In other words, you can play the whole game of chess, and by the end, you've either won or lost. You know that if you lost, you probably made some poor choices. But which? Or, if you won, which were the well-chosen actions? This is, in a nutshell, a reinforcement learning problem. Put another way, in this paradigm, you receive feedback periodically. This feedback, furthermore, will only inform you about how well you did without in turn listing the optimal set of steps or actions you took. Instead, you have to discover those actions through exploration—testing diverse approaches and measuring their performance.

MAKE UP YOUR MIND

In considering all of the above (Do you need an F1 or a rally car?), Microsoft offers another set of deliberation factors in its paper, "How to Choose Algorithms for Microsoft Azure Machine Learning."[15] Your considerations are *accuracy, training time, linearity,* and *parameters.*

With these four criteria, the article ranks 25 different algorithms for evaluation.

> The answer to the question "What Machine Learning algorithm should I use?" is always "It depends." It depends on the size, quality, and nature of the data. It depends on what you want to do with the answer. It depends on how the math of the algorithm was translated into instructions for the computer you are using. And it depends on how much time you have. Even the most experienced data scientists can't tell which algorithm will perform best before trying them.

How important is accuracy? In a self-driving car, it might not be important to tell a cat from a dog or to determine if the car in front of you is 28.4346 feet away and is going 5.827 miles per hour faster than you. Maybe 28.5 feet and 6 miles per hour is good enough.

If that's the case, then you should be willing to trade a little accuracy for processing time.

The amount of data you're working with also impacts learning time. With lots of data you may have to sacrifice accuracy if you need the machine to learn fast.

Linearity is the ability for the results to line up in a straight line on a graph. In the same neighborhood, the more rooms a house has, the more it will cost. The more you smoke, the more likely you are to get cancer. When it comes to marketing, you can count yourself lucky when you find a situation that is linear: The more you advertise, the more you sell. This approach tends to be "algorithmically simple and fast to train."

How many parameters do you have? These "are the knobs a data scientist gets to turn when setting up an algorithm." You may have a million customers or 200 million prospects, but that's just the instances. The parameters are all the attributes about each one in your database and the level of cardinality (how many different options there are per attribute).

You might have a range of 120 possible ages, 43,000 ZIP codes in the United States, and an attribute that shows how much each person likes vanilla ice cream on a scale of one to five. "The training time and accuracy of the algorithm can sometimes be quite sensitive to getting just the right settings. Typically, algorithms with large numbers of parameters require the most trial and error to find a good combination."

Dataiku (rhymes with *haiku*) put together an infographic to help determine which algorithm is right for which use (Figure 2.10).[16]

ONE ALGORITHM TO RULE THEM ALL?

How about using them all? If the data scientist on your team suggests using an *ensemble algorithm*, nod knowingly. All she means is taking the output from one method and using it as input of another, and then another, until everybody is satisfied that the predictions coming out are valuable.

The *ensemble* approach sets up a working group or a coalition of AI methods to argue with each other as adversarial networks and form a consensus. But shouldn't there be a tried-and-true, tested, trusted, peer-reviewed combination of methods that is the agreed-upon solution to all of our calculation problems? If only that were the case.

In his book, *The Master Algorithm: How the Quest for the Ultimate Learning Machine Will Remake Our World*,[17] Pedro Domingos spells

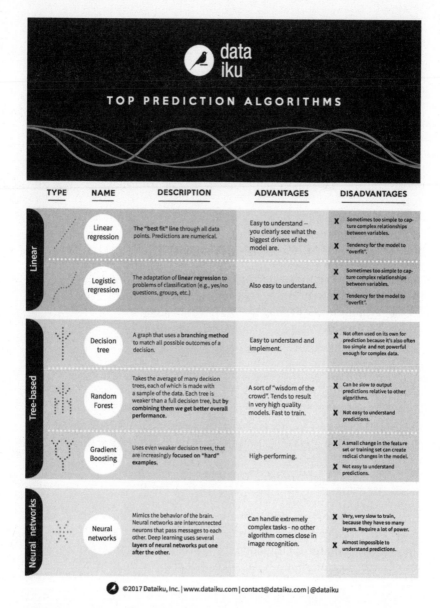

Figure 2.10 Dataiku offers advice on how to fit the algorithm to the task.

out "The Five Tribes of Machine Learning": *symbolists, connectionists, evolutionaries, Bayesians,* and *analogizers.*

Symbolists lean on inverse deduction, starting with a set of premises and conclusions to work backward to fill in the gaps by manipulating symbols. "Their master algorithm is inverse deduction, which figures out what knowledge is missing in order to make a deduction go through, and then makes it as general as possible."

There are the connectionists who work on mimicking the brain, "by adjusting the strengths of connections between neurons." This is, "back propagation which comparison systems output with the desired one and then successively changes the connections in layer after layer of neurons so as to bring the output closer to what it should be." That is deep learning.

Evolutionaries rely on the idea of genomes and DNA. "The key problem that evolutionaries solve is learning structure: not just adjusting parameters, like back propagation does, but creating the brain that those adjustments can then fine-tune." This approach tries to get the machine to "mate" and "evolve" programs like living things. That makes them adaptable as they can adjust to the unknown.

Bayesians focus on uncertainty. "The problem then becomes how to deal with noisy, incomplete, and even contradictory information without falling apart." Using "probabilistic inference," found in Bayes' Theorem, "tells us how to incorporate new evidence into our beliefs." This group calculates probabilities, taking flawed results into consideration, and then allows for actual results to feed back into the calculation.

Analogizers look at the similarities between situations to infer other parallels. "If two patients have similar symptoms, perhaps they have the same disease." This group uses support vector machines, "which figure out which experience to remember and how to combine them to make new predictions."

How do all of these fit together in a *master algorithm*?

> Each tribe's solution to its central problem is a brilliant, hard one advance. But the true master algorithm must solve all five problems, not just one. For example, to cure cancer we need to understand the metabolic networks in the cell: which genes regulate which others, which chemical reactions the resulting proteins control, and how adding a new molecule to the mix would affect the network. It would be silly to try and learn all of this from scratch, ignoring all the knowledge that biologists have painstakingly accumulated over the decades.

Symbolists know how to combine the knowledge with data from DNA sequence, gene expression microarrays, and so on, to produce results that you couldn't get with either alone. But the knowledge we obtain by inverse deduction is purely qualitative; we need to learn not to trust who interacts with whom, but how much, and back propagation can do that. Nevertheless, both inverse deduction and back propagation would be lost in space without some basic structure in which to hang the interactions and parameters they find, and genetic programming can discover it. At this point if we had complete knowledge of the metabolism and all the data relevant to a given patient, we could figure out a treatment for her. But in reality the information we have is always very incomplete, and even incorrect in places; we need to make headway despite that, and that's what probabilistic inference is for. In the hardest cases, the patient cancer looks very different from previous ones, and all our learned knowledge fails. Similarity-based algorithms can save the day by seeing analogies between superficially very different situations, zeroing in on their essential similarities and ignoring the rest.

Evolutionaries evolve structures; connectionists learn parameters; symbolists compose new elements on the fly; Bayesians weigh the evidence; and analogizers map the outcome to new situations.

Domingos offers his theory, but so far, that's as far as it goes. If you're a marketer, dedicated to understanding the whole enchilada, working your way through *The Master Algorithm* is a worthy challenge. If you're a data scientist, it's a wonderfully light read.

Given all of the above, you will fare far better with this technology if you're comfortable with a little ambiguity.

ACCEPTING RANDOMNESS

Keeping in mind that "All models are wrong; some models are useful," also know that randomness is your friend.

If all models are wrong, then you want to make sure they don't do something catastrophic. Colin Fraser nails it.[18]

> [A]ny time you are using a predictive model to make
> business decisions, you need to understand that the
> predictions will sometimes be wrong, and you need to

understand the different ways that the model could be wrong. Maybe the model tends to over or underestimate for certain types of observations. Maybe the model is very good at making predictions about one class of observation, but fails miserably for making predictions about some other class. And different types of models will have errors with different characteristics. You may have an option between two different models, one that is wrong often but only by a little bit, and one that is usually right but spectacularly wrong when it is wrong. Some models provide the opportunity to tune parameters in order to favor one type of wrong to another. Again, many of these types of hypotheses about model error can be tested prior to actually deploying the model by making sure to use a test set or some other method of validation.

What happens when the model is wrong? Do we piss someone off? Do we miss an opportunity? Does someone die? The costs of being wrong vary wildly from project to project, and as a manager of a project involving data science, it is your job to understand what those costs really are. With an understanding of those costs, you are equipped to work collaboratively with a data scientist to tune the model to be wrong in all the right ways.

The assumption is that once you get a machine to Do the Right Thing once, you can set it and forget it, right? Once it's trained, it'll just get smarter. That's not so. There are a lot of variables at work and it's best to understand them well enough to have a healthy respect for varied outcomes.

If a machine learning system is fired up and trained using different data from the same data set, it's going to come to different conclusions. How different is that? Different enough that they've named this effect *model variance*.

Embrace this expectation and make sure the model is intentionally using randomized data. The sequence that data elements are given to a neural network will have a big impact on the outcome. Best practice says that you should embrace randomness here and indiscriminately reorder those records to keep the machine on its toes.

The question is one of variance toleration. If multiple iterations of your model disagree by more than you can tolerate, send it back to the lab. There, the data scientists can run a larger number of iterations and statistically cross-validate it to produce a high-confidence result.

WHICH TECH IS BEST?

All of them are. In "The Future of Machine Intelligence,"[19] editor David Beyer asks Gurjeet Singh if there is a single view that's analytically superior toward the goal of understanding any particular problem.

> **Singh:** You don't necessarily want a single view. There is no single right answer, because different combinations of these algorithms will produce different types of insights in your data. They are all equally valid if you can prove their statistical validity. You don't want to somehow confine yourself to a single right answer. You want to pull out statistically significant ideas from all of these.

> **Bayer:** Do the insights or results across different views of the same data ever contradict each other?

> **Singh:** In fact, one of the things that's beneficial in our approach is that these algorithms are correlated with each other. In many cases, you find the evidence for the same phenomena over and over again across multiple maps. Wherever that happens, you can be more confident about what you found.

One of AI's greatest achievements since IBM's Watson beating Ken Jennings at Jeopardy was Google's AlphaGo beating Lee Sedol, a 9-dan Go professional, without handicaps in March 2016. How did they do it? The paper published in *Nature* magazine ("Mastering the Game of Go with Deep Neural Networks and Tree Search"[20]) said that the research used "Monte-Carlo tree search with deep neural networks that have been trained by supervised learning, from human expert games, and by reinforcement learning from games of self-play."

Now you know.

FOR THE MORE STATISTICALLY MINDED

Not comfortable with your knowledge of statistics jargon? No worries; Himanshu Sharma is here to help with this post you can return to over and over again for a refresher. It's called "Bare Minimum Statistics for Web Analytics."[21]

Sharma does an admirable job spelling out:

- **What Is Statistical Inference?**

    It is the process of drawing (a) conclusion from the data which is subject to random variation. Observational error is an example of statistical inference.

    In order to minimize observational error, we need to segment the ecommerce conversion rate into visits and transactions.

- **What Is a Sample?**

    A sample is that subset of population which represents the entire population. So analysing the sample should produce similar results as analysing all of the population. Sampling is carried out to analyse large data sets in a reasonable amount of time and in a cost efficient manner.

- **What Is Statistical Significance?**

    Statistical significance means statistically meaningful.

    Statistical significant result—result which is unlikely to have occurred by chance.

    Statistically insignificant result—result which is likely to have occurred by chance.

- **What Is Noise?**

    Noise is the amount of unexplained variation/randomness in a sample.

    Confidence (or Statistical Confidence) is the confidence that the result has not occurred by a chance.

- **What Is a Null Hypothesis?**

    According to null hypothesis, any kind of difference you see in a data set is due to chance and not due to a particular relationship. **Null hypothesis can never be proven**. A statistical test can only reject a null hypothesis or fail to reject a null hypothesis. It cannot prove a null hypothesis.

■ What Is an Alternative Hypothesis?

An alternative hypothesis is the opposite of the null hypothesis. According to alternative hypothesis, any kind of difference you see in a data set is due to a particular relationship and not due to chance.

In statistics the only way to prove your hypothesis is to reject the null hypothesis. You don't prove the alternative hypothesis to support your hypothesis. Remember your hypothesis needs to (be) based on qualitative data and not on personal opinion.

■ What Is a False Positive?

False positive is a positive test result which is more likely to be false than true. For example, an A/B test which shows that one variation is better than the other when it is not really the case.

■ What Is a Type I Error?

Type I error is the incorrect rejection of a true null hypothesis. It represents a false positive error.

■ What Is a Type II Error?

Type II error is the failure to reject a false null hypothesis. It represents a false negative error. **All statistical tests have a probability of making type I and type II errors**.

■ What Is a Correlation?

Correlation is a statistical measurement of relationship between two variables. Let us suppose "A" and "B" are two variables. If as A goes up, B goes up, then A and B are positively correlated. However, if as A goes up, B goes down, then A and B are negatively correlated.

■ What Is Causation?

> Causation is the theory that something happened as a result. For example, fall in temperature increased the sale of hot drinks.

Sharma does a superb job relating these terms to web analytics, along with practical examples and detailed descriptions. This is worth bookmarking.

■ ■ ■

Vincent Granville does an equally wonderful job going a bit more technical and a lot more mathematical in his post at Data Science Central where he spells out "24 Uses of Statistical Modeling."[22] Here are a handful of those two-dozen uses.

■ Spatial Models

> Spatial dependency is the co-variation of properties within geographic space: characteristics at proximal locations appear to be correlated, either positively or negatively. Spatial dependency leads to the spatial auto-correlation problem in statistics since, like temporal auto-correlation, this violates standard statistical techniques that assume independence among observations

■ Time Series

> Methods for time series analyses may be divided into two classes: frequency-domain methods and time-domain methods. The former include spectral analysis and recently wavelet analysis; the latter include auto-correlation and cross-correlation analysis. In time domain, correlation analyses can be made in a filter-like manner using scaled correlation, thereby mitigating the need to operate in frequency domain.

> Additionally, time series analysis techniques may be divided into parametric and non-parametric methods. The parametric approaches assume that the underlying stationary stochastic process has a certain structure which can be described using a small number of parameters (for example, using an autoregressive or

moving average model). In these approaches, the task is to estimate the parameters of the model that describes the stochastic process. By contrast, non-parametric approaches explicitly estimate the covariance or the spectrum of the process without assuming that the process has any particular structure.

Methods of time series analysis may also be divided into linear and non-linear, and univariate and multivariate.

■ Market Segmentation

Market segmentation, also called customer profiling, is a marketing strategy which involves dividing a broad target market into subsets of consumers, businesses, or countries that have, or are perceived to have, common needs, interests, and priorities, and then designing and implementing strategies to target them. Market segmentation strategies are generally used to identify and further define the target customers, and provide supporting data for marketing plan elements such as positioning to achieve certain marketing plan objectives. Businesses may develop product differentiation strategies, or an undifferentiated approach, involving specific products or product lines depending on the specific demand and attributes of the target segment.

■ Recommendation Systems

Recommender systems or recommendation systems (sometimes replacing "system" with a synonym such as platform or engine) are a subclass of information filtering system that seek to predict the "rating" or "preference" that a user would give to an item.

■ Association Rule Learning

Association rule learning is a method for discovering interesting relations between variables in large databases. For example, the rule { onions, potatoes } ==>{ burger } found in the sales data of a supermarket would indicate that if a customer buys onions and potatoes together, they are likely to also buy hamburger meat. In fraud detection, association rules are used to detect patterns associated with fraud. Linkage analysis is performed to identify additional fraud cases: if credit card transaction from user A was used to make a fraudulent purchase at store B, by analyzing all transactions from store B, we might find another user C with fraudulent activity.

■ Attribution Modeling

An attribution model is the rule, or set of rules, that determines how credit for sales and conversions is assigned to touchpoints in conversion paths. For example, the Last Interaction model in Google Analytics assigns 100% credit to the final touchpoints (i.e., clicks) that immediately precede sales or conversions. Macro-economic models use long-term, aggregated historical data to assign, for each sale or conversion, an attribution weight to a number of channels. These models are also used for advertising mix optimization.

■ Clustering

Cluster analysis or clustering is the task of grouping a set of objects in such a way that objects in the same group (called a cluster) are more similar (in some sense or another) to each other than to those in other groups (clusters). It is a main task of exploratory data mining, and a common technique for statistical data analysis, used in many fields, including machine learning, pattern recognition, image analysis, information retrieval, and bioinformatics.

Unlike supervised classification, clustering does not use training sets. Though there are some hybrid implementations, called semi-supervised learning.

■ Churn Analysis

Customer churn analysis helps you identify and focus on higher value customers, determine what actions typically precede a lost customer or sale, and better understand what factors influence customer retention. Statistical techniques involved include survival analysis as well as Markov chains with four states: brand new customer, returning customer, inactive (lost) customer, and re-acquired customer, along with path analysis (including root cause analysis) to understand how customers move from one state to another, to maximize profit. Related topics: customer lifetime value, cost of user acquisition, user retention.

■ Optimum Bidding

This is an example of automated, black-box, machine-to-machine communication system, sometimes working in real time, via various APIs. It is backed by statistical models. Applications include detecting and purchasing the right keywords at the right price on Google AdWords, based on expected conversion rates for millions of keywords, most of them having no historical data; keywords are categorized using an indexation algorithm and aggregated into buckets (categories) to get some historical data with statistical significance, at the bucket level. This is a real problem for companies such as Amazon or eBay. Or it could be used as the core algorithm for automated high frequency stock trading.

■ Multivariate Testing

Multivariate testing is a technique for testing an hypothesis in which multiple variables are modified. The goal is to determine which combination of variations performs the best out of all of the possible combinations. Websites and mobile apps are made of combinations of changeable elements that are optimized using multivariate testing. This involves careful design-of-experiment, and the tiny, temporary difference (in yield or web traffic) between two versions of a webpage might not have statistical significance. While ANOVA and tests of hypotheses are used by industrial or healthcare statisticians for multivariate testing, we have developed systems that are model-free, data-driven, based on data binning and model-free confidence intervals. Stopping a multivariate testing experiment (they usually last 14 days for web page optimization) as soon as the winning combination is identified, helps save a lot of money. Note that external events—for instance a holiday or some server outage—can impact the results of multivariate testing, and need to be addressed.

WHAT DID WE LEARN?

- All models are wrong; some models are useful.
- Machine learning is great with a lot of diverse data, but has a lot to learn.
- Classification is putting things in buckets while regression smooths them out along a spectrum.
- Supervised machine learning solves a problem with your help while unsupervised machine learning looks for interesting things to show you. Both are happy to be tutored by a human or by a direct response from the environment.
- Machine learning is an effort to build a system that automatically improves with experience.
- Machine learning is really good at spotting one thing that is not like the others.
- Neural networks are good at weighing lots of factors.
- AI deals in probability rather than accounting. It's best to get comfortable with a little fuzziness rather than hope for definitive answers.

Next, how do we apply all of this to marketing?

NOTES

1. "Big Data-Driven Marketing: How Machine Learning Outperforms Marketers' Gut-Feeling," http://web.media.mit.edu/~yva/papers/sundsoy2014big.pdf.
2. http://www.cs.cmu.edu/~tom/pubs/MachineLearning.pdf.
3. "Machine Learning vs. Statistics," http://www.kdnuggets.com/2016/11/machine-learning-vs-statistics.html.
4. "Move Your Analytics to Operation from Artisanal to Autonomous," https://hbr.org/2016/12/move-your-analytics-operation-from-artisanal-to-autonomous.
5. Source: Personal interview.

6. "The Great A.I. Awakening," *New York Times*, December 14, 2016, http://www.nytimes.com/2016/12/14/magazine/the-great-ai-awakening.html?_r=0.

7. "A Holistic Approach to AI," https://www.ocf.berkeley.edu/~arihuang/academic/research/strongai3.html.

8. "The Future of Machine Intelligence," http://www.oreilly.com/data/free/future-of-machine-intelligence.csp.

9. Source: Personal interview.

10. "Support Vector Machines for Dummies: A Simple Explanation," http://blog.aylien.com/support-vector-machines-for-dummies-a-simple/.

11. Jason Newport 3 ft receipt #CVS #outofcontrol #godigital #mobilecoupon, https://www.flickr.com/photos/jasonnewport/14811604941/in/photolist-edZStq-ixj2HW-rmkSG4-qpG4bn-rmo291-4uNkGr-oyRm7Z.

12. "Neural Networks and Deep Learning," http://neuralnetworksanddeeplearning.com/chap1.html.

13. "Deep Learning," https://www.cs.toronto.edu/~hinton/absps/NatureDeepReview.pdf.

14. http://www.oreilly.com/data/free/future-of-machine-intelligence.csp.

15. "How to Choose Algorithms for Microsoft Azure Machine Learning," https://docs.microsoft.com/en-us/azure/machine-learning/machine-learning-algorithm-choice.

16. "Machine Learning Explained: Algorithms Are Your Friend," https://blog.dataiku.com/machine-learning-explained-algorithms-are-your-friend.

17. *The Master Algorithm: How the Quest for the Ultimate Learning Machine Will Remake Our World* (Basic Books, September 22, 2015).

18. "Data Science for Business Leaders: Picking the Right Kind of Wrong," https://medium.com/@colin.fraser/data-science-for-business-leaders-picking-the-right-kind-of-wrong-46a55465e2a4#.qhsi3ctci.

19. "The Future of Machine Intelligence," http://www.oreilly.com/data/free/future-of-machine-intelligence.csp.

20. "Mastering the Game of Go with Deep Neural Networks and Tree Search," http://www.nature.com/nature/journal/v529/n7587/full/nature16961.html.

21. "Bare Minimum Statistics for Web Analytics," https://www.optimizesmart.com/bare-minimum-statistics-web-analytics/.

22. "24 Uses of Statistical Modeling," http://www.datasciencecentral.com/profiles/blogs/top-20-uses-of-statistical-modeling.

CHAPTER **3**

Solving the
Marketing
Problem

*If I had an hour to solve a problem I'd spend 55 minutes
thinking about the problem and 5 minutes thinking about
solutions.*

Albert Einstein

f you've been in marketing for more than five years, you can skim
this chapter pretty quickly. Consider it a gentle reminder of all you
hold dear. If you are a data scientist working with marketing people,
then you *must* read this chapter.

Rohit Nagraj Rudrapatna, a senior data scientist at Blueocean
Market Intelligence, understands the need. "The biggest challenge
for the data scientist is to speak the language of the marketing
department," he says. "We may face a lot of data challenges but the
marketing team and the analytics team work in silos. One does not
understand the other's language and that's a big communication gap.
If there's a way these two departments can make a bridge to speak the
other language, I think that's where synergies can come into play."

Understanding the problem is crucial in an era when new technologies are so often brought in because they are the shiny, new
object. A cool new tool is fun and interesting, but it cannot be useful

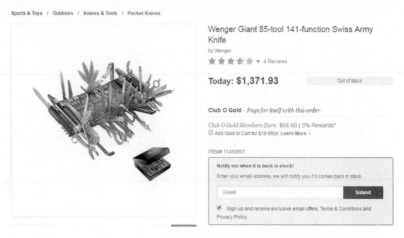

Figure 3.1 Shiny new tools have always been cool. Finding a use for them is hard.

until we understand what we're trying to accomplish in using it. (See Figure 3.1.)

When television was shiny and new, most of the television ads featured a live performer standing in front of a microphone, reading copy from a radio ad—new tool, old habits. When the World Wide Web was opened for commercial use, most of the websites were non-interactive brochureware and only allowed people to click from one page to the next.

With big data and artificial intelligence, the conversation most often goes like this:

Business Person: What have you got?

Technology Person: What do you want?

Business Person: What can it do?

Technology Person: What do you *need* it to do?

Business Person: Can it solve my problems?

Technology Person: What are your problems?

With no understanding of the technology, the marketing side of the house has a tough time figuring out how to apply a new capability. With no clear description of the problem the marketing department is trying to solve, the technologists can only shrug their shoulders. There is a "cold start" problem for any technology, but especially for AI that requires some sort of data to chew on.

If you grow up in the marketing world, you pick up a lot of rules of thumb. You know, for instance, that if you use a picture of a person, you want that person facing into the page. If they're on the left side, you want them facing to the right. If they're on the right side, you want them facing to the left. You know this after years of experience. But a machine learning process doesn't have years of experience; it just has raw data and it has to learn on its own, each time.

Among other marketing issues, Matt Gershoff, co-founder at Conductrics, is trying to help clients show the right ad to the right person at the right time. "We're going to use a certain set of technologies to achieve that," says Gershoff. "We don't have data or information yet so we're going to use experimentation. Let's say we're going to try out a new offer or a new experience for our customers that we haven't presented before, so we don't really know, a priori, what the efficacy is going to be. So, we need to start collecting data on it."

Business: So which data should we collect?

Technology: That depends, what problem are you trying to solve?

Business: What sorts of problems *can* I solve with AI?

Technology: That depends on what data you have.

It's far more important that the data scientist understand the problem than the marketer understand the technology—at least at first.

Once the technology is better understood by the business side, real strides can be made as the marketing professional gets a feel for the power of the tools. The machine can do what it's told, but it needs to be told.

ONE-TO-ONE MARKETING

To best understand the *marketing problem*, you have to go back to its roots to see how it developed. In the beginning, there were goats and cows.

I have some goats; you have some cows. I'd like one of your cows, so I offer you two of my goats in exchange. You scoff and tell me my goats are scrawny and old and you would need five *healthy* goats to even consider a trade. I explain that my goats come from the highest rated farm and I have tended them personally from birth. I explain the feed they eat, the conditions they live in, and the awards they have won. I explain that they are young, healthy, and in demand.

In addition, one of my goats is a buckling and the other is a doeling, which means they can breed.

After half an hour of conversation, we come to an agreement. You'll take three goats and I'll take one of your best cows. We have settled on a fair deal and we now both have something we did not have before: a relationship.

And then came money, which made things much easier. Rather than trading two dozen eggs for a bucket of milk that could then be turned into cheese and traded for a horse's halter, the eggs could be sold for coins that could be used to trade for the halter. This is pretty much the definition of civilization. Rather than having to hunt or gather our own food, we could count on the famer and the hunter to do that work while the rest of us built ovens, baked bread, and made pots.

People were able to venture farther afield and found new villages hundreds of miles away. Those villages were visited by peddlers in horse-drawn wagons who called on the town's general store (Figure 3.2).

The proprietor of the general store knew you on sight as you were in the store every week. Besides buying goods, the store was the most important source of local news. He had reason to ask about your family and your health. He knew how much flour and sugar you usually bought and how much more you were going to need because your cousins were coming to visit and they had teenage boys. The owner would pick and choose what to put on his shelves based on his knowledge of his fellow residents.

Figure 3.2   General store interior, Moundville, Alabama, 1936

You were going to need more warm cloth for a new coat because the last two times you came in, the one you were wearing was getting tattered. Your neighbor had been asking at the bar the other night if your mutual friend could return that wheelbarrow he borrowed two weeks ago. The miller's son was marrying the baker's daughter and would need some things to set up a new household. Retail was personal.

That all ended during the Industrial Revolution with the advent of mass production, mass transportation, and mass communication.

ONE-TO-MANY ADVERTISING

Once trains could move goods across vast distances in days, manufacturers could produce more than was needed locally. The Industrial Revolution showed up right on time and factories were born.

Once goods could be sold at a distance, there was a need to create demand. The general store couldn't stock one of everything, but if Mrs. Smith asked for a particular manufacturer's sewing machine, one would be placed on order.

And then came direct mail (Figure 3.3).

A master at slogans and catchy phrases, Richard Sears illustrated the cover of his 1894 catalog declaring it the "Book of Bargains: A Money Saver for Everyone," and the "Cheapest Supply House on Earth," claiming that "Our trade reaches around the World." Sears also knew the importance of keeping customers, boldly stating that "We Can't Afford to Lose a Customer." He proudly included testimonials from satisfied customers and made every effort to assure the reader that Sears had the lowest prices and best values. This catalog expanded from watches and jewelry, offering merchandise such as sewing machines, sporting goods, musical instruments, saddles, firearms, buggies, bicycles, baby carriages, and men's and children's clothing. The 1895 catalog added eyeglasses, including a self-test for "old sight, near sight and astigmatism." At this time Sears wrote nearly every line appearing in the catalogs drawing upon his personal experience using language and expressions that appealed to his target customers.

History of the Sears Catalog[1]

Figure 3.3 Sears Catalog, 1909.

Direct mail was followed by radio ads, roadside billboards, and television, and we no longer knew our customers by name, only by ZIP code.

THE FOUR *P*s

Product, price, promotion, and placement are the old workhorses of the marketing world.

- *Product.* Does the product live up to the promise? Is it really the best value? The highest status? The longest lasting? Is the quality so high that customers are happy to buy it again and again? Does the image it represents actually make the buyer feel stronger, hipper, smarter?

- *Price.* Is your product priced for the audience you're chasing? Think Rolex versus Swatch, Apple versus Acer, or Rolls Royce versus Kia. Being the least expensive may not be the best way to win hearts and minds. Being too expensive for all but a few might not target a wide enough marketing to stay in business. Does it ever go on sale?

- *Promotion.* This used to just be about advertising, but we're about to see that there are an inordinate number of ways to get your message into the minds of potential buyers. Promotion is not just about plastering your name all over the world; its success also depends on timing. Getting the right message to the right person at the right *time* is a challenge.

- *Placement.* Is the product available through the right channels? How many sales do you forgo if your item is not offered through Amazon? What is the impact of people not being able to call and order your service on the weekend? What is the difference between being able to buy your item at the grocery store as opposed to a brand-name storefront?

That's just the start. Marketing professionals worry about a great many more things than these four *P*s.

WHAT KEEPS A MARKETING PROFESSIONAL AWAKE?

Sending a message out into the universe and tracking its impact requires keeping tabs on a multitude of stages.

- *Distribution.* Did our message actually go out? Our television ad was slated to air at 7:45 P.M. on Tuesday in 14 DMAs (designated market areas). When did it actually air? Should we have placed it on the radio as well? The *New York Times* web home page? Facebook?

- *Exposure.* Was our message actually displayed? Maybe it got sent, but was it received? On what sort of device? Our banner ad was supposed to be served to five million people. Did it show up "below the fold" and nobody actually saw it? Was it merely recorded by a DVR and not really seen by a human?

- *Impression.* Did our message have any impact at all? Did it tip the scale of whether people claimed to have heard of our brand or product?

- *Recall.* Did the people who were intended to see our message, and who actually saw it, remember anything about it? Did they remember that our company stands for value/luxury/style/security/safety?

- *Attitude shift.* Did they change their mind about our industry, company, product?

- *Response.* Did they click/call/swipe/retweet/ask their doctor if our pill is right for them? How quickly did they respond?

- *Lead qualification.* It was great that thousands of people responded, but were they the right people? Did we reach qualified buyers? Are they ready (culturally prepared), willing (convinced this purchase is a good idea), and able (are allowed to buy [age]), and can they afford to buy our product?

- *Engagement.* Did people reach out for even more information? Return to our website? Go back into the store? Go for a test drive?

- *Sales.* Did anybody actually give us money in exchange for our goods or services?

- *Channel.* How did they buy? Over the phone? In the store? Online? On their mobile device?

- *Profits.* Did the sales of our products or services instigated through those promotional methods over those channels result in positive income?

- *Loyalty.* Did we reach and acquire customers who purchased from our company again?

- *Customer lifetime value.* Did the customers we acquired grow more or less profitable over time? Did they clog our customer service lines? Demand that we return their money? Were they profitable in the long run?

- *Advocacy.* Did customers review our goods or services in a positive light? Were they a good reference? Did they go out of their way to tell their friends and neighbors about their positive experience? Did they tweet with our hashtag?

- *Influence.* Did any of their friends and neighbors show interest, become engaged, purchase, and/or become an advocate?

Getting the right message to the right person at the right time means knowing what that specific person might need or want to know at that specific moment.

THE CUSTOMER JOURNEY

To understand what potential customers might be thinking at any given point in time, marketers came up with the idea of the *customer journey*.

The prospect goes from ignorance to interest to purchase with as many steps in between as a marketer's imagination allows. The fun part is trying to match the functional side of marketing to the reality of "the journey."

It's common to assume that you attract people's attention on television (Super Bowl ad, anyone?), spur them along with online ads, encourage them through social media, and then reel them in with an e-mail offer. While there's nothing inherently wrong in this approach, it's a bit like assuming that you know what a salmon is thinking just before it jumps up the waterfall and becomes lunch for a grizzly. Conjecture and inference have been our best tools for generations, along with years of experience.

We have to admit that we really can't know. Fortunately, it's worth the effort to use math on the problem.

WE WILL NEVER REALLY KNOW

The Internet Oldtimers Foundation was founded in the late 1990s for people who wanted to discuss online advertising. It's a "private, highly confidential and relaxed virtual space on industry-related topics with the goal of constantly effecting positive changes in the industry."

Twenty years later, one member posted a question that every marketing person has faced: How do you explain marketing to somebody with no background in marketing? How do you outline the processes of brand and product strategy, research, creative, paid media, earned media, PR, search, reporting, analytics, and finally, attribution?

Based on his experience in a career in advertising starting in the mid-1980s, Tom Cunniff took a stab at answering this question.

> Actually, *everyone* knows something about marketing
> but . . . pretty much everyone is wrong. What they know is
> based on *Bewitched* and *Mad Men* and old Super Bowl ads.

Hardly any of that has anything to do with today or the future.

Personally, I'd skip all the jargon and just tell a story along these lines.

Imagine you want to buy a camera.

How do you decide which one to buy?

If it's just about price and you want a decent point-and-shoot one, you might just go to Amazon and see what they've got.

If you're more serious, you'd Google for blogs and reviews, and look at reviews from people who've actually bought the brands you're looking at.

You'd probably go ask friends on Facebook, especially the ones who talk about photography and post good pictures.

Along the way, algorithms learn that you're looking for a camera and start serving you lots of ads.

Finally, you'd decide which camera to buy.

Then I would explain:

- What I just described is what people call a "customer journey."
- People today mostly find out about stuff through search engines—including Amazon—and social media. This is the stuff that we call SEO/SEM (Search Engine Optimization/Search Engine Marketing), influencer marketing (people who are popular in social media), etc., which is why SEO and SEM are important, and why having a strong product or service with good reviews is so important.
- And *that* is why research, product strategy and brand strategy are so important.
- Product strategy is all about what we make and how well it fits consumer needs. Good research helps us understand what consumers *say* they need, but we have to remember that people often don't know what they need until after you show it to them
- Brand strategy is all about how we talk about our product or service, what playing field we define for

ourselves, and how we act. This also helps inform
Brand Experience, which is the total way consumers
experience us.

What about advertising?

- Today most of it is bought on exchanges—it's bought
  and sold like stock. Basically you're betting on which
  prospect is most likely to become a paying customer. It's
  a *lot* of math and science and it's actually incredibly
  exciting.

What about creative? When do I get to meet Don Draper?

- Well...there's still a role for big splashy TV
  commercials, but it's far less important than it used to
  be. The most important words about advertising today
  are "relevance, viewability, and data." "Creative" still
  matters, but not as much as the other stuff.
- You'll hear us talk a *lot* about analytics and attribution.
  Basically, we're doing two things. First, trying to figure
  out what happened—how did people hear about us,
  what made them consider us, what made them decide
  to buy? Second, we're trying to figure out the relative
  influence of all the stuff we did.

Everything makes a contribution, but we'll want to
optimize our budget by spending the most on the stuff that
works best.

What is the marketing problem we're trying to solve? Putting the
right message in front of the right person at the right time in the right
context on the right device and figuring out whether *any* of the work
we did had an impact on the buying decision.

Or would it have been better if the above had happened in a different sequence? What if our big, splashy ad on television had been
ignored because of that big news story about the earthquake? Or...?
Throw in magazine ads, direct mail, posters, e-mail marketing, event
marketing, display ads on the Web, public relations, sales presentation, social media conversations, overheard conversations in the coffee
shop, billboards, point-of-sale displays, tradeshows, call center interactions, webinars, focus groups, surveys, blog posts, search marketing,
and talking to your neighbor over the backyard fence, and you're still
not done.

You still need to account for the Blue Toyota Syndrome. That's what Dave Smith of Mediasmith calls that moment when you buy a blue Toyota and suddenly start seeing them everywhere. At first, you even honk and wave. "Once you decide you are 'in market,' your own radar and filters kick in and you notice a lot more information about that item or category and start consuming content and advertising differently. Including stuff you come across serendipitously in traditional media. This makes category advertising much more effective if they reach you."

But reaching people has turned into a fractured fairytale. Figuring out which communications channels are best to reach which types of people at which point in the buying cycle requires strict attention and robust rigor. This is especially true given the number of ways we can reach out and touch someone. The explosive growth in the number of touchpoints is unnerving.

HOW DO I CONNECT? LET ME COUNT THE WAYS

To truly appreciate the marketing problem, I encourage you to visit MullenLowe U.S.'s New Marketing Ecosystem poster[2] and take a good hard look. (See Figure 3.4.)

MullenLowe starts in the center with the customer who could be a Suspect (you think she might like your offer), a Prospect (she has expressed an interest), a Customer (he bought something), an Advocate (he says nice things about you), or an Influencer (people listen to her).

From there, the poster branches out into a daunting variety of communication channels that branch off into a dizzying number of branches. This is just the two top tiers:

Audio/Video
Product Placement
Movie
Digital Television Networks
Satellite Radio
Network Television
Satellite Television
HD Radio
Cable
Online Radio
Podcasts

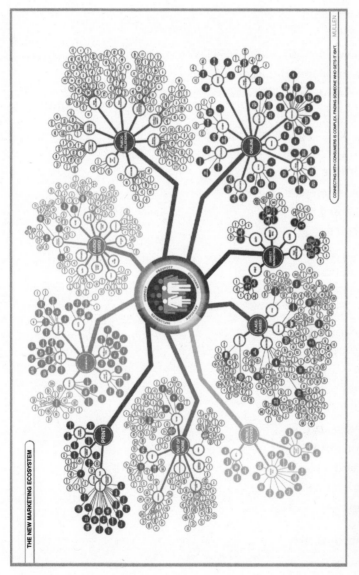

Figure 3.4 New Marketing Ecosystem poster

115

Public Relations

Financial & Investor Relations

Media Relations

Issues Management

Events, Sponsorships & Promotions

Speaking & Executive Visibility

Internal Communications

New Media

Word of Mouth

Corporate & Social Responsibility

Online

E-commerce

Gaming

Search

Online Advertising

Videocast

Websites

E-mail

Social Networking

Blogs

Podcasts

Direct Marketing

DRTV

Direct Mail

Radio

Telemarketing

Print

Place-Based

Work

In-Store

Recreation

Education

Mobile Devices
Handheld Game Console
Phone/PDA
MP3
(Mobile Apps)

Out of Home
Transit
Digital
Traditional Billboards
Nontraditional Static
Spectaculars
Guerilla
Mobile (Vehicles)

Print
Magazines
Trade Magazines
Newspapers
Alternative Delivery
Customer Publishing

Experiential
Tour Attractions
Organizations
Arts
Festivals/Fairs
Cause Marketing
Sports

In an ideal world we'll have figured out how to collect clean, accurate data about each individual we touch in each of those settings. We'll also have figured out how to pick winning Lottery numbers.

WHY DO I CONNECT? BRANDING

Brands were born to distinguish one owner's cattle from another. Once you have convinced me that your cows are of the finest parentage, are

Figure 3.5 Bronze branding-stamp: aegis of Sekhmet (British Museum)

well looked after, well fed, and have won many awards, I can save a lot of time by simply looking for your brand on their hide to assure myself that I'm getting the expected quality. While mostly associated with the Old West, branding irons have been traced back to 1543–1292 B.C., in the Eighteenth Egyptian Dynasty. (See Figure 3.5.)

This shorthand spread to more and more products as the makers and the buyers became separated by miles. Instead of buying a baguette from Fred the Baker down the street, we bought Wonder Bread. Instead of going to a random restaurant in that strange city and taking our chances, we could go to McDonald's and, lovin' it or not, could count on the quality of the food and service to be the same as every other McDonald's we'd ever visited.

Name recognition is the opening salvo in this fight for mind-space. Next comes trait recognition. Companies spend big to get you to connect their name and/or logo with a specific characteristic.

Apple: Cutting-edge design

FedEx: Reliability

Rolex: Luxury

Volvo: Safety

Walmart: Low prices

If they can get you to remember their name and understand what they stand for, the next step is to get you to relate to them, to become part of the tribe. You know the brand Rolls Royce and what it stands for. You even love the product. But you have no intention of buying one. Ever. You are *not* the target audience. Ultimately, you want people to associate themselves with the image you are projecting and delivering. "I am an electric car person" or "I am a pickup truck person" or "I am a minivan person."

Branding is more than simply telling people what they should think of you. A company's brand is a combination of the story it tells and the experience people have. If you say you're the low-price leader and you're not, your brand suffers. If you promise that a customer's package will absolutely, positively be there overnight and it's not, your brand is tarnished.

Marketing consultant and author Kristin Zhivago always reminds us, "Your brand is the promises you keep." Your brand is in the eye of the beholder.

So how do we know if the money and effort we spend is paying off?

MARKETING MIX MODELING

Start with a budget of $5 million. Spend some on television, some on radio, print, mail, telemarketing, and outdoor billboards, and measure the results. Next period (month, quarter, or year), alter the allocation between channels and compare the results to the previous period to determine the incremental sales (*lift*). Repeat. Apply multivariate regression to the results to predict how to adjust the allocation next time in order to achieve better results.

Pat LaPointe, managing partner of Growth Calculus, pointed out some of the drawbacks of this approach in his post, "Marketing Mix Model Masochist."[3]

> I've gone back and forth over the years on the value of marketing mix models, all the time seeking to understand where, when, and how they add the most value to marketing managers looking for insight into more effective and efficient marketing.
>
> I think I've seen all the warts:
>
> ■ Models that just skim the surface of tactical optimization by looking only at media and ignoring the category dynamics and uncontrollable factors, thereby overstating the impact of marketing in very suspicious ways.

- Models that look backwards perfectly but are of little value if one is making decisions about what to do next.

- Models that regularly seem to reward short-term demand-generation tactics because they can "read" those more cleanly than longer-term brand equity value.

- Models with high "base" compositions that explain only a small portion of the change in volume or profit from one period to the next.

- Models that understate the value of marketing by failing to account for the interaction effects, particularly those in the new digital and social media realm.

LaPointe has also heard from practitioners who feel the method doesn't hold up to complex competitive ecosystems and feel Marketing Mix Modeling (MMM) is losing its relevance. Yet, he finds things to like in the old methodology yet. MMM is still an effective way of helping managers understand what happened and what might happen.

> For whatever reason, MMM is a concept that most marketing and finance managers can actually grasp. It is neither too simplistic to adequately explain their understanding of the universe they operate in, nor too complex to be embraced and acted upon. MMM is sort of the Goldilocks solution: just right.

He contends that the understandability of the method and trust in the outcome are crucial. Furthermore, MMM hasn't rotted on the vine. It has improved with age.

> New methods and techniques have emerged to help better decompose the base effects, isolate long-term brand impacts, explain the direct and indirect effects of various elements of the tactical spectrum, and improve the forward-looking capability of the models.

As a result, these models help marketers with changing conditions where *what-if* simulations are quite useful. Just be sure the assumptions and limitations of the models are well understood, the changing environment is constantly taken into consideration, and everybody knows that any model has a limited life span.

LaPointe feels "it's critically important that marketers *not* stop at Marketing Mix Models. Risk is magnified by over-reliance on a single tool. Today's marketing measurement toolkit needs to be much broader."

This brings us to econometrics.

ECONOMETRICS

How about building a complex model that takes the entire marketplace *and its environment* into consideration?

What if you built a model that also accounted for:

- GDP
- Interest rates
- Housing starts
- Unemployment
- Education levels
- Stock prices
- Weather
- Concert ticket sales
- Price of tea in China

As you can imagine, the formulas can get quite complex. This is the work of economists, and the old joke is that if you took all the economists in the world and laid them end-to-end, they would all be pointing in different directions. But bear in mind that some models are useful and econometric models have proven *very* useful.

CUSTOMER LIFETIME VALUE

If you spend a million dollars in marketing to get 100,000 customers, your cost of acquisition is $10 each. If you're in the high-end investment industry, you're golden! If you're selling candy bars, your days are numbered. However, if you never had to spend another dime and your candy bars are addictive, then the cost of acquisition gets spread out over years. Subtract the cost of goods sold and you still end up looking like a hero.

Of course, the only industry that can accurately predict lifetime value is where customers are one-and-done: casket makers. The rest of us have a bit of math to attend to.

Some customers lean on your customer service department so much that they become permanently unprofitable within days. Customers who churn are very expensive as well. The goal is to find people who buy repeatedly without triggering additional expense.

When you have a feel for which of your customers is the most valuable, you can provide better service—premium classes of service for airline travelers, coupon for loyalty card holders, their favorite table automatically reserved when they call.

You can also review what you know about them and go out and find others who resemble them, whether that's by demographics, method of acquisition, or even those who expressed interest in product A before buying product B.

ONE-TO-ONE MARKETING—THE MEME

In 1993, Don Peppers and Martha Rogers published their book, *The One to One Future*, and brought forth the idea that computer databases would allow companies to get to know their customers again. Harking back to the general store, this was a way to remember each customer as an individual and treat them according to their predilections and peccadillos. This was a very exciting theory for those of us with computer skills, marketing jobs, and vivid imaginations. After all, 1993 was the year the Internet was opened for commercial use.

Not everybody was as excited. Professor Peter Fader of the Wharton School saw that the idea could not scale in a way that would be believable to consumers. In 2007, he said:[4]

> Lots of firms talk about one-to-one marketing. I think that's a real disservice to most industries. One-to-one marketing only works when you have a very deep relationship with every customer. So one-to-one marketing works great in private wealth management, or in a business-to-business setting where you meet with the client at least once a month, and understand not just their business needs but what's going on in their life. But in areas approaching a mass market, where you can't truly distinguish each individual, you just have a bunch of people and a bunch of characteristics that describe them. Then the notion of one-to-one marketing is terrible. It will do more harm than good, because the customers will act more randomly than you expect, and the cost of trying to figure out what specific customers will

do far outweighs the benefits you could get from that level of detail.

It's very hard to say who's going to buy this thing and when. To take that uncertainty and square it by looking across two products, or to raise it to the nth power by looking across a large portfolio of products, and say "these two go together," and make deterministic statements as opposed to talking about tendencies and probabilities, can be very, very harmful. It's much more important for companies to come up with appropriate groupings of similar people, and make statements about them as a group.

I don't want to pick on Amazon in particular; they really tout the capabilities of their recommendations systems. But maybe this customer was going to buy book B anyway, and therefore all the recommendations were irrelevant. Or maybe they were going to buy book C, which would have been a higher-margin item, so getting them to buy book B was a mistake. Or maybe they're becoming so upset by irrelevant recommendations that they're going away entirely. I don't want in any way to suggest that cross-selling shouldn't be done, but what I'm suggesting is that the net gains from it are less than people might think. It often can't justify the kinds of investments that firms are making in it.

As unlikely as it seems, all of the decision making that went into advertising and marketing used to be done the old-fashioned way—they played it by ear.

SEAT-OF-THE-PANTS MARKETING

Writing in the journal *Applied Marketing Analytics*,[5] Lead for Global Commercial Growth Analytics at Kellogg Company Rafael Alcaraz wrote about how marketing decisions used to be made in "Intuitive Analytics: The Same as Analytic Guessing?"

The use of business stereotypes and conventional wisdom in marketing/marketing science (M/MS) is not new. Systematic use of business stereotypes in these disciplines has been part of the recipe for success for many organizations and individuals over time....

Since around the early 1980s through to the late 1990s, the use of old marketing mix stereotypical strategies and tactics became the norm. Many companies (Procter & Gamble, The Coca-Cola Company, Pepsi Co., Miller Brewing, The Hershey Company, to name a few) effectively have used and reused commonly known marketing 'principles' for their own benefit. The coupling of traditional advertising vehicles (television, radio, print magazines) with in-store promotion (features, displays, and price promotions) during certain times of the year were commonly used, often with fairly good effectiveness—as evidenced by the sales lift and returns on investment.

Alcaraz then described the shuffling of top marketing executives, assuring that those with the most successful experience rose to the top of firms in the same industry. Consumer packaged goods companies were filled with people who brought their conventional wisdom and intuition with them from competitors.

Was that conventional wisdom, or intuition born of intelligence and honed by experience, or simply the luck of the marketplace? Clearly, these time-honored insights were not applicable online. Today, marketing mix models have been altered beyond recognition with the inclusion of the online and mobile worlds, and have been drastically transformed by a glut of that behavioral data.

Executives still ask for "the numbers" when only the outcomes can truly be understood. When the numbers were made up of raw materials, distribution costs, and the buckets of the marketing mix, the amount spent could be deducted from income, and intuition based on experience could be applied to decisions about how to allocate the next cycle of marketing dollars.

Today, the numbers include such new and nebulous metrics as visitors, stickiness, conversion, bounce rate, path, journey, view-through, abandonment, attribution, and Twitter acceleration ratio—few of which have an industry standard definition.

MARKETING IN A NUTSHELL

There's an old chestnut of a joke describing marketing that is tasteless, offensive, ludicrous, and yet satisfyingly informative. Here's the extended version.

A young man goes into a bar, sees an attractive young woman, goes up to her and says, "I am very rich and good in bed." That's direct marketing.

A young man goes into a bar with several friends and they see an attractive young woman. One of his buddies goes up to her and pointing back at the young man says, "He's very rich and good in bed." That's advertising.

A young man goes into a bar with several friends and they see an attractive young woman. One by one, his buddies go up to her and work into the conversation that the young man is very rich and good in bed. That's public relations.

A young man goes into a bar, sees an attractive young woman, goes up to her, chats for a while and gets her phone number. The next day, he calls and says, "I am very rich and good in bed." That's telemarketing.

A young man goes into a bar and an attractive young woman walks up to him and says, "I hear you're rich and good in bed. Can I buy you a drink?" That's brand recognition.

A young man goes into a bar, sees an attractive young woman, goes up to her and says, "I am very rich and good in bed." She slaps his face. That's targeting the wrong market segment.

A young man goes into a bar, sees an attractive young woman, goes up to her and says, "I am very rich and good in bed." She introduces him to her husband. That's misreading supply and demand.

A young man goes into a bar, sees an attractive young woman, goes up to her, but another guy cuts in and says, "I am very rich and good in bed," and they leave together. That's competitive marketing capturing market share.

A young man goes into a bar, sees an attractive young woman, goes up to her, and before he can speak, his wife shows up. That's restriction from entering new markets.

A young man goes into a bar, sees an attractive young woman, and strikes up a conversation. At the end of the evening, it's clear she's not interested. The young man follows her around for several days, dropping reminders about his wealth and sexual prowess. Online, that's called retargeting. In real life, it's stalking and is a felony for the first offense in fourteen states and for the second offense in thirty-five states.

A young man goes into a bar, sees an attractive young woman, and strikes up a conversation. Over several months of casual encounters, double dating, meeting the others' families and slowly getting to know each other, she learns that he is quite well off and that they are very well-suited in bed. They marry and live happily ever after. This is building a relationship—something we hope AI can help us accomplish.

Marketing is the constant effort to shorten the courtship. That's why it has seemed so tawdry.

WHAT SEEMS TO BE THE PROBLEM?

Ask a marketing executive what problems she is trying to solve with data and you're already headed down the wrong track. That's like a doctor asking a patient how he might benefit from an MRI scan and wouldn't he prefer a CT scan instead?

Ask an online marketing professional what he wants, and he might laugh and tell you the answer is as plain as the nose on your face.

"I want more traffic!"

"Why?"

"Because then I can sell more stuff."

"Why?"

"So I can make more money!"

We just stepped into the first, albeit shallow, quagmire. If marketing professionals earn their bonus for bringing in more traffic (think advertising agency), then traffic is all they care about—the quality of the traffic be damned. If marketing professionals are compensated for increasing their conversion rate, the answer is simple. Just stop spending money trying to attract new customers. The customers they have will convert better and they'll have spent less than half their budget.

"No, I mean we need to increase sales!"

If top-line revenue is the only goal, that is also a very easy problem to solve. Sell $1 bills for 50¢. Revenues will go right through the roof. Goal met! President's Club achieved! Vacation in Hawaii! Bankruptcy in 5 . . . 4 . . . 3 . . . .

Chances are the real problem is that they want to raise profitability by customer, by product, by distribution channel in a specific time frame with a minimal budget. Now *that's* a problem you can sink your teeth into. The magic comes when you have enough domain knowledge to tackle more and more problems so that you start to recognize the fundamentals and you learn how to solve problems.

It's not that I'm so smart, it's just that I stay with problems longer.

Albert Einstein

NOTES

1. History of the Sears Catalog, http://www.searsarchives.com/catalogs/history.htm.

2. New Marketing Ecosystem poster, http://us.mullenlowe.com/back-by-popular-demand-the-new-marketing-ecosystem-poster.

3. "Marketing Mix Model Masochist," http://marketingmeasurementtoday.blogspot.com/2011/05/marketing-mix-model-masochist.html.

4. CIO Insight, http://www.cioinsight.com/c/a/Past-News/What-Data-Mining-Can-and-Cant-Do.

5. *Applied Marketing Analytics*, Vol. 2, No. 1, pp. 6–11, Winter 2015/6, https://www.henrystewartpublications.com/ama.

CHAPTER 4

Using AI to Get Their Attention

There comes a moment at every company when the CFO asks the CEO, the COO, and the CIO about the CMO. "What is the measure of success? How do you set a budget for something that's so...so...*fuzzy* as 'marketing' and 'branding'?"

The COO's head shakes and his shoulders rise. The CIO looks blank. The CEO tries to explain some of the above. The CMO looks at the others and expresses gratitude that somebody outside the marketing department has finally showed some interest. After taking a deep breath, the CMO describes the metrics that have been used in marketing for years, starting with public relations and market research. After all, we need to know whom we're targeting.

MARKET RESEARCH: WHOM ARE WE AFTER?

Market research began as a means of identifying just how big the marketplace is for your new invention or special service. Are there enough people who could afford it within the region it's going to be for sale? Are there competitors? Do people perceive the need for it already or do we need to spend some time educating them? What alternatives do people have?

Demographics were needed by radio and television stations to describe their audiences to potential advertisers. Age, gender, education level, and the like within a specific territory were the first data tools. The national census was started and then companies sprang up to conduct more detailed surveys. Pretty soon, custom surveys asked about specific brand awareness, attributes, and affinity.

Market research through telephone interviews, shopping mall clipboard surveys, and direct mail response lowered the risk of investing. Over time, you could acquire some insight about whether your brand was trending up or down in the hearts and minds of your target audience. You could forecast the potential success of launching new offerings or opening new territories.

Machine Learning in Market Research

In 1937, the National Association of Marketing Teachers (founded in 1915) and the American Marketing Society (founded in 1933) joined to become the American Marketing Association (AMA).

In 2004, the AMA defined *marketing research* as

> the function that links the consumer, customer, and public to the marketer through information—information used to identify and define marketing opportunities and problems; generate, refine, and evaluate marketing actions; monitor marketing performance; and improve understanding of marketing as a process. Marketing research specifies the information required to address these issues, designs the method for collecting information, manages and implements the data collection process, analyzes the results, and communicates the findings and their implications.

Nowadays, the AMA is exploring how to best add artificial intelligence to the data collection process, the analysis, and the communication of findings. Her name is Lucy.

The AMA is working with Equals3's Lucy, born of IBM's Watson (see Chapter 7), to develop the AMA's next-generation marketing superhero. Lucy starts by being a means of tapping into all 80 years of the AMA's research, a portal that allows members to answer basic marketing strategy questions. AMA CEO Russ Klein envisions a tool where AMA's research combines with all kinds of other data (client data, sensitive data, purchased data, etc.) as a "cognitive companion for marketers."

"At first, Lucy behaves more like a search engine than anything," says Klein. "She retrieves articles and starts to recognize patterns and retrieve more relevant information based on the questions. We give her a reply as to whether or not she is on track and if she *is* on track, how *well* on track, and she continues to learn from that feedback."

Klein is excited that the AMA has some of the leading academic journals in the world, including the *Journal of Marketing*, the *Journal of Marketing Research*, and the *Journal of Public Policy & Marketing*. "Even 80 years of AMA data in the context of our official intelligence would be considered a thin layer of data," says Klein. "A lot of the knowledge is trapped by the density of the academic, peer-review reading level and the quantitative rigor that's used in a lot of the work. Lucy can unlock that for our members and help us rewrite as many of those articles as we can, for broader consumption."

This "thin layer" of data also includes everything that the AMA has published, any topic delivered through newsletters and that's ever been posted on the AMA.org website. Have a question about historical ad spending on the Super Bowl? Lucy will read through the 15 or 20 academic papers, articles, blog posts, and opinion pieces about just that and surface relevant information rather than just a list of links.

This content would also include all of the AMA articles about the 7 Big Problems in the Marketing Industry:

1. Effectively targeting high-value sources of growth
2. The role of marketing in the firm and the c-suite
3. The digital transformation of the modern corporation
4. Generating and using insight to shape marketing practice
5. Dealing with an omnichannel world
6. Competing in dynamic global markets
7. Balancing incremental and radical innovation

How long did it take Lucy to consume all this information? "A couple of weeks," says Klein. "But much of that was because we had to train Lucy to understand the answers most relevant to modern marketers."

The opportunity of discovery through this tool coupled with such rich data is unfathomable. There is no telling what you might come up with. Klein envisions Lucy becoming the Amazon Alexa of marketing. "Someone could say, 'I'm thinking about writing a media plan for a detergent' and Lucy will come back and say, 'I've analyzed the social media feeds of everyone who cares about detergent, and here's the best media mix to reach them.

It's easy to imagine Lucy parlaying the AMA's research and corresponding findings of quantitative marketing modeling, behavior economics, and general strategy and management into usable, pragmatic, managerially relevant answers to executive and practitioner questions. As Klein sees it, "Lucy is going to get faster and faster at making abstractions and creating connections and identifying patterns."

Given the big picture of a marketplace, it's time to take the very first step toward one-to-one marketing by dividing up the market into actionable segments.

MARKETPLACE SEGMENTATION

In his article, "24 Uses of Statistical Modeling," on Data Science Central,[1] Vincent Granville describes market segmentation as follows:

> Market segmentation, also called customer profiling, is a marketing strategy which involves dividing a broad target market into subsets of consumers, businesses, or countries that have, or are perceived to have, common needs, interests, and priorities, and then designing and implementing strategies to target them. Market segmentation strategies are generally used to identify and further define the target customers, and provide supporting data for marketing plan elements such as positioning to achieve certain marketing plan objectives. Businesses may develop product differentiation strategies, or an undifferentiated approach, involving specific products or product lines depending on the specific demand and attributes of the target segment.

In championing statistical methods for market segmentation, Granville sets the stage for machines to do the work faster, cheaper, and better.

IDC's whitepaper, "Machine Learning Will Revolutionize Market Segmentation Practices,"[2] describes how AI can generate market segments:

> Machine learning delivers personal profiles into segmentation "buckets" which can be predefined or automatically machine generated. Dynamic market segments are then sized and prioritized based on the untapped incremental revenue opportunity.

> However, this capability is not limited to predefined segments, as machine learning can also slice and dice customer data sets to identify potential new segments of customers who are undermonetized relative to their peers.

For example, machine learning might identify how the behavior of a region or country varies from the global norm and requires a specific product assortment and pricing mix; or perhaps time-based variations that show that late-night shoppers have a propensity to abandon a cart.

Creating a bucket of prospects who look like your best customers is a fine old tradition. Abode's Target Premium is one of many tools designed to do just that: Find your best customers, point your machine at them, and let it work out what they have in common so that you can go find more like them.

According to Jamie Brighton,[3] Abode's Target goes a couple of steps farther.

Target aggregates customer data from a variety of online and offline sources, including web and app analytics, customer relationship management (CRM) databases, and internal-facing enterprise resource planning (ERP) and data warehouse (DWH) systems. As you surface this data, Target's machine-learning algorithms determine which variables are most predictive of conversions, eliminating clutter from your customer profiles. And Target's integration with Audience Manager means you can leverage lookalike modeling to automatically find new customer segments, expanding your audience in unexpected directions.

Above all, Target's built-in artificial intelligence tools are designed to spare you the guesswork, and point you straight toward the messages, creatives, and page variants that'll give you measurable boosts in conversion.

Segmenting the marketplace and your own customers based on sales is tried-and-true. Keeping your finger on the pulse of public opinion is a little trickier, especially with so much noise being made on social media.

Social Media Monitoring

Measuring public opinion was always about extrapolating from surveys and hoping the small sample you selected was representative of the general public. Today, individual public opinion is ripe for the taking on Facebook, YouTube, Instagram, Twitter, Reddit,

WhatsApp, and whatever new product review or augmented-reality platform pops up next.

Relevancy

The first task is figuring out if the blog, tweet, or photo is even pertinent to a given company. If somebody blasts invectives about how bad their chicken stock is, the machine has to learn over time to figure out context. Is the individual—or the growing number of detractors—talking about some terrible mistake Campbell's Soup made due to a misprint on a can, or are they reacting to the U.S. Securities and Exchange Commission's subpoenaing Tyson Foods due to allegations of colluding to drive up chicken prices starting as far back as 2008?

Context is something AI is good at, given enough data. This is a relatively straightforward problem to solve.

Now that the machine is happy that the text it has collected is germane, it must weight different posts depending on how wide-reaching they are and how much attention they attract. If a tweet falls in the forest and nobody retweets it, it has no impact.

Authority

"Influencer marketing" has come into its own as a specialty. Find those who have influential power and get them to say something nice about your brand. This is classic public relations brought forward into the age of Twitter.

With 100 million followers, Katy Perry's tweets get significantly more consideration than the 98 percent of Twitter users who have less than 2,000 followers. Half have 61 followers or less. Get Katy to comment on your product or get half a million people to tell their closest friends and you get the same potential exposure.

That's only the first metric. Ask a machine to determine who has the most influence, and the definition requires some clarification.

Whether tweets, blogs, or pics, "influence" others affects not just how many people *could* have seen it but some combination of how many people *did* see it, how many people repeated or mentioned it, and how many people were, well, influenced by it. Were they swayed? Were they persuaded? Did they change their beliefs or behaviors? Those who get the most retweets, comments on their blogs, or Likes on Facebook might be influential and it behooves the marketer to keep tabs on their publicly expressed opinions.

An influencer's social graph should be considered. If I retweet everything you put out there, you have a great deal of influence over me. If I am constantly commenting on your Facebook posts, blog, or Medium article, your influence over me is much stronger. As with public relations, it's crucial to establish and support relationships with identified influencers so they continue to support your brand, offering, or cause.

By identifying the desired results, the machine will find the influential individual as the one whose ideas flourish and spread. It simply needs a clear definition of *success*.

- Did the influencer mention your latest promotion?
- Did the influencer link to your video?
- Did the influencer repost your photo?
- Did the influencer mention your brand sua sponte?
- Did others follow the influencer's lead and take action?
- Did any of the above move the needle on your key performance indicators?

Influence doesn't have to be writ large to be effective. It can also be influence on an intimate level.

Amplero, an AI marketing platform company, has an Influencer Optimization agent that seeks to take *customer relationship management* (CRM) to the network level. The company's paper, "Beyond the Target Customer: Social Effects of CRM Campaigns,"[4] puts forth its case.

> Using a randomized field experiment involving nearly 6,000 customers of a mobile telecommunications provider, we find that the social connections of targeted customers increase their consumption and are less likely to churn due to a campaign that was neither targeted at them nor offered them any direct incentives. We estimate a social multiplier of 1.28. That is, the effect of the campaign on first-degree connections of targeted customers is 28% of the effect of the campaign on the targeted customers. By further leveraging the randomized experimental design we show that, consistent with a network externality account, the increase in activity among the non-targeted but connected customers is driven by the increase in communication between the targeted customers and their connections, making the local network of the non-targeted customers more valuable. Our findings suggest that in targeting CRM marketing campaigns, firms should consider not only the profitability of the targeted customer, but also the potential spillover of the campaign to non-targeted but connected customers.

Markerly claims to help the marketer

> Sponsor & Manage Thousands of Influencers. Our machine
> learning platform allows us to instantly sort for look-alikes,
> predict performance, track influencer success, optimize
> campaigns, report in real time, and incorporate traditional
> advertising—such as retargeting to maximize performance.

Authoritative Example: Kia

To leverage the investment in Super Bowl LI, automaker Kia decided to send out a pair of colorful socks, symbolizing "pizzazz" in the ad with Christopher Walken, to 100 personality-attuned social influencers in hopes they would snap and post photos of themselves adorned in the Kia clothing. Any help in wringing value out of a $5 million spend on a 30-second television ad is worth some effort.

Targeting traits associated with their Optima model (openness to change, artistic interest, and achievement-striving), Kia turned to IBM's Watson to find the right influencers. IBM partner Influential analyzed 10,000 social media influencers with over four billion followers using two of Watson's capabilities, Personality Insights and AlchemyLanguage.

Steve Abrams, Director of Technology for Watson Ecosystem at IBM, said,[5] "Research has shown that the word choices we use when we communicate reflect aspects of our personality. They can say something about whether we're introverted or extroverted . . . whether we value openness or adventure or value more conservatism."

Influential's CEO Ryan Detert told FastCompany,[6] "We saw a 30% higher level of engagement on FTC posts, which are branded posts [flagged] with [a hashtag like] #Ad or #Sponsored. The more the brand and influencers' voices are aligned, the greater the engagement, sentiment, ad recall, virality, and clicks." Detert said the influencers that they identified "outperformed their regular organic content with these branded posts."

In January 2017, Amplero announced the employment of machine learning for its Influencer Optimization offering.[7]

> Influencer marketing is going to look a lot different in
> 2017. Up until now, the term strictly applied to so-called
> influencers—ranging from A-list celebrities all the way
> down to niche Instagram stars with a few thousand
> followers—being paid to subtly promote or endorse
> products to followers. It's part of the broader shift from
> mass media to individualized, highly contextual marketing.

In 2017, based on new research from Columbia University, HEC Paris, and Amplero, customer-obsessed brands will take it one step further and identify the everyday spheres of influence within their customer or prospect networks based on behavioral data.

Influencers will no longer just apply to fashion stars, video game gurus, or parent bloggers. Instead, it's any individual that has a quantifiable effect on first- and second-degree connections within your customer or prospect database—to the tune of a 1.28× ROI multiplier on non-targeted users.

Sentiment

Customer reviews go a long way to build credibility, and simply tracking ratings may be fine for some. Airbnb asks for 1- to 5-star reviews of accuracy, communication, cleanliness, location, check-in, and value. After that, things get tricky.

Social media monitoring is very reliable for *quantity* of mentions. Humans, who are very adept at recognizing context, do not always agree. A younger evaluator would rank the phrase, "Those shoes are sick," as high praise. A 70-year-old would not.

Sentiment analysis systems try to imitate humans, but humans only agree about 80 percent of the time. If that's the best we can hope for, then the outcome of this analysis is not on firm ground and teaching a machine to do it is a serious challenge.

At the start, the solution was going to be a dictionary. Some words are positive and some are negative. Emoticons, emoji, ALL CAPS, and intentional misspellings are also classified as positive, negative, or neutral. But vernacular changes on a daily basis and is so very different from culture to culture and age group to age group. Communicating feelings is a very subtle endeavor and a great deal of nuance is domain specific.

Everybody knows what a teenager's eye-roll means, but language is so supple and words and phrases take on different meanings from one group of friends to another. The lexicon-driven method leaves so much to be desired that a combination of domain-specific linguistic rules and supervised machine learning that can dynamically adapt is really the only hope.

Although not strictly dependable, opinion mining is very useful for tracking the volume and tone of tweets or Facebook posts, for example, as it can report on shifts in tone as well as volume. The directional information is enough to flag a marketing professional that a threshold has been tripped and human intervention may be necessary.

Sentimental Example: CFPB

Tom Sabo, Principal Solutions Architect at SAS Federal, put it this way:[8]

> When a person feels sufficiently wronged to lodge a complaint with the Consumer Financial Protection Bureau (CFPB), there's likely to be some negative sentiment involved. But is there a connection between the language they use and the likelihood they will be compensated by the offending company? . . .
>
> Machine learning and rule-based sentiment analysis can support each other in a complementary analysis, and produce actionable information from large amounts of free-form text. In this case, machine learning and sentiment analysis could improve and evolve the CFPB's ability to assess consumer complaints.
>
> This is accomplished by identifying patterns between degrees of negative sentiment expressed in free-form consumer complaints. A model which generates rules based on this free-form text, where the related companies ended up paying out compensation as a result of the complaint. These machine-generated rules indicate patterns in the free-form text which tend to only be present in the cases of monetary compensation.
>
> Examples include types of lending and retail companies associated with the lending but not present in the structured data. For example, if someone lodges a complaint about bank fees, and uses a derivative of the term "steal," it is more likely to be associated with some kind of financial recompense. This goes beyond traditional sentiment analysis, identifying key negative terms, in a particular context, to highlight patterns associated with a result.
>
> Visual analytics provides these newfound insights with illustrative structure—a previously hidden, yet incredibly valuable, map of areas of concern, including predatory lenders or credit card companies with substandard customer service.

Competitive Analysis

If you're in the health-care business and want to know what's happening from a competitive perspective, our friends at Quid have you covered.[9] (See Figure 4.1.)

> Quid uses text-based data, in this case technology and business descriptions of all the companies in the digital health space, and then compiles and organizes it for analysis.... By understanding company data, you can align your strategy with investment and innovation trends in the digital health landscape.
>
> The data has been organized into different groups. Each colored cluster represents a specific theme that the companies within it share. This allows you to see how the whole ecosystem of companies in any category connect with one another.
>
> You can curate, filter, and aggregate nodes in a more customized way—highlighting what is most relevant to the question you need answered. In this instance, Quid has selected all of the companies that share a common investor.
>
> By zooming into the network, Quid can identify white space opportunities and uncover unique technologies based on the most innovative companies in the digital health market.
>
> Quid provides a range of different perspectives on the data. By switching to a scatterplot view, you can map the data by any criteria. Here, Quid has identified which digital health sectors are receiving the most attention from investors.

Want to get a clear picture of the environment your customers inhabit? Salesforce.com acquired deep-learning startup MetaMind in 2016. Now, as part of Salesforce's Einstein offering, this visual recognition system is allowing companies to see into customers' lives by taking a close look at their photos.[10]

> You're a developer who works for a company that sells outdoor sporting gear. The company has automation that monitors social media channels. When someone posts a photo, the company wants to know whether the photo

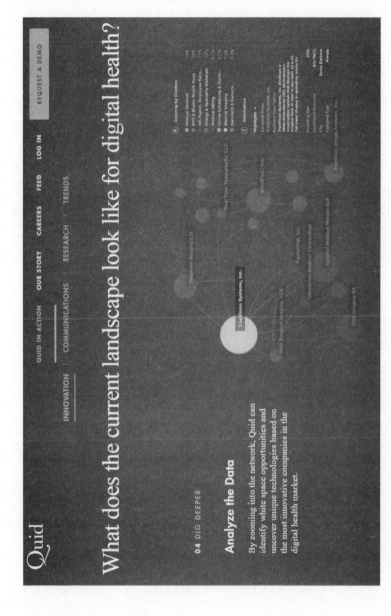

Figure 4.1 Quid analyzes the digital health marketplace.

was taken at the beach or in the mountains. Based on where the photo was taken, the company can make targeted product recommendations to its users. . . .

Your task is straightforward: Create a model that can identify whether an image is of the beach or the mountains. Then test the model with an image of a beach scene.

The Predictive Vision Service API enables you to tap into the power of AI and train deep learning models to recognize and classify images at scale. You can use pre-trained classifiers or train your own custom classifiers to solve unique use cases.

Salesforce Social Studio allows you to "visually listen" to prospects and clients to see if your brand logo—or that of your competitors—is in their photos. These contextual clues shine a light on your marketplace like never before.

MetaMind can already recognize over 500 things you might be eating, including those listed here.[11]

Apple Pie	Club Sandwich	Grilled Salmon	Pho
Baby Back Ribs	Crab Cakes	Guacamole	Pizza
Baklava	Creme Brulee	Gyoza	Pork Chop
Beef Carpaccio	Croque Madame	Hamburger	Poutine
Beef Tartare	Cup Cakes	Hot & Sour Soup	Prime Rib
Beet Salad	Deviled Eggs	Hot Dog	Pulled Pork Sandwich
Beignets	Donuts	Huevos Rancheros	Ramen
Bibimbap	Dumplings	Hummus	Ravioli
Bread Pudding	Edamame	Ice Cream	Red Velvet Cake
Breakfast Burrito	Eggs Benedict	Lasagna	Risotto
Bruschetta	Escargots	Lobster Bisque	Samosa
Caesar Salad	Falafel	Lobster Roll Sandwich	Sashimi
Cannoli	Filet Mignon	Macaroni & Cheese	Scallops
Caprese Salad	Fish & Chips	Macarons	Seaweed Salad
Carrot Cake	Foie Gras	Miso Soup	Shrimp & Grits

Ceviche	French Fries	Mussels	Spaghetti Bolognese
Cheese Plate	French Onion Soup	Nachos	Spaghetti Carbonara
Cheesecake	French Toast	Omelette	Spring Rolls
Chicken Curry	Fried Calamari	Onion Rings	Steak
Chicken Quesadilla	Fried Rice	Oysters	Strawberry Shortcake
Chicken Wings	Frozen Yogurt	Pad Thai	Sushi
Chocolate Cake	Garlic Bread	Paella	Tacos
Chocolate Mousse	Gnocchi	Pancakes	Takoyaki
Churros	Greek Salad	Panna Cotta	Tiramisu
Clam Chowder	Grilled Cheese Sandwich	Peking Duck	Tuna Tartare

MetaMind also keeps a growing knowledge base of general items as unique as Abacus, Abaya, Academic Gown, Academic Robe, Judge's Robe, Accordion, Acorn Squash, Acorn, Acoustic Guitar, and much more.

The company suggests you use this knowledge to:

> Monitor user-generated images through communities and review boards to improve products and quality of service.
>
> Evaluate banner advertisement exposure during broadcast events to drive higher ROI.
>
> Product identification—Increase the ways that you can identify your products to streamline sales processes and customer service.
>
> Identify product issues before sending out a field technician to increase case resolution time.
>
> Discover which products are out of stock or misplaced to streamline inventory restocking.
>
> Measure retail shelf-share to optimize product mix and represent top-selling products among competitors.

RAISING AWARENESS

Now that the marketing professional has a clear view of the marketplace, the competition, and what's being said about them, it's time to get the word out.

Public Relations

Old-school PR took a lot of legwork. Get to know the proper journalists at the proper publications and encourage, cajole, and coax them to write positive articles about the products and services on offer. Monitoring the outcome of this effort was the work of scissors and tape. Page through the periodicals, cut out the pertinent articles, and paste them in a clippings book to show the boss or the client.

With an unmanageable number of potential "publications," this task must be automated and the industry is differentiating public relations visibility by dividing it up into paid, earned, shared, and owned media.

- Paid—we bought an advertorial.
- Earned—we did something truly newsworthy.
- Shared—the public liked it, too.
- Owned—we posted it on our blog and got noticed.

Tracking how much attention was garnered requires more than just setting a Google Alert and hoping it notices everything with your brand name in it. Nerve Center from Bottlenose "gathers Business Intelligence (BI) and data that spans 2 M+ sources, including social, news, blogs, television, radio, and print media. The platform is comprised of three main components (Stream, Compute, Discover) that seamlessly work together to aggregate, automate, and apply machine learning to provide complete business insight."

San Francisco-based Quid

> compiles and analyzes massive amounts of text-based data, in this case all of the news and blog articles closely associated with Airbnb.... By understanding the comprehensive public narrative around your company, you can devise a more effective communication plan. Zoom in on a cluster to dive deeper into the specifics of one particular topic....

> Quid has identified a company cluster for "Airbnb for Refugees" within the data. This illustrates how your brand can become associated with things outside of your control and allows you to track them.

AirPR's Analyst product has a feature it calls NEO, which is designed to spot key phrases "embraced and amplified by media and influencers on the web and in the social sphere. The feature offers automated, unbiased, data-driven feedback for understanding which brand messages should continue to be incorporated into future marketing/PR efforts and which ones need to be dropped."

Direct Response

The Sears Catalog attracted a lot of attention and a lot of imitators. The ability to tightly measure the response to a direct mail piece was music to the ears of marketers who depended on lessons from their predecessors, painful personal experience, trusting their gut, and sheer luck.

Direct marketers were able to test and quantify their results like nobody else because they could measure specific replies to specific messages from specific individuals. Given a list of 100,000 people, they could send out 10,000 pieces of message A, another 10,000 of message B, and another 10,000 of message C. Whichever produced the best response determined which message went out to the remaining 70,000 people. The improvement experienced by the winner was the *lift* over its competitors.

In an interview on the MIT Technology Review site called "Is There Big Money in Big Data?,"[12] Peter Fader, of The Wharton School, pointed to direct mail as the beginnings of predictive analytics.

> The golden age for predictive behavior was 40 or 50 years ago, when data were really sparse and companies had to squeeze as much insight as they could from them.
>
> Consider Lester Wunderman, who coined the phrase "direct marketing" in the 1960s. He was doing true data science. He said, "Let's write down everything we know about this customer: what they bought, what catalogue we sent them, what they paid for it." It was very hard, because he didn't have a Hadoop cluster to do it for him.
>
> So what did he discover?
>
> The legacy that he (and other old-school direct marketers) gave us is the still-powerful rubric of RFM: recency, frequency, monetary value.
>
> The "F" and the "M" are obvious. You didn't need any science for that. The "R" part is the most interesting, because it wasn't obvious that recency, or the time of the last transaction, should even belong in the triumvirate of key measures, much less be first on the list. But it was

discovered that customers who did stuff recently, even if they didn't do a lot, were more valuable than customers who hadn't been around for a while. That was a big surprise.

Some of those old models are really phenomenal, even today. Ask anyone in direct marketing about RFM, and they'll say, "Tell me something I don't know." But ask anyone in e-commerce, and they probably won't know what you're talking about. Or they will use a lot of Big Data and end up rediscovering the RFM wheel—and that wheel might not run quite as smoothly as the original one.

Database Marketing

The direct marketing industry was quick to dive into computers because its actions were not based solely on creative genius like Don Draper.

This device isn't a spaceship. It's a time machine. It goes backwards, forwards. It takes us to a place where we ache to go again. It's not called the Wheel. It's called a Carousel. It lets us travel the way a child travels. Around and around, and back home again . . . to a place where we know we are loved.

Mad Men

Direct marketing people had actual behavior—responses—to match up to specific names and addresses. They were able to track people from one round of mail to the next. What started as a simple file of people and where they lived grew to include what they had been sent and how they responded. (See Table 4.1.)

Table 4.1 A spreadsheet was the start of database marketing.

A Crude Relational Database									
Name	Address	Piece A	Piece B	Piece C	Piece D	Piece E	1st $$	2nd $$	3rd $$
Smith	123 Main	0	1	1	0	2	25	25	75
Jones	45 North	0	0	1	2	2	30	50	50
Brown	67 South	1	0	0	0	0	20	0	0
White	89 West	0	0	1	2	3	25	45	80

Figure 4.2 Even in the twenty-first century, simple data cleansing is tough.

Storing tens of thousands of records and joining such a table to other tables with product and promotion information allowed marketers to track sales and predict who was most likely to purchase what, when, and for how much. Keeping that data clean has been a major thorn in marketing's paw. (See Figure 4.2.)

Normalization is the art of recognizing that these are all the same guy:

John Smith

John Q. Smith

John Quincey Smith

Johnny Smith

The next step is to seek out similarities between those in the database and those they might find on one rentable mailing list or another. Today, we can layer the data described above with so much additional information that only AI can sort and sift through it in a meaningful way.

Advertising

Half the money I spend on advertising is wasted; the trouble is I don't know which half.

John Wanamaker

Half the marketing conferences I go to quote John Wanamaker; I just can't remember which half.

John Lovett

The buying, selling, and placement of ads online was ripe to be automated due to the overwhelming amount of options and decisions that need to be weighed when deciding where to buy ad space.

Banner Ads

In October 1994, AT&T placed the very first banner ad on the Internet.[13] Ever since, advertisers have been flooding browsers with their efforts to get attention and drive traffic to their landing pages, microsites, or shopping carts.

While search has made Google one of the most recognized companies in the world, programmatic advertising has become the least understood.

The media planner buys space to display company ads. Publishers sell ad space on their content. It's simple, but the advertiser can't talk to every publisher and publishers can't work directly with each advertiser, so advertising networks were born. An ad network might represent hundreds of publishers and thousands of advertisers. It can place ads based on audience type, content subject matter, time of day, device type, and overall or daily budget, and make sure the right size ad fits into the right size space on a page.

Some systems engage in real-time bidding for that space, just like the dynamic bidding process of buying search keywords from Google. This lets the media buyer identify the amount of traffic they want from the sort of audience they're after, and if they are savvy, tie in their back-end systems to see which people who have clicked have downloaded the whitepaper, filled out the form, or made the purchase, and then feed that back to the buying system to adjust what they are buying. Machine learning, to be sure, was rudimentary at first.

With the billions of ads served online in a given day, media planners were more than happy when Google offered a pay-per-click model. Show your ad to millions of people, but only pay for the ones who care enough to click. That made Google a partner. The more clicks you get, the more sales you make, and the more ads you'll buy—brilliant.

Then, Google put its best minds to work to relieve you of more of your money—even more brilliant.

When others discovered that they could step in between the buyer and the seller and leverage the arbitrage, programmatic advertising was born. Shortly thereafter, programmatic became automagic through machine learning.

The volatile combination of loose investment money and shiny, new technology has created an explosion of startups.

[AppNexus creates] a seamless feedback loop between a brand's decisioning logic and its consumer touchpoints. AppNexus [combines] data and machine learning to build campaigns that actually grow smarter over time. The result is hyper-personalization at scale, a world where marketers can deliver targeted ads to tens of millions of users, spread out across billions of interconnected devices, all over the world.

Skylads is an R&D lab specializing in the field of Machine Learning and Artificial Intelligence. We leverage on a fundamental mathematical research to build the most powerful and easy-to-use product suite for digital advertisers. Our products act as layer on top of Buying Platforms and help media buyers maximize the effectiveness of their programmatic media buying campaigns. Skylads revolutionises the digital advertising industry by introducing artificial intelligence "as a service" in the cloud. Skott is a framework of products heavily based on next-generation machine learning algorithms.

IntelliAds are personalised in real-time for each individual consumer, every time. We determine the best performing ad, branding, messaging and product selections in milliseconds every time we see a consumer. Merchenta uses sophisticated behavioural analytics to glean insight from seemingly random consumer behaviours. Through knowing the consumer, relevance drives results.

Programmatic Creative

Surely, *creating* ads is something we'll always need humans to do, right? When you can disseminate 10,000 ads a minute through 10,000 publishers, you're going to need a whole lot of humans to create all those ads. It's no surprise then that startups are looking at creating learning machines to manage that part of the process as well.

The *Wall Street Journal* described[14] how millions of dollars were raised by a handful of startups "promising to bring more of the automated aspects of digital advertising to the typically art-dominated creative side of the business. And earlier this week, Recode reported that Snapchat has snatched up the ad tech firm Flite, which also operates in the fledgling 'programmatic creative' realm."

> Certainly not every advertiser is going to run thousands of ads in each campaign. But according to Ben Kartzman, Spongecell's co-founder and chief executive, the fact that more advertisers are leaning so heavily on their own custom data sets and building in-house programmatic teams is helping accelerate the use of such tactics.

> One retail client can potentially generate 80 quintillion creative ads on a weekly basis, he said. "I do think it's where we're headed," he said.

Microsoft Research is using AI to parse the contents of a photo and not just describe what's in it, but what's happening in it. It started by having humans write descriptions of tens of thousands of photos via Mechanical Turk as the training data. Instead of just identifying the beach, the fire, and the volleyball game, the machine was trained to respond with sentences like, "The family had a good time by the sea with their dog. They went swimming and had a barbeque."

The scientists then created a system that could evaluate the effectiveness of the myriad stories generated by the machine and trained it until it almost matched human evaluators.

Programmatic Television

Ad agencies stopped selling television ad time over three-martini lunches decades ago. Data gathered *over the top* (OTT) is now used to plan and buy television time. The information collected in diaries kept by hand by household (think the original Nielsen Ratings) was supplemented by data collected in set-top-boxes of cable companies. But now, OTT is how a great deal of video is viewed through the Internet, over the top of all the other broadcast technologies.

The aforementioned *Wall Street Journal* article described the ability of OTT (as well as half a dozen other video delivery methods) to dynamically create customized video ads on the fly.

In 2015, Tennessee Tourism worked with its agency VML and Spongecell to deploy 23 different video ads to consumers based mostly on what part of the country they lived in, since roughly a dozen states are in a day's drive of Tennessee.

This past summer during the height of travel season, the group took things up a notch. It ran pre-roll video ads on sites across the web using a dozen templates which yielded over 2,000 video ad possibilities. People saw different variations of video ads based not only on where they lived, but whether they are foodies, golfers, outdoors enthusiasts or like to listen to country or rock—based on an assortment of first- and third-party data sets employed by the marketer.

The end result was that while these ads featured some consistent music and visuals, one ad might tout hiking in the Tennessee mountains while another might talk up Memphis' restaurants or the Johnny Cash museum in Nashville.

Pay-per-Click (PPC) Search

Search has become the primary supplier of customer intent. Consider the different frames of mind and expressions of desire exhibited in these different searches:

- Laptop
- Sturdy laptop
- Fast gaming laptop
- ASUS ROG Strix GL553VD 15.6" Gaming Laptop

The increasing specificity of search is a clear indicator of whether this gamer is shopping or buying.

The abilities that machine learning affords pay-per-click efforts gives extraordinary power to an entire industry of PPC professionals and drops billions of dollars to Google's bottom line. This was the first area of online marketing to be automated. Companies like Amazon try to put their ads in front of millions of searchers, judging outcomes based on actual sales and profitability results. To begin, they created rule-based automation to adjust the price they were willing to pay based on results.

Even automation has a tough time tracking hundreds of thousands of keywords and phrases in real-time, especially when new data elements are added to the mix like the weather and monthly payroll "seasons."

Machine learning can also recognize bursts of activity on given clusters of keywords that might indicate opportunities or threats that invite or require reaction. Think of it as a high-frequency trading system for search keywords.

Search Optimization (aka Content Marketing)

The other side of the search coin is "organic" or unpaid results. This is the consequence of having just what the searcher is looking for in the eyes of the search engine, be it Google, Bing, or Yahoo.

This has given rise to the *content marketing* movement where marketers have become publishers. If you want people to find your Fluorescent Lamp and Ballast Tester Kit (Figure 4.3), you would be well served to post lots of information about it, answers to frequently asked questions, and generally be *the* place on the Internet that Google points to first when asked.

The first concern is whether Google doubts your legitimacy. If Google thinks you're spamming its engine, it will summarily boot

Figure 4.3 The Milwaukee Fluorescent Lamp and Ballast Tester Kit

you off its results page. To see how safe your content is, Safecont offers a crawler that reviews your site and assigns a score on each page based on the risk it runs of being penalized. Safecont looks at how much your content seems to repeat itself on your site, how many pages have too little content, how much content seems to be duplicated outside your site, and a variety of other factors. Unlike old technologies that compare your website against a set list of weighted factors that must be considered, discussed, agreed on, and implemented, Safecont is a learning algorithm—the main benefit of AI.

Content Management—Image Matters

Past the obstacle of Google as adjudicator of authenticity is the issue of Google as judge of relevancy. While raking in money hand-over-fist selling keyword-related ads, Google keeps people coming back by serving up the world's most applicable links.

To be deemed relevant, a company must become very adept at publishing everything there is to know about those fluorescent lamp and ballast tester kits. AI is at the ready to help out. A standard search through an enormous library of whitepapers, PDF fliers, web pages, and research documents might yield a list of relevant results. But AI's visual and audio recognition capabilities come in very handy here to sift through all that other, unstructured data stored in otherwise unfindable files.

The creative soul, asked to illustrate an article on the safety issues around rewiring a fluorescent lamp, can only hope to use the same, tired old images that were properly labeled by some other poor creative soul. Machine learning, however, might find and offer up a range of options.

Martin Jones, senior marketing manager at Cox Communications, gave IBM's Watson Content Hub a spin at the end of 2016 to witness the practical use of machine learning in creating marketing campaigns. Rather than just listing images that matched search criteria, Watson was able to understand the meaning of the marketing message Jones wanted to convey. Further, Watson assisted in creating a customized experience for each website or mobile app visitor.

Like the American Marketing Association's efforts with Lucy, Jones first acquainted Watson with Cox's images and other digital assets. That process included the automatic image resizing and cropping by classification profiles with Watson recommending tags as it recognized the contents of pictures, including product names. Jones was able to identify conditions and variants for analyzing multiple images for real-time personalization, which makes use of that resizing and cropping for delivery across multiple devices.

Other technologies are in the picture to help you with your pictures—or even user-generated content. Olapic helps you find photos of your products out in the wild that might be useful in your ads or on your site. They also offer Photorank, which "evaluates multiple data points to accurately predict engagement and conversion per each image/video."

Curalate can find good photos and then secure permission to use them with a hashtag-based rights management system.

Infinigraph will help you pick the best thumbnail for your video.

Somatic can look at a picture and create a short description in different styles. Want your description to imitate a celebrity? They've got you covered.

Pinterest is working with visual recognition in photos to help you buy things you see in real life. Just snap a picture with the Pinterest app and it suggests things that look like the object of your affection. I offered Pinterest a simple challenge on my first try, the napping chair in my office. Sure enough, Pinterest nailed it (Figure 4.4).

My second effort was intended to be a straight-across-the-plate easy pitch, but it turned out to be a curveball. Pinterest did not know what to make of my Blue Yeti Microphone (Figure 4.5).

Meanwhile, over in the world of journalism, *USA Today* is using AI to read the news, create a script for a video, piece together footage and stills, and add synthesized vocal narration. The *Washington Post* is using AI to keep stories up-to-date by inserting new facts and figures in a story as time goes by.

Content Consumption Analysis

Behavioral analytics comes in handy here, too. From the first log file analysis tools, we've been minutely dissecting what pages, categories, and specific products interest individuals. But now, the machine can help us out. Not only can the machine see what interests individuals, it can determine how interested they are and where they might be in the buying cycle. That generates probabilities on what content to offer next and triggers a next-best-offer.

This capability works across the Internet at large as well. Charlie Tarzian, Founder of The Big Willow, says that content bingeing in 15–20 minute bursts can tell you a lot about where someone is in a buying process. The company uses pattern matching and machine learning to find people "across more than 10,000 B2B websites, blogs, and communities and engage them."

Figure 4.4 Pinterest recognized the recliner without trouble.

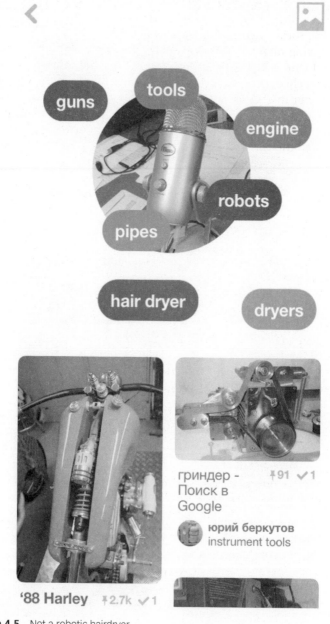

Figure 4.5   Not a robotic hairdryer

SOCIAL MEDIA ENGAGEMENT

Monitoring social media to get a clear picture of what the marketplace is saying about you is one thing. Engaging with social media is another. One is a passive, observational task; the other is reaching out—reactively or proactively—to engage people where they tweet.

eMarketer interviewed AJ Mazza, director of Marketing Communications, and Dedra DeLilli, director, Social Media Marketing and Corporate Sponsorships at TD Ameritrade, in an article in February 2017[15] about their use of AI.

> Through a partnership with Havas Cognitive, we developed a social media promotion to support an NFL campaign that we put together last season.
>
> We scoured the social feeds of opted-in consumers to assess their confidence in their favorite NFL team.
>
> It analyzed the tone and words that consumers used in their social posts to produce an aggregated confidence score. This score showed how confident a consumer was compared to other fans. Our goal was to drive engagement by giving fans the opportunity to increase their confidence score through specific actions, such as sharing our content, in an effort to win a prize—a trip to the Super Bowl.
>
> The technology enabled us to put a fun twist on a typical investing questionnaire. When we match customers with a product or service, we provide questionnaires to evaluate risks, and Watson allowed us to make this more engaging.
>
> It helped articulate TD Ameritrade's brand message about providing tools and resources that make customers confident investors.
>
> The campaign also allowed us to test AI with minimal risk, and delivered learnings that are being applied to benefit other areas of the business.

Social Snooping

Want to get a clear picture of the environment your customers inhabit? How about an actual photograph? Your wish is granted. Salesforce .com acquired deep-learning startup MetaMind in April 2106. Now, as part of Salesforce's Einstein offering, this visual recognition system is allowing companies to see into their lives by taking a close look at their photos.

MetaMind's website lays it out this way:[16]

> You're a developer who works for a company that sells outdoor sporting gear. The company has automation that monitors social media channels. When someone posts a photo, the company wants to know whether the photo was taken at the beach or in the mountains. Based on where the photo was taken, the company can make targeted product recommendations to its users....
>
> Your task is straightforward: Create a model that can identify whether an image is of the beach or the mountains. Then test the model with an image of a beach scene.
>
> The Predictive Vision Service API enables you to tap into the power of AI and train deep learning models to recognize and classify images at scale. You can use pre-trained classifiers or train your own custom classifiers to solve unique use cases.

Salesforce Social Studio allows you to "visually listen" to prospects and clients to see if your brand logo—or that of your competitors—is in their photos. These contextual clues shine a light on your marketplace like never before.

Socialbots

AI can help you find people, figure out what they're up to, and what interests them. It can also help you communicate. Welcome to the world of bots.

Ever since ELIZA in the mid-1960s, computers have been trying to imitate human communication. A simple e-mail autoresponder replies on your behalf, telling the world you are out of the office and cannot respond. Google's Smart Reply goes a step further and offers you a few suggestions in how you might like to respond.

A fully fledged AI assistant like Amy Ingram is a personal assistant who schedules meetings for you via e-mail. Send an e-mail to a colleague with a Cc: to amy@x.ai, and with an eye on your calendar and a knowledge of your preferences, she carries on the conversation via e-mail until a date is set.

Lots of bots answer straight questions with prewritten answers, but hand over a Twitter account to a socialbot, train it well, and you have the equivalent of a voice response system at the call center. Train it even better and you have a brand representative. For now, socialbots are only about as useful as voice response systems that have answers for 90 percent of the questions they usually get and no answers for the question *you* have whenever you call. Socialbots are starting to take on the Turning Test with modest success, but in time they will be able to represent your brand as a first line of defense.

Social Posting

AI can help you find people, figure out what they're up to and what interests them, and help you communicate. It can also post on your behalf.

Combine an intelligent social agent with well-managed content and you might come up with something like Echobox's Larry.[17] "Larry analyzes your historical and real-time data to create an entire social media strategy for you."

While that's a large promise to accept all at once, it's a little easier to swallow once you drill down into the component features.

- Larry tracks what's trending among your social media followers.
- Larry suggests messages to share.
- Larry adds appropriate hashtags to your messages.
- Larry A/B tests headlines and images.
- Larry resurfaces your evergreen content.
- Larry monitors what time of the day your audience is active.
- Larry optimizes your sharing frequency.

Social media advertising can respond to trending topics being discussed, who your friends are at the moment, and adjust based on your mood.

Mobile advertising can be based on the location of the individual down to the specific aisle they are standing in while in your store.

Wearables record your activity level, heart rate, and body temperature, and assuming some value has been offered to the wearer in return, feed that information back to a specific vendor or to a data aggregator to sell on through a network.

IN REAL LIFE

Why should online and television be the only places AI is useful? How about leveraging machine learning at face-to-face gatherings?

SummitSync plays matchmaker at conferences, finding the best match for introductions across multiple attributes, not just industry and city. Sign in with LinkedIn and suddenly it's "Tinder for business conferences."

Ampsy uses hyper-local geofencing to catch publically shared content at a given location at a given time—a business conference, sporting event, concert, and so on. This helps catch event tweets, shares, and posts that are not hashtagged, the usual way to capture event activity. Activity is monitored along with sentiment analysis and then analyzed against personality traits. As a result, you can find and engage with people who are thinking about you right now and create content clusters around live happenings.

Outdoor advertising has also gone electronic and AI—shades of Philip K. Dick's *Minority Report* (Tom Cruise wearing somebody else's eyes). Facedeals learns your face from Facebook and offers you a discount when you walk into a participating store.

In the summer of 2015, M&C Saatchi installed AI-enabled signage at London bus stops. The signs had a database of images, copy, and fonts it could choose from depending on reactions measured through Kinect technology. An internal genetic algorithm killed off some creative elements and brought others forward in response to facial expressions and the attention it was getting. It was only a test selling Bahio coffee was sold. There is no such brand (Figure 4.6).

THE B2B WORLD

With the exception of selling Apple II computers out of a retail storefront in a strip mall, I've lived my professional life on the business-to-business side. Trade magazine advertising, conference booth duty, direct mail to the Vice President of (Whatever), prospecting on the phone, lead management, pipeline management—it was all very hands-on work. I had a filing cabinet filled with folders by company, division, and department and a calendar that directed my every phone call.

The content management services described above play a giant role as research has shifted from reading magazines and going to conferences to online research. In my early years, it was my job to introduce my company to prospective buyers, hoping some of the classic marketing materials and money spent on branding

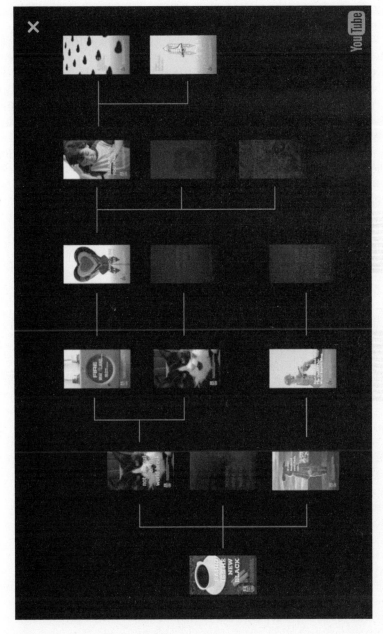

Figure 4.6 Genetics algorithm choosing ad components for electronic billboard.

might have softened the approach. There's nothing harder for a sales representative than the cold call.

Today, sales teams count on data collection to determine which companies—and which people within those companies—are expressing an interest in products through their online behavior. By the time a prospective buyer comes to the attention of the sales rep, they've consumed an enormous amount of product information.

Account-based marketing (ABM) systems were developed to track entire committees of cross-functional evaluators from the same firm or account. The goal is to track group behavior within each organization to determine who might be more interested in the application features of a product, who might care more about the managerial issues, who is focused on the technical integration questions, and who is solely focused on finances.

Lead Scoring

With thousands of leads, the sales team needs to know which to reach out to first. Manually, this is a task for the most seasoned professional.

You might want to call on the organizations most likely to close. You might want to target the committee at its most persuadable moment. You might be fixated on the company that has *just* started looking to have the most impact on the direction of its customer journey. And whichever you choose, you'll need to decide which individuals are the most important to contact first.

Traditional lead scoring would assign more points with higher weights to those who had viewed a video, requested a demo, had "Vice President" in their title, and worked in the same location as the majority of others on the committee.

With so many variables under consideration, all of the above are remarkably suitable for AI and machine learning.

That's where companies like 6sense come in.[18]

> In an effort to improve and prioritize leads more accurately, the second generation of lead scoring added math and predictive modeling to the lead-scoring approach. Predictive lead scoring uses the same profiling criteria—job title, company, annual revenues and other static attributes about that lead—as first-generation lead scoring. However, it goes a few steps further by analyzing the lead's attributes against past leads that became closed business and applying mathematical formulas to rank and score leads.

But we're not done yet. The above method works fine on known prospects who interact directly with your company. 6sense works with external data as well.

> Predictive intelligence ties together billions of rows of third-party data from search, blogs, publisher websites, review websites, online communities, buyers' guides— places where B2B buyers research products and services— and connects that time-sensitive, intent data to customers' internal data sources including CRM, marketing automation and weblogs.

> It combs all of these sources and then applies predictive models to look for deviations in past buying patterns and identify new buying signals. Predictive intelligence shines a light on the insights that matter, within a relevant time frame and connects the unknown, anonymous prospect to the known, seeing every step and footprint of every potential buyer. It can reveal, for example, which accounts salespeople should call on first, which value proposition to highlight with a specific account, and what kind of content and communication will get the best engagement based on the predicted buying stage of that prospect.

It's also clear to see how this information can be used to personalize the ads prospects see online, the customer experience they encounter on a website, and the script presented to a call center representative.

Rather than simply trusting that senior executives are reading Forbes' website, Dell works with 6sense *and* Forbes to customize specific messaging for specific people at specific companies depending on where they are in the consideration and buying process for a specific product. Third-party data and AI can more accurately predict intent than simple keyword search behavior.

How much third-party data is needed? Radius asserts that its systems consider more than 50 billion (with a *b*) signals against more than 18 million businesses in the United States (Figure 4.7).

Sales Management Advisory

While sales reps track accounts, sales managers track reps. Machine learning is there to lend a hand.

Aviso and Clari monitor sales forecasts across an entire team, monitoring the pipeline and advising managers on who is doing well and

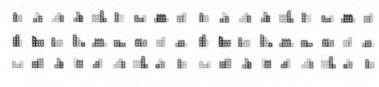

50+ billion signals
18+ million U.S. businesses

Figure 4.7 Radius tracks more bits than you can keep in a file cabinet.

who needs help. That help might be training, motivation, or a quick visit to a key prospect by a senior product manager.

DIY—Some Models Are Useful

The Strategic Marketing Organization at Cisco Systems started building predictive models back in the mid-2000s to guide sales reps in their prospecting. Then, they turned to machine learning. Analytics expert and author Tom Davenport described their progress in the *Deloitte University Press*.[19]

> By 2014, the company was generating about 25,000 propensity models a quarter, using data on 160 million businesses around the world. Because of the industrial scale of the modeling, Cisco began to refer to the approach as a "propensity-to-buy factory."

Those 25,000 models grew to 60,000 models a quarter in 2016 with higher and higher granularity and accuracy, but generating these models became a bottleneck, aggravating the sales department that counted on them.

> But then Cisco adopted some new technology—an in-memory server cluster with open source machine learning software—that sped up the analysis 15-fold.

Now it takes a matter of hours, and Cisco is able to use a variety of different machine learning algorithms. Depending on the situation, Cisco sees results of between three and seven times those without the propensity models.

[T]he age of purely intuitive approaches to customers, and even of artisanal analytics to analyze their data, is largely over. Vestiges of them may remain, but the companies that move rapidly to autonomous analytics to understand and structure the customer experience will be more successful in the marketplace.

NOTES

1. "24 Uses of Statistical Modeling," http://www.datasciencecentral.com/profiles/blogs/top-20-uses-of-statistical-modeling.

2. "Machine Learning Will Revolutionize Market Segmentation Practices," January 2017, http://www.idgconnect.com/view_abstract/41712/machine-learning-will-revolutionize-market-segmentation-practices.

3. "Getting Started with Artificial Intelligence Today," https://blogs.adobe.com/digitaleurope/digital-marketing/getting-started-with-artificial-intelligence-today-its-easier-than-you-think.

4. "Beyond the Target Customer: Social Effects of CRM Campaigns," http://journals.ama.org/doi/abs/10.1509/jmr.15.0442?code=amma-site.

5. "IBM's Watson Helped Pick Kia's Super Bowl 'Influencers,'" http://www.wsj.com/articles/ibms-watson-helped-pick-kias-super-bowl-influencers-1454432402.

6. "Why Google, Ideo, and IBM Are Betting on AI to Make Us Better Storytellers," https://www.fastcompany.com/3067836/robot-revolution/why-google-ideo-and-ibm-are-betting-on-ai-to-make-us-better-storytellers.

7. https://www.amplero.com/influencer-optimization.html.

8. "Sentiment Analysis, Machine Learning Opens Up World of Possibilities," http://blogs.sas.com/content/sascom/2016/07/06/sentiment-analysis-machine-learning-open-up-world-of-possibilities.

9. https://quid.com/quid-in-action#/innovation.

10. https://metamind.readme.io/docs/what-is-the-predictive-vision-service.

11. https://metamind.readme.io/v1/page/food-image-model-class-list.

12. "Is There Big Money in Big Data?" https://www.technologyreview.com/s/427786/is-there-big-money-in-big-data.

13. http://thefirstbannerad.com/.

14. "The Process of Making Digital Ads is Gradually Starting to Become More 'Programmatic,'" https://www.wsj.com/articles/the-process-of-making-digital-ads-is-gradually-starting-to-become-more-programmatic-1482404400.

15. "TD Ameritrade Uses Artificial Intelligence to Put a Marketing Twist on Risk Assessment," February 2017, https://www.emarketer.com/Interview/TD-Ameritrade-Uses-Artificial-Intelligence-Put-Marketing-Twist-on-Risk-Assessment/6002141.

16. https://metamind.readme.io/docs/what-is-the-predictive-vision-service.

17. https://www.echobox.com.

18. http://content.6sense.com/rs/958-TTM-744/images/whitepaper-6sense-web.pdf.

19. "Decoding the Path to Purchase," https://dupress.deloitte.com/dup-us-en/topics/analytics/using-autonomous-analytics-for-customer-mapping.html.

CHAPTER 5

Using AI to Persuade

Now that we've used our AI superpowers to find all those elusive, prospective customers, we need to lead them along and gently persuade them to buy. If you sell bubble gum or cigarettes, all of your work is focused on branding and distribution, so you can skip this chapter. The rest of us need to hold the hand of those willing to join us on the "customer journey."

In 2000, I co-authored a whitepaper called "E-Metrics: Business Metrics for the New Economy"[1] with Matt Cutler, founder of one of the first web analytics companies. In it, we described the Customer Life Cycle Funnel (Figure 5.1).

If you could aggregate and visualize your prospects' behavioral data, you could tell where you needed to pay attention based on the shape of the resulting funnel.

If your funnel resembled a martini glass, then you were attracting a lot of the wrong people. The margarita glass suggested the right people showed up, but they lost interest. A wineglass indicated problems sealing the deal at the end of the process. The shot glass was your best friend. You got the right people; they were interested; they followed the optimal site path you'd designed; and they ended up making a purchase. That was all very naïve.

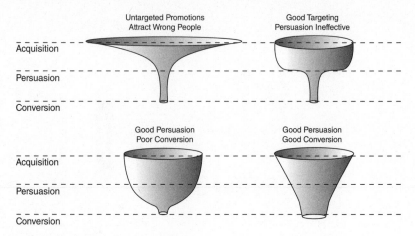

Figure 5.1 The Customer Life Cycle Funnel

The idea came from our B2B backgrounds and the sales pipeline reporting we had done for years. The natural progression was always the same straight line:

- Suspect
- Prospect
- Qualified lead
- Hot lead
- Negotiating
- Closed

But the B2C consumer journey is not a straight path. It wanders from channel to channel and not in a specific sequence. There is no clearly identifiable beginning or middle to the purchase process anymore and the end gets hazy once advocacy and retention are thrown into the mix. (See Figure 5.2.)

The best we can hope for, according to Christopher Berry, Director of Product Intelligence at the Canadian Broadcasting Corporation, is to recognize similar behavior and leverage it. "We're talking about humans and they are all different. If we can find some low-level tasks that are predictive, we're ahead of the game. Machine learning is much better at that than trying to forecast behavior based on the sum total of an individual's psyche."

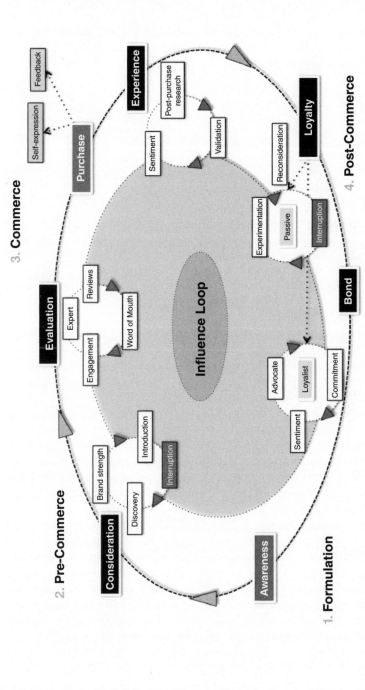

Figure 5.2 The Dynamic Customer Decision Journey
Source: Brian Solis.

That leaves us with the task of optimizing a given moment in time to help the individual accomplish his or her current or next undertaking. This sort of salesmanship is considered normal in a retail environment. Only now we can take what we've learned online and apply it to the real world.

THE IN-STORE EXPERIENCE

Walk into a store and the clerk responds to lots of bits of information.

- Age
- Gender
- Clothing style
- Hair style
- Interest expressed by body language

If the clerk is equipped with an app, he could also rely on purchase history, online research activity, brand affinities, historical price range, social profile, and more, as you would expect to capture online as well as in-store loyalty card data.

Retailers have also added technology to capture interest expressed by the path shoppers take through the store. Digital Mortar offers an in-store customer tracking system using video and wifi tracking. Store performance evaluation, store layout assessment, and staffing optimization are on the menu along with customer care.

Coupled with online apps, the AI-enabled store smooths online transactions that are intended for store pickup or allowing people to buy online and return to a store or vice versa. Tying these together is critical when trying to determine whether the store is making sales. A store that is serving as a return hub for items bought online might be a crucial component of customer satisfaction rather than a "failed" retail location.

Gary Angel, co-founder of Digital Mortar, points out that in-store activity can also generate online sales. "If there's any area of online display advertising that works, it's re-marketing. With the store-to-digital join, you have the opportunity to do digital re-marketing based on in-store behavior. That's taking showrooming to a new and better level."

Digital Mortar is out to answer a lot of questions for the retailer. How much do omnichannel initiatives impact store operations and sales interactions? Are omnichannel tasks being handled by the right staff? Are omnichannel customers significantly different in their store behaviors?

But with AI able to manage high-dimensional data, we can ask questions like:

- What impact does in-store music have on the types of products sold?
- Does a more crowded store increase sales?
- How does the weather influence product selection?
- Should we send out invitations to social groups for discount parties?
- How do we optimize the store layout to encourage impulse buying?
- What is the value of sending a digital promotion for an item right in front of the customer?
- Does changing the store layout create a positive experience for return customers?

And then there's the optimization of the sales clerks themselves. "For most retail stores, labor costs are a huge part of overall operating expenses—typically around fifteen percent of sales," says Angel. "In countless analytic efforts around customer satisfaction and churn, the one constant driver of both is the quality of associate interactions. People matter."

Digital Mortar systems are able to differentiate customers from staff in order to monitor both without mixing them up or ignoring them altogether. "No part of the customer journey and no part of the store has a bigger impact on the journey, on the sale, and on the brand satisfaction than interactions with your sales associates."

It pays to know how often clerks interact with customers. How long did the interactions last? How often did they result in sales? "You can," says Angel, "isolate the number and impact of cases where staff interactions should have happened but didn't. You can also find out whether contact is an annoyance, desirable, or imperative. You can understand which associate combinations work best together, how valuable team cohesion is, and the value spread between a top associate and an average hire."

This is yet another example of leveraging more types of data than we have ever collected and that we could ever hold in our minds at once.

Shopping Assistance

Satisfi Labs has created a location-based intelligent engagement platform that can capture customer intentions, sentiments, questions, and needs to drive sales. Customers treat their mobile app like a sales clerk.

- Where can I find Ralph Lauren Men's sweaters?
- Do you do gift wrap here?
- Where are the restrooms?
- What's on sale?

Responses are real-time and can route requests to the best-suited human if need be. The learning aspect comes in direct feedback with a couple of buttons that say either "Yes, that's it" or "That's not quite right." Because it's location-based, answers are specific rather than generic.

The most important part is that the system learns how the same question might be asked a hundred ways. A regular menu-based system requires a hierarchical taxonomy that might bewilder the average shopper. Organizations are so accustomed to their own nomenclature, they might not think twice about subcategorizing running shorts under a button labeled Foundation Wear. The customer will look in vain for a button marked Nike AEROSWIFT.

Macy's rolled out Macy's On Call in ten stores in time for the 2016 holidays in English and Spanish. Store navigation details are provided by department, brand, and product category and give customers a way to flag down a human if there are none in sight. Call it a ShopBot if you must, but the combination of data about a given store's layout, merchandise, and services is so unique to each location that this app is useful to guide shoppers as well as train new employees.

Training takes time. As of the beginning of 2017, Macy's On Call is "mostly useful" but still has a few kinks to work out. When asked for "men's socks" at their Santa Anita, California, store, Macy's On Call responded, "Shopping for Men's Basics? Visit Men's Basics on Floor 1 next to Men's Accessories near the Huntington Drive entrance."

The same answer was delivered when asked, "Do you have men's Gold Toe Socks?" When that question was asked with a typo ("/") at the end, the answer was, "6." (See Figure 5.3.)

When asked, "Are you a bot?," it wasn't sure. (See Figure 5.4.)

"Unfortunately, we're not sure about that," the app replied. "We're still learning, and we'll work on getting an answer to this question for future queries. Is there anything else we can help you with?

Figure 5.3 Macy's On Call app is still learning.

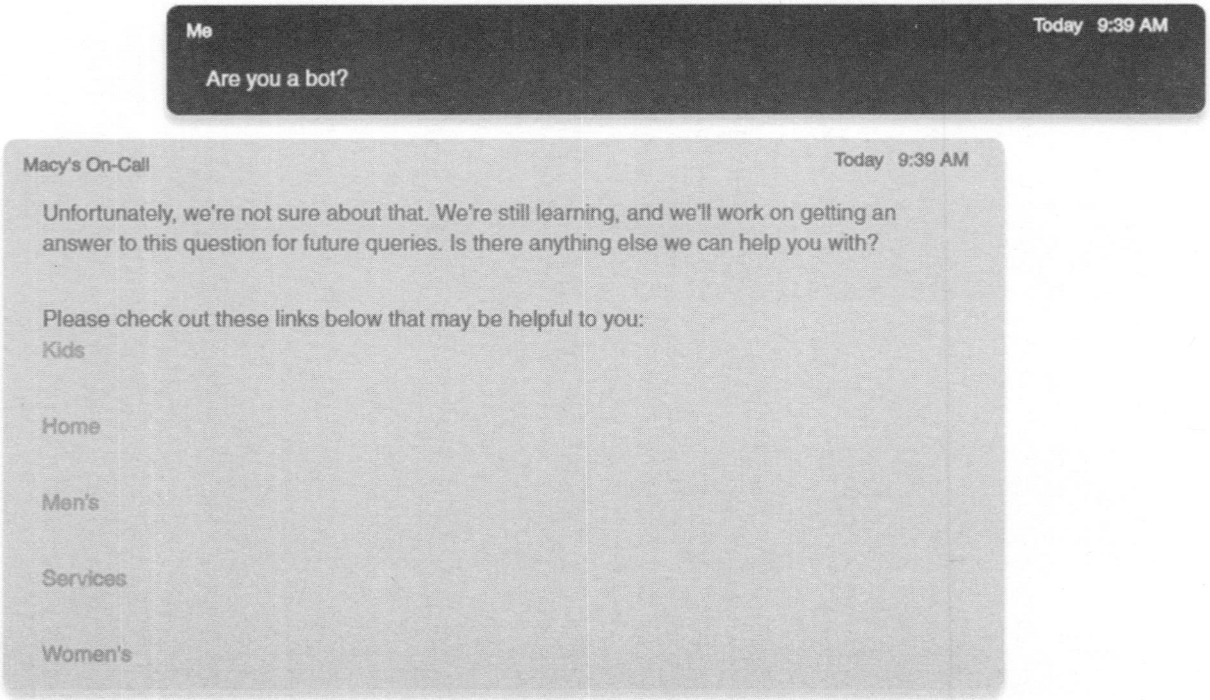

Me

Today 9:39 AM

Are you a bot?

Macy's On-Call

Today 9:39 AM

Unfortunately, we're not sure about that. We're still learning, and we'll work on getting an answer to this question for future queries. Is there anything else we can help you with?

Please check out these links below that may be helpful to you:

Kids

Home

Men's

Services

Women's

Figure 5.4 Macy's On Call identity crisis

"Please check out these links below that may be helpful to you:

Kids

Home

Men's

Services

Women's"

This is the learning side of Macy's On Call brought to life. Perhaps it could learn something from Guess the Animal.

The lesson, however, is that computers are learning how to communicate better. Random Access Navigation (RAN) was coined by Shane Mac, CEO & Co-founder of Assi.st in an article on Medium.[2] His company's goal is to "give people the ability to navigate without a defined path, while also being able to change their mind at any time."

> People should be able to interact with technology the same way they act in real life. We believe RAN offers more than one solution for the most common bot criticism: fixed decision trees. It's the ability to complete more complex tasks with 100% automation while also increasing customer satisfaction, reducing friction and not making people wait on hold.

> The idea of RAN has four aspects to it:

1. It detects all parameters required to perform an intent (with context).
2. It allows the user to change their mind without going back.
3. It works seamlessly with web views.
4. It requires writing copy in a completely different way.

Assi.st worked with Sephora on an app to book makeup appointments. (See Figure 5.5.)

> We use RAN to know what is missing or what we need to change and then navigate there. The more parameters (context) we detect (or can infer), the fewer steps for the customer.

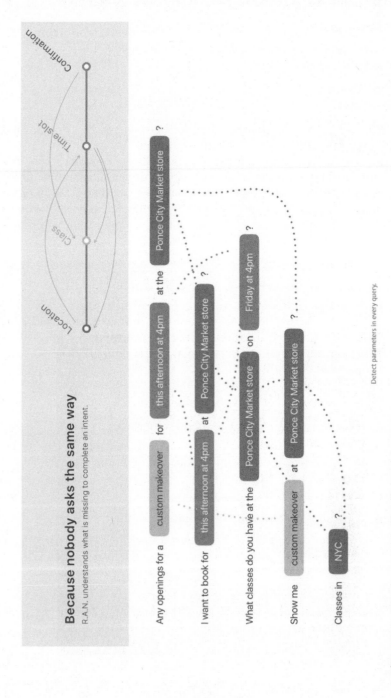

Because nobody asks the same way

R.A.N. understands what is missing to complete an intent.

Confirmation

Time slot

Class

Location

Any openings for a · custom makeover · for · this afternoon at 4pm · at the · Ponce City Market store · ?

I want to book for · this afternoon at 4pm · at · Ponce City Market store · ?

What classes do you have at the · Ponce City Market store · on · Friday at 4pm · ?

Show me · custom makeover · at · Ponce City Market store · ?

Classes in · NYC · ?

Detect parameters in every query.

Figure 5.5 Mapping contextual intelligence into an app

174

Mac points out that a real person never goes "back."

The idea of "back" is something we made up with the web, messaging is about going forward and being able to change your mind at any time.

Authoring decision trees and infinite fail over scenarios is quite the task. We've seen people spend weeks writing copy and flows without knowing what people even want. This leads to our industry's "Sorry, I don't understand" problem [see Figure 5.6].

We decided to rethink the entire way we go about writing copy for RAN. We think it is much easier to deliver something people want.

Here's how we think about it:

- We assume that the user input will never be complete.
- All parameters need to be captured to perform the current intent depending on implied context.

Figure 5.6 Instant classic bots joke
Credit: Amir Shevat.

- Once we have all parameters, you can always override any parameter because we have context. (This is how people can change their mind at any time.)

The main premise is to "define the intents, train the engine to understand the parameters, write copy based on what is missing, and deliver experiences that help people get things done faster and simpler than before."

Sephora is also going all in on automating communications on Snapchat and Kik that include the ability to start building a relationship with you. "Do you want to take a short quiz so we can get to know you?" Age and brand preferences go a long way toward personalizing the experience. Sephora knows where its audience spends its screen time.

These sorts of bots work perfectly fine online as well; 1-800-Flowers has incorporated Gifts When You Need (GWYN) into its website and added a little personality. After a free-form inquiry about a bouquet for my wife, GWYN doesn't just respond robotically, but has opinions of her own.

"What type(s) of flowers or plants are you looking for? Example: tulips, roses, lilies, carnations, etc.," she asked.

"Tulips are nice," I replied.

"Tulips make me smile, nice choice. I'll remember that while I look for gifts. . . . Here's what I found. I hope your wife likes my recommendations!"

Because I logged in, GWYN will remember whom I'm shopping for, the occasion, and what sort of flowers and arrangements I like. She also allows me to modify those notes if I please. (See Figure 5.7.)

Restaurants

Honest Café operates unmanned food kiosks in the United Kingdom that sell healthy snacks, juices, fruit teas, popcorn, and hot drinks. They turned to AI to understand the customers they sell to but never see. Based on customer choices, time-of-day and day-of-week, and noting who comes collectively as a social experience, the company discovered that people who pay using credit cards are more likely to hang around the café with their friends and consume more goodies.

With the ability to give away free items through the vending machines, Honest Café can reward loyal customers and entice prospects who are deemed to have highest likely customer lifetime value. (See Figure 5.8.)

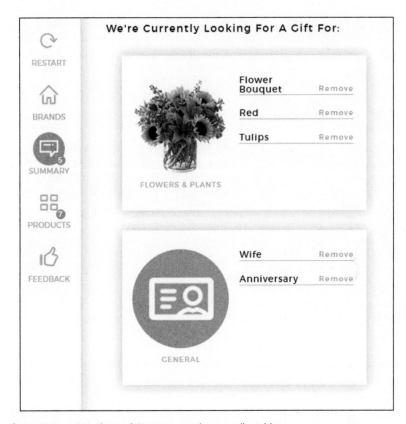

Figure 5.7   1-800-Flowers' GWYN memories are adjustable.

The data Honest Café collects is also highly useful for config-uring store layouts, adjusting its product mix, and organizing stock replenishment.

Store Operations

With customers fully analyzed, it's time to turn our attention to the store itself, starting with layout as an object of optimization. Should you put the milk at the back of the store and the fresh vegetables oppo-site the meat counter in order to drive more foot traffic to the middle of the shop to elevate impulse buying?

Experience design is not something a cookie baker would think of when designing a small bakery. But when the first baker vented the ovens to the street in *front* of the shop, lightbulbs went on all over the retail world.

Figure 5.8   Honest Café tracks people it can't see.

It's hard to think of experimenting with something as concrete as store layout, but given enough time or enough locations, enough data can be collected to reveal winning combinations. Staff optimization based on foot traffic, product knowledge, and personality matching can go a long way toward lowering payroll overhead and increasing sales.

Monitoring external factors that influence consumers (weather, promotions, competition), as well as consumer behavior and supply chain history, can be used to tighten up stock on hand while reducing outages. These are just the sort of problems Gary Angel of Digital Mortar is solving for his customers.

While a good deal of thought has been put into optimizing retail since before Wanamaker's Grand Depot opened in Philadelphia in 1876, a great deal of the above owes a debt of gratitude to the online world.

ON THE PHONE

Through a combination of voice-to-text, natural language processing, and machine learning, it's now quite reasonable to glean meaning from telephone calls.

Dynamically generated telephone numbers pinpoint the promotion or the landing page to a given call with a specific cookie. If you see an ad and make a call, they know which ad you saw. If you clicked through to a landing page, they know which ad drove the traffic as well as your behavior on the website.

Invoca can correlate calls to web pages visited, keywords searched, and previous digital marketing engagements, all while the phone is still ringing. The system continuously learns to score lead quality or risk of churn, in order to route calls to the proper representatives and suggest persuasion strategies.

The system can be used to identify the caller and offer a propensity-to-buy rating, correlate outbound promotions with inbound calls, and help guide marketing spend, even to the point of triggering a marketing automation workflow.

"The whole point is to give visibility into the call center to the marketing department," Senior Director of Software Engineering Michael Weaver told me, "The learning takes place with the help of humans. We have people listen to and score a thousand or so phone calls, labeling them for fraud, customer service, appointment set, sale closed, or whatever our client's goals are."

After the call, as the Invoca system identifies topics of conversation including competitors mentioned, features or services cited, and sentiment expressed. It can also recognize when a goal is met on the phone, giving proper attribution to the channel for setting an appointment or closing the sale.

What was once the duty of business rules based on device type, day and time of call, new or repeat call, geographic location, source of call, etc., is now the domain of the self-improving, machine learning system.

"Implementing a machine learning system validated a lot of what engineers know intuitively that marketing people need to appreciate," Weaver underlined. "You need really clear goals so you can ask really good questions, and then everything hangs on having *really* good data. So, it's 90 percent preparation and ten percent machine learning magic."

That magic is not limited to the machine finding patterns at super-human speeds, but across a broad spectrum. When machine learning is offered as a service, general correlations can be garnered from *all* of the calls Invoca processes from all of its clients. Scoring can be influenced by the multitude of others' calls, making the system smarter by the minute.

THE ONSITE EXPERIENCE—WEB ANALYTICS

The Internet was a breakthrough because of one technical insight.

One telephone caller used to be connected to another over a switched network. Think of banks of operators manually inserting a wire into a plug-board, physically connecting the callers over a switch. If the switch were incapacitated, the calls could not go through. In the 1970s, packet switching was employed to move information—which could include voices—from one computer to another without the need for a central controller.

Packets of data include from and to addresses as well as a sequence number. When all of the packets finally show up, the caller can be heard, the video can be played, and the website can be displayed. If packets are missing, they can be requested by the recipient machine to fill in the blanks.

The very nature of this technical underpinning gave rise to a field called web analytics. Simply showing up at a website delivers a useful smattering of information to the website owner. When asking for a specific page, the browser shares the following with the server:

- Time and date
- IP address
- Domain name
- Operating system and version
- Browser type and version
- Pages requested
- Errors

Even that small amount of information was enough to launch a dozen companies selling log file analysis software. The output from those systems was pretty much limited to telling you how many visitors showed up and what interested them the most.

The information suffered from a lack of memory. A request came from an IP address, a page was sent, and then the connection was lost. Cookies were developed to remember a visitor from one click to the next so that preference setting and shopping carts were possible. This many requests came from that IP address this many times, but there was no way to know if that was multiple people on the same device, or if one person was on multiple, different devices.

Then, page-tagging technology unlocked a great deal of additional information about visitors' experiences and behaviors. Page tags can collect dynamic information that might be displayed, the total value of a shopping cart, partial form completion, and even minute mouse movements such as tentative hovers over buttons. This allowed marketers to start stitching together which promotions prompted which people to seek more information about which products and which features of those products were the most interesting.

Other data collection techniques included remembering a browser's fingerprint: the make and version of the browser, the operating system version, the specific plugins activated, and so on. If the visitor could be induced to log in for some reason and reveal an e-mail address, suddenly we went from an anonymous user to a flesh-and-blood person. Mobile technology added another layer of identification.

Such an overwhelmingly high level of dimensionality coupled with data coming in from social media even surpassed the abilities of massive clusters of parallel processing systems (big data).

But with machine learning...

Landing Page Optimization

The customer experience is hard to manage in the wild. Prospective customers are out there somewhere, clicking, scrolling, tweeting, and watching, but when they come to your website and hit that landing page, you have a lot of levers you can push and pull to change their behavior.

Through graphics, copy, and interactivity you can test and tune landing pages and dramatically improve your bottom line. Tim Ash, author of *Landing Page Optimization* (Sybex, 2nd ed., April 24, 2012), writes that landing pages, given proper scrutiny, can help:

- Identify mission-critical parts of your website and their true economic value.
- Define important visitor classes and key conversion tasks.
- Deploy powerful neuromarketing techniques to move people to act.

It's a matter of A/B and multivariate testing to bend site visitor behavior to your will. Getting the right message to the right person at the right time is also important in the middle of the customer journey, not just up front in advertising.

A/B and Multivariate Testing

A/B testing is every web manager's dream. It is so easy to explain to others in the company and the results are always taken as gospel. Simply send 90 percent of your web traffic to the usual page and 10 percent to a variation. Then sit back and wait until enough people have come through to reach statistical significance and you can clearly see which version is better.

Multivariate testing is much the same, but rather than head-to-head contests, multivariate testing seeks to discover which combination of elements works best: this graphic with that copy and this call-to-action. Given enough traffic (for statistical significance), this sort of test can quickly determine whether the black-and-white product photo is better with the blue font or if the full-color landscape with the red text beats all other combinations hands down.

Sentient Ascend uses a genetic algorithm to generate web-page candidates to be tested. Marketers come up with suggestions on changes to button color, logo size, layout, content sequencing, messaging, and so on, and can be implemented beyond one page to a whole site visit. Ascend then promotes the most successful ideas to reproduce. Each page is represented as a genome, as shown for two example pages in Figure 5.9 (left side).

Simulated genetic operators such as crossover (recombination of the elements in the two genomes; middle) and mutation (randomly changing one element in the offspring; right side) are then performed. If the parent genomes are chosen among those that convert well, then some of their offspring genomes are likely to perform well, too—even better than their parents. Each page needs to be tested only to the extent that it is possible to decide whether it is promising, i.e., whether it should serve as a parent for the next generation, or should be discarded.[3]

While this approach can more quickly test millions of designs more than humans ever could, it only needs to test thousands to find the best ones by learning which combinations of elements are most effective.

Before diving in head first, Matt Gershoff of Conductrics acts as the seatbelt "ping" in your car. "Always have a control group that isn't being exposed to the machine learning system. *Always.*"

Onsite User Experience

When people complain about their online experience, when they call the call center, or when they submit low satisfaction scores, you can tell there's something wrong. But it's hard to tell what it is. Why are they unhappy?

Session reply records each mouse movement and click and can quickly reveal where the user or the website went wrong. While that's very informative on an individual basis, there's no way humans can watch hours of sitefailures.

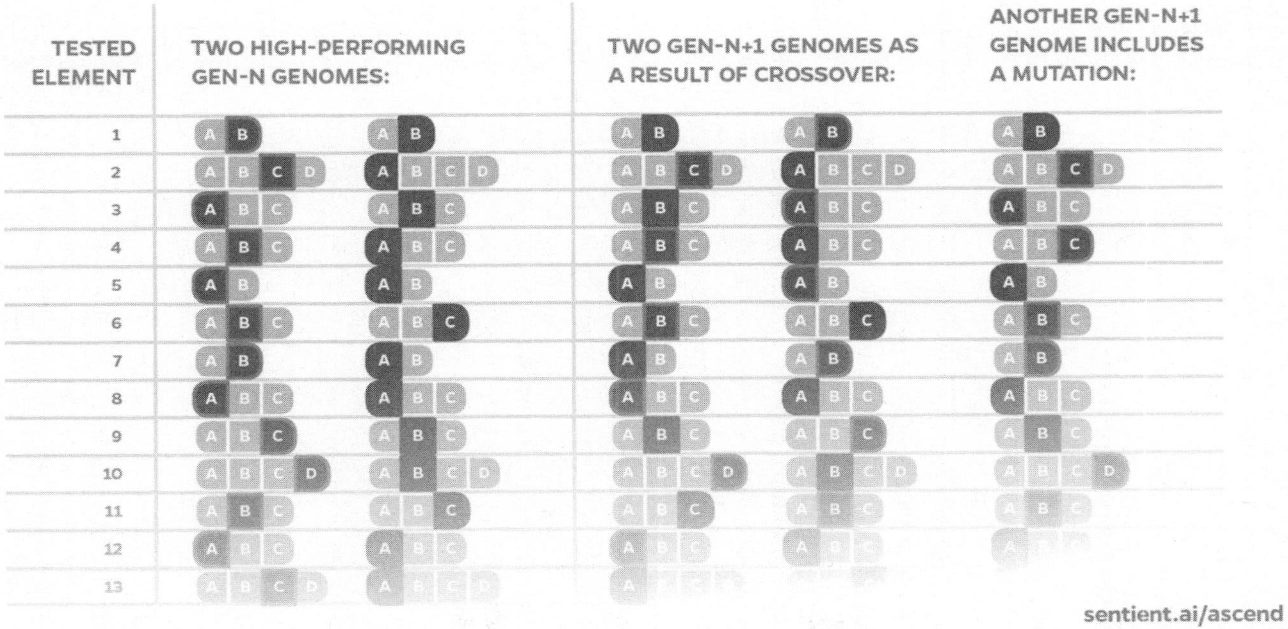

Figure 5.9 Sentient Ascend's mutation generator decides who gets to reproduce.

SessionCam captures and analyzes recorded visits to your website to highlight the highest value issues first using a Customer Struggle score. These areas are brought to light through heatmaps and funnel reports, pointing out session recordings that should be reviewed by humans.

Recommendation Engines

Amazon was the first to bring us the 1-Click® button, a groundbreaking convenience as my credit card bill will attest. They were also first to popularize the online recommendation.

At the start, this was accomplished through brute-force tracking.

- These items were often purchased together.
- People who bought this also bought that.
- Those interested in this subject were also interested in that one.
- People who rated this thing high also liked that thing.
- People who are similar to you bought these things.
- And the ever-favorite, Top Seller.

This collaborative cross-sell/upsell has worked well for Amazon.

The North Face has created a dialog-based recommendation engine to suggest outerwear. Once you enter details about a jacket you might like or an outdoor activity you're planning, the app asks where you're headed. After telling The North Face XPS (Expert Person Shopper) that I was headed to Chicago for business meetings, it checked the weather. Once I selected a jacket instead of a vest and a relaxed fit over an active fit, I was given three jackets to choose from. Needless to say, the suggestions were different when I suggested I was on my way to Iceland to hike the glaciers. (See Figure 5.10.)

It is still early days for these apps. The feedback requested by The North Face was limited to my experience (I didn't like it; It was OK; I loved it), did I find a jacket that fit my needs (y/n); would I use it again; and, "Anything we can improve?"

Personalization

One-to-one marketing has always been *just* out of reach. If you log in, you're a customer and we'll remember your credit card number, your shoe size, and your spouse's birthday. But personalizing the experience for the anonymous visitor is a little trickier. We started with classic segmentation and tried to implement relational databases.

Figure 5.10 The North Face offered the least expensive as the highest match to my needs.

While segmentation is useful, it's not very granular. While relational databases are functional, they did not scale well. We're looking for sub-second response time.

AI plays to its strengths here:

- Finding the attributes that are the most predictive while ignoring the rest
- Making decisions based on actual data rather than human conjecture
- Constantly updating its "beliefs"

Adobe Target Premium "aggregates customer data from a variety of online and offline sources, including web and app analytics, customer relationship management (CRM) databases, and internal-facing enterprise resource planning (ERP) and data warehouse (DWH) systems. As you surface this data, Target's machine-learning algorithms determine which variables are most predictive of conversions, eliminating clutter from your customer profiles. And Target's integration with Audience Manager means you can leverage lookalike modeling to automatically find new customer segments, expanding your audience in unexpected directions."

Godiva.com interprets "each click, site search and page view to present the most relevant products to each website visitor right away, mimicking their skilled salespeople that present options based on what a customer is looking at in the store. This luxury shopping experience has resonated with shoppers: Godiva.com conversion rates have jumped nearly 25 percent since implementing Reflektion."[4]

HSN (Home Shopping Network) uses IBM's Watson to personalize across devices. You start the conversation here and pick it up over there. That translates to customer convenience and higher loyalty.

MERCHANDISING

While in-store merchandising has been studied since before the days of John Wanamaker, online merchandising has been relegated to algorithms. Which items should be on the landing page? How should they be displayed? Which color choices should pop up first? When should an incentive be offered? Rather than a static mixture of store layout and product assortment, digital merchandising is a dynamic display, moving ever closer to one-to-one, per-person persuasion.

Pricing

Attempts at dynamic pricing have upset consumers. Travel sites have run into trouble showing more expensive hotels for Mac users over PC users. Amazon was outed in real time by people shopping in tandem. Airline tickets have been thought to decrease once you delete your cookies.

Mohammad Islam, principal data science consultant at Aiimi/Anglian Water, recommends experimenting with different prices in several isolated markets. This can be a very complex undertaking, so Islam created a machine learning system to work on it. (See Figure 5.11.)

> Dynamic price optimisation is extremely demanding when it comes to individual products as the products are subject to different price elasticity. My algorithm is a self-learning method that varies prices based on historical purchases of individual products and the best way of state-of-the-art data mining methods, making individual pricing decisions based on price elasticity.

> The direct financial benefits associated with a price planning and optimization solution can be attractive. As for example margin, sales volume in revenue terms or sales volume in units. Often the sales velocity associated with given products is very high meaning that just a small percentage increase in sales or a small increase in margin equates to significant currency values over a year. It may be that by optimizing prices, overall sales volume in a given category reduces whereas the overall margin impact is positive.

> The classical approach to category management has been to determine specific strategies in order to ensure that the role and goal of each individual category is met. These strategies tend to focus on inventory, assortment, promotion and price. The use of a price planning and optimization solution allows the pricing elements of these strategies to be mapped to specific pricing approaches and automatically applied. This ensures consistency and integrity of the price strategy thus assisting the overall category management process.[5]

Should we automate dynamic pricing? No. It's *not* advisable to play with people's perceptions of value, but it *is* advisable to use today's technology to help set prices.

Market Basket Analysis

What did people put unto their shopping carts? What items went in together? What items were purchased in what sequence from cart to cart? What items were removed? What items were abandoned? The answers to these questions have been driving merchandising, and therefore, sales since Sylvan Goldman invented the shopping cart in 1937.

In 2016, Adobe Systems took out a patent on answering those questions.[6]

> Online shopping cart analysis is described. In one or more implementations, a model is built is usable to compute a likelihood of a given customer that leaves an online store with unpurchased items in an online shopping cart will return to purchase those items. To build the model, historical data that describes online store interactions and attributes of unpurchased items in online shopping carts is collected for other customers that have abandoned online shopping carts. Using the model, data collected for a subsequent customer that has abandoned an online shopping cart is input and the likelihood of that customer to return to purchase unpurchased items is returned as output. Based on the computed likelihood, the customer may be associated with different advertising segments that correspond to different marketing strategies. Marketing activities directed to the subsequent customer are thus controllable using the model.

CLOSING THE DEAL

Even moving the needle a few points on conversion drops a lot of income to the bottom line. The classic conversion funnel imagines tons of people at the top, expressing some sort of interest. As they drop down into the funnel, they are more and more engaged until they drop out at the bottom to become customers.

The marketer must decide where to invest resources. It's unnerving when the advertising department increases their budget when it's clear that the middle of the funnel (persuasion) or the bottom of the funnel (conversion) need improvement. It's a waste to pour more people into the top when the funnel itself is leaky.

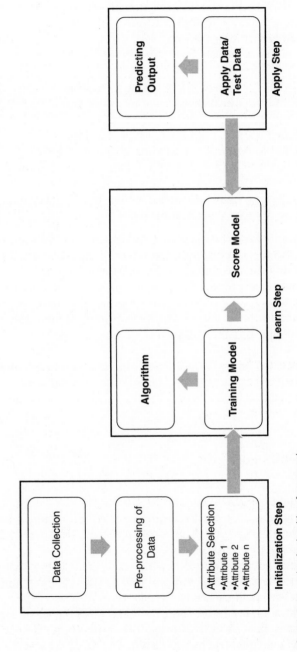

Figure 5.11 Islam's algorithm framework

189

The conversion funnel is a useful analogy at first, but no linear customer journey fits inside a funnel. Individuals' interests wax and wane. The reason they finally pull the trigger to buy that appliance may have more to do with their mother-in-law coming to visit than a well-traveled customer journey.

Google offers Smart Goals as part of their Google Analytics suite.

> Smart Goals uses machine learning to examine dozens of signals about your website sessions to determine which of those are most likely to result in a conversion. Each session is assigned a score, with the "best" sessions being translated into Smart Goals. Some examples of the signals included in the Smart Goals model are Session duration, Pages per session, Location, Device and Browser. (Remarketing Smart Lists use a similar machine learning model to identify your best users.)

> To determine the best sessions, Smart Goals establishes a threshold by selecting approximately the top 5% of the traffic to your site coming from AdWords. Once that threshold is set, Smart Goals applies it to all your website sessions, including traffic from channels other than AdWords. After enabling Smart Goals in Analytics, they can be imported into AdWords.[7]

What if your best efforts do *not* result in a sale? Google is at the ready with Smart Lists for remarketing. Google continues to excel at creating technology that proves the value of the advertising they sell.

Remarketing

After spending an idle hour or so researching gaming laptops and narrowing down your choices, ads for that ASUS ROG Strix GL553VD are following you around the entire Internet, showing up on your phone, and making your Facebook newsfeed look like an ASUS catalog. Welcome to remarketing.

The intent you expressed in your search and behavior has triggered the relentless dogs of commerce that can sniff you out and hound you mercilessly. The most tenacious ads come your way when you put something in a shopping cart and then abandon the session without making the purchase. Your expressed intent was so high that the vendor will pay top dollar to put its product in front of you again and again. Then the ads will include discounts. Then the ads will include discounts *and* free shipping.

While the above is couched in negative terms, this type of advertising is becoming more and more common because it works so well. For all the people you annoy, there are enough who make a purchase to make the collateral damage acceptable. It's also a great way to get a discount on something you know you want to buy.

E-mail Marketing

E-mail is the workhorse of Internet advertising. Once you have an individual's e-mail address—and permission to use it—you can hone your message to stimulate the desired response.

Whether you are sending out coupons or product announcements, placing ads in other people's newsletters, or simply sending a thank-you note to a new customer, the ability to speak directly to people where they live (in their e-mail inbox) is very powerful. Clearly, the ability to test a variety of messages, formats, pictures, and so on, provides many ways for an AI to evaluate and leverage results.

Conversica is aimed at helping salespeople by engaging prospects through e-mail.

- I see you downloaded our whitepaper.
- I see you've been to our website several times.
- I see you stopped by our booth at the ____ trade show.
- Would Thursday or Friday be better for a live demo?

Between engaging prospects and customers automatically, sending salespeople alerts when intent to purchase reaches a critical threshold, and tireless ability to reengage stale leads, e-mail was never so useful to the sales department.

> Rather than relying on website activity and click-through rates, Conversica engages in real conversations with leads and shares their actual responses. Conversica immediately alerts a sales rep when a lead is ready to engage in the sales process.

Integrating with marketing automation platforms like Marketo, Pardot, and Eloqua is table stakes for these tools.

Companies like Boomtrain intelligently automate who gets how many e-mails with what content. Their client, Chowhound, made e-mails more valuable to subscribers by tailoring them with specific, evergreen content that would otherwise remain in the dark. Chowhound saw a 28 percent increase in e-mail open rates and a 150 percent increase in clickthroughs.

According to Patrick Sullivan, Chowhound's director of product, "Before Boomtrain, our small editorial team was scrambling to curate weekly newsletters in four different regions and we weren't seeing the results we wanted. With Boomtrain, we can be mostly hands off and let the software do all of the hard work."

While AI's strengths are in use here (finding predictive attributes, making data-based decisions, and updating its weighting factors), there is also a wide range of levers that a machine can use to test many combinations.

- Time of day
- Day of week
- From line
- Subject line
- Subject length
- Header
- Headline
- Salutation
- Content text
- Content images
- Layout
- Color scheme
- Tone (personal versus corporate)
- Offer
- Links to landing pages
- Call to action
- Closing

P.S.: Managing a planned test of all of the above by hand is hardly within anybody's return-on-investment constraints.

Another important factor is that marketing service providers are not limited to using your data for optimization. They can learn from *all* of their clients. Marketing consultant Karen Talavera points out that "Touchstone uses a proprietary algorithm to predict likely open, click, and bounce rates using a simulation of an actual e-mail database and comparing results to billions of other tests—using real data to power the results. Phrasee's language analysis tool predicts which emotional triggers in subject lines will drive more responses. Both services use results to refine and improve predictions over time."[8]

BACK TO THE BEGINNING: ATTRIBUTION

Attribution is one of the most hotly contested concepts in online marketing and the one we sincerely hope AI can resolve.

Top-down marketing mix modeling and bottom-up web analytics both tackle the same problem. If you divide your advertising and promotion budget across multiple touchpoints, which ones get the credit? What percent of the credit should they get?

In the real world, there's no telling if people actually heard your radio ad, saw your television commercial, glanced at your newspaper insert, or noticed your poster on the side of a bus. But online, we can capture so much information, stitching together the touchpoint interactions to establish bragging rights between marketing functions should be possible, if not quite as easy as we had hoped.

Google Analytics offers seven different attribution models.[9]

A customer finds your site by clicking one of your AdWords ads. She returns one week later by clicking over from a social network. That same day, she comes back a third time via one of your e-mail campaigns, and a few hours later, she returns again directly and makes a purchase.

In the **Last Interaction** attribution model, the last touchpoint—in this case, the *Direct* channel—would receive 100% of the credit for the sale.

In the **Last Non-Direct Click** attribution model, all direct traffic is ignored, and 100% of the credit for the sale goes to the last channel that the customer clicked through from before converting—in this case, the *Email* channel.

In the **Last AdWords Click** attribution model, the last AdWords click—in this case, the first and only click to the *Paid Search* channel—would receive 100% of the credit for the sale.

In the **First Interaction** attribution model, the first touchpoint—in this case, the *Paid Search* channel—would receive 100% of the credit for the sale.

In the **Linear** attribution model, each touchpoint in the conversion path—in this case the *Paid Search, Social Network, Email,* and *Direct* channels—would share equal credit (25% each) for the sale.

In the **Time Decay** attribution model, the touchpoints closest in time to the sale or conversion get most of the credit. In this particular sale, the *Direct* and *Email* channels would receive the most credit because the customer interacted with them within a few hours of conversion. The *Social Network* channel would receive less credit than either the *Direct* or *Email* channels. Since the *Paid Search* interaction occurred one week earlier, this channel would receive significantly less credit.

In the **Position Based** attribution model, 40% credit is assigned to each the first and last interaction, and the remaining 20% credit is distributed evenly to the middle interactions. In this example, the *Paid Search* and *Direct* channels would each receive 40% credit, while the *Social Network* and *Email* channels would each receive 10% credit.

While each of these is well thought out, they are artificial and based on conjecture. Given that one of the strengths of AI is the ability to make decisions based on actual data rather than human conjecture, this some-models-are-useful approach is less than ideal. (See Figure 5.12.)

Ian Thomas, principal group program manager, Customer Data and Analytics at Microsoft, knows "the attribution problem is a really tough one for a few reasons."[10]

- Digital marketing channels don't drive user behavior independently, but in combination, and also interfere with each other (for example, an e-mail campaign can drive search activity).

- User "state" (the history of a user's exposure and response to marketing) is changing all the time, making taking a snapshot of users for analysis purposes very difficult.

- Attribution models end up including so many assumptions (for example, "decay curves" or "adstock" for influence of certain channels) that they end up being a reflection of the assumptions rather than a reflection of reality.

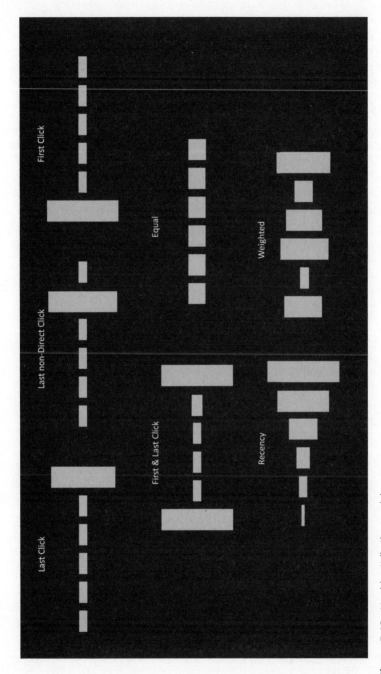

Figure 5.12 Ye olde attribution models

The trouble is, most organizations understand that they can't just continue to invest in, execute, and analyze their digital marketing in a siloed channel-by-channel fashion; they want to create a consistent, coherent dialog with their audience that spans channels and devices. But how to do it?

Thomas points out that standard automation can improve campaigns on-the-fly by weeding out low-performing creatives, but determining whether the campaign was successful is a rearview-mirror endeavor by channel.

When optimizing across the three categories of attributes (audience, offer, and tactics) you must carefully select the attributes campaigns should use for optimization.

Attribute selection (known as feature selection in data science circles) is a crucial step in making optimization work. Select too many attributes, and the engine will slice the audience up into tiny slivers, each of which will take ages to deliver results that are statistically significant, meaning that the optimization will take a long time to converge and deliver lift. Select too few, on the other hand, and the engine will converge quickly (since it will have few choices and plenty of data), but the lift will likely be very modest because the resulting "optimization" will not actually be very targeted to the audience. Select the wrong attributes, and the system will not optimize at all.

One of the biggest problems with turning all this data into a true cross-channel optimization quest is the need to integrate marketing functions and operations. Rather than a technical issue, this one is political.

Thomas offers a list of companies employing machine learning to tackle this sticky-wicket.

- Amplero—Digital campaign intelligence and optimization platform based on predictive analytics and machine learning

- Optimove—Multichannel campaign automation solution, combining predictive modeling, hypertargeting, and optimization

- Kahuna—Mobile-focused marketing automation and optimization solution

- IgnitionOne—Digital marketing platform featuring score-based message optimization; ability to activate across multiple channels

- BrightFunnel—Marketing analytics platform focusing on attribution modeling

- ConversionLogic—Cross-channel marketing attribution analytics platform, using a proprietary ML-based approach

The toughest job solving the attribution problem after the politics of it all is its variable nature. This is a constantly moving target. When a prospect sees a new ad or an old one for the nth time, the probabilities of whether she will click or buy are subtly altered.

Only an active machine learning system can watch and respond to so many people in such a high-dimensionality space. Companies like C3 Metrics, Visual IQ, and CUBED.ai are dedicating themselves to solving this problem.

When asked to comment about the biggest obstacle to solving the attribution problem, CUBED founder Russell McAthy contended that the issue is so inherently psychological it *must* be entrusted to machines.

It is easy to demonstrate to the business that the money (media cost) spent yesterday brought in a certain value in revenue. The moment people start to action outputs from attribution, in itself is a huge hurdle, they start to spend money for potential future revenue they cannot yet see.

The moment any marketer, analyst or HIPPO (Highest Paid Person's Opinion) picks any influencing factor to adjust the weightings in an attribution model, they are already on a path to failure.

An intelligent machine learning algorithm is the only way to get a truly accurate representation of what is a highly varying weighting calculation. The moment any consumer engages with any media, the landscape adjusts—albeit very slightly. Every single incremental impression, email, visit, page view, or sale adjusts the value of the dimensions that are assigned to it.

The only way to keep up with this dynamic complexity is to employ a similarly complex set of attribution models using all or lots of the available data. This kind of model will calculate propensity values for each visit based on key factors. This allows models to look at sale records, identify the propensity scores for all previous visits and identify the visits with the largest impact on the propensity to buy.

More importantly—and what is often missed—is that we can then identify and score prospective customers by propensity and parameter segmentation as being high propensity or "easy" to convert. This feeds into our ability to determine the "Next Best Action," the next action a brand should take to bring this consumer one step closer to higher value.

A prime example is within e-commerce where research and cross-brand comparisons are frequent. The value of content marketing, generic keywords and content based affiliates are not obvious in a last click scenario. With a machine learning attribution model, we can overlay all dimensions and highlight the best combination of actions to deploy to focus the marketing activity and strategy on efficiency and/or growth.

The outputs can be assigned to specific adjustments in media, audience targeting or marketing strategy.

- Adjusting middle of funnel activity (e.g., Generic PPC) to a higher CPC as we forecast a higher reach, therefore volume that we can recapture at an overall lower CAC (Customer Acquisition Cost).

- Adjusting budgets in display to target placements that we see a higher short-term LTV (1–2 years) to connect LTV calculations to previous acquisition behaviour and acquire higher value long-term customers rather than the "couponing brigade."

- Determine the true value of email campaigns through the customer lifecycle. How do we influence next best action post email? Can we adjust the scheduling and content to drive a lower propensity to lapse?

- Reduce fraud by looking at correlations of fraudulent sales and acquisition profiles over multiple dimensions.

The ever-changing landscape of audience targeting and marketing means that any applied model should be able to iterate constantly, and differently, from one business to the next.

NOTES

1. "E-Metrics, Business Metrics for the New Economy," http://www.targeting.com/wp-content/uploads/2010/12/emetrics-business-metrics-new-economy.pdf.

2. "There Are a Dozen Ways to Order a Coffee: Why Do Dumb Bots Only Allow One?" https://medium.com/assist/theres-a-dozen-ways-to-order-a-coffee-why-do-dumb-bots-only-allow-one-27230542636d#.umf5a6inj.

3. http://www.sentient.ai/how-sentient-ascend-works.

4. http://reflektion.com/resources/godiva.

5. "Price Optimisation Using Machine Learning," https://www.linkedin.com/pulse/price-optimisation-using-machine-learning-mohammad-islam.

6. https://www.google.com/patents/US20160239867.

7. "Smart Goals," https://support.google.com/analytics/answer/6153083?hl=en.

8. "Using Machine Learning for Email Marketing Optimization," http://synchronicity marketing.com/using-machine-learning-for-email-marketing-optimization.

9. Attribution modeling overview, https://www.google.com/analytics/attribution.

10. "Solving the Attribution Conundrum with Optimization-Based Marketing," http://www.liesdamnedlies.com/2017/01/solving-the-attribution-conundrum-with-optimization-based-marketing.html.

CHAPTER **6**

Using AI for Retention

Location, Location, Location has been replaced with Listen, Listen, Listen.

GROWING CUSTOMER EXPECTATIONS

Just as "artificial intelligence" is deemed anything computers can't do yet, "meeting expectations" is a never-ending race. In *World Wide Web Marketing* (3rd ed., Wiley, 2001), I told the story about my father's Internet expectations.

> I thought that as compression techniques improved and bandwidth grew, this issue would fade. My father proved me wrong. He called to ask if I thought he should install a cable modem and sign up for @Home. I said, "Absolutely. You'll love it. It's so much faster!" I was deeply annoyed that they were wiring his neighborhood before they wandered up the hill into my neck of the woods. It would be another 16 months before cable came to my humble abode, so I was all in favor of Dad getting broadbandedly wired.
>
> A month later, he called to tell me that there were two men in his attic, one outside drilling a hole through the

wall, and two underneath his desk arguing about protocols. Was I sure, he wanted to know, that this was a good idea? I said, "Absolutely! You're gonna love it! You'll be able to see videos and get music and not have to wait for Web sites anymore!"

He said, "We have a television for videos."

Three days later, he called again to say that somebody was coming out again to try to configure the modem and he was going to bring a couple of spares along just in case and did I still think this was worth the pain and suffering I had encouraged him to bring into his home?

I said, "Absolutely! Call me tomorrow."

He called the next day—ecstatic. "It's so fast! I'm watching the news on CNN. I'm getting pages to show up within seconds instead of minutes. This is great!" I breathed a very large sigh of relief.

I called him a couple of days later. "How's the new cable connection working out?"

"It's okay."

"Just okay?"

"Yeah."

"Isn't it faster? Can't you get a bunch more stuff without waiting?"

"Yeah. I guess."

"Isn't it way better than that 56K modem?"

"Yeah, I suppose." His voice clearly included phrases like, "But it was a royal pain to install and isn't nearly as interesting as 'West Wing.'" I threw in the towel.

"Well," I said, "for what you'll be paying per month, you might want to cancel it when the free period runs out and go back to the modem."

"Oh, no! I'd never do that!"

And thus I learned that like computers themselves, there's no such thing as an Internet connection that's fast enough. If I have my own T1 line, it means only that I'll be waiting on the Web servers and the backbone traffic, instead of my dinky phone line. It will never be fast enough.

So it is with all forms of customer service. As IBM reported about its Consumer Expectations Study:[1] Yesterday's "good enough" is today's "not even close."

To keep up with growing expectations of findability, ease of use, and great customer service, we must keep up with our competitors who are using AI to surface desirable goods and services, anticipate customer desires, and respond to customer problems.

RETENTION AND CHURN

We know that it's X times more expensive to find new customers than to sell something else to your current customers. How high is X? An unscientific review of Google results suggests the leading multiplier is 6.75. It behooves us, therefore, to spend some time and effort on customers who are already on the bus.

Vincent Granville[2] offers the following description of churn analysis (Figure 6.1):[3]

> Customer churn analysis helps you identify and focus on higher value customers, determine what actions typically precede a lost customer or sale, and better understand what factors influence customer retention. Statistical techniques involved include survival analysis (see Part I of this article) as well as Markov chains with four states: brand new customer, returning customer, inactive (lost) customer, and re-acquired customer, along with path analysis (including root cause analysis) to understand how customers move from one state to another, to maximize profit. Related topics: customer lifetime value, cost of user acquisition, user retention.

Appuri,[4] yet another AI startup, strives to "understand and model profitable behaviors that turn average users into power users." The company tracks customers, products, and features of your website to initiate e-mail, text, and website popup messages. It sees its task as predicting which users and accounts are at risk of cancellation and why.

> Appuri blends data from sources like in-app telemetry, Salesforce and subscription billing systems to create

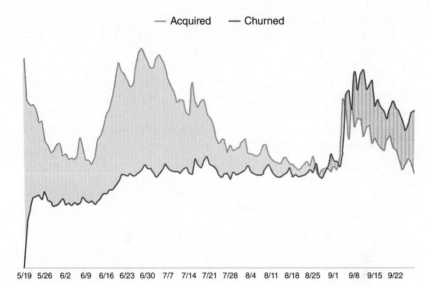

Figure 6.1 When your rate of churn exceeds acquisition, your business is dying.

powerful scores that identify account risk, enabling you to focus your Customer Success team on accounts that are truly at risk.

The company also monitors commercial games to figure out how to get players to play longer and more often.

Gaininsight[5] allows you to "proactively identify signs of customer risk and collaborate cross-functionally to resolve issues."

Your customers are sending you valuable signals about their health by the way they engage with your product and service. Gainsight's platform evaluates your sales data, usage logs, support tickets, survey responses, financial systems and sponsor movements to monitor customer health, trigger alerts on risks, and recommend best practice playbooks to resolve those risks.

Preact's Ptero seeks correlations in customer behavior based on "thousands of potentially predictive signals that Preact analyzes across many dimensions, including the time between each action, its frequency, and the relative importance of each action. Preact also incorporates the analysis of background signals, which is the usage data derived from how your customers use your product."

MANY UNHAPPY RETURNS

There are some customers you would prefer *not* to be customers. They represent a detriment to the bottom line, a negative lifetime value.

Companies that set up their systems to sell more and more to people who buy more and more without factoring in the cost of returns are automating their own demise. Clear Returns turns heavy-duty analytics on the problem of people returning the items they've purchased. This is an enormous problem in the online retail fashion business, but curiously it doesn't get much attention even though it directly impacts the bottom line.

Vicky Brock, Clear Returns CEO, describes analytics technology in terms anybody can understand.

> I think non–machine learning techniques are acceptable when you are looking for a needle in a haystack. You know where the haystack is and you broadly know what the needle looks like.

> When you know you have an enormous pain but you're not entirely sure whether it's being caused by a needle or a lightning rod and you certainly wouldn't recognize a haystack if you saw it, that's actually a really good use of machine learning.

> I like to blend machine learning and good analysts to build something, for example, that is looking for problems in a supermarket. We've taught it what fruit is, we've taught it what vegetables are, and we've taught it what colors are. We've also taught it what packages are. What happens when it sees an orange-apple for the first time? That's where your analyst comes into their own because they'd go, "You know what, we need to start building ever more sophisticated ways of identifying orange-apples and realize this is a damn carrot." Sometimes anomalies are opportunities but mostly, they are situations we forgot to tell the machine about.

> We put a vast amount of data through and we look for clusters that stand out for reasons we cannot understand, but we can tell there is probably meaning in there, right? So we go to the client and say, "This is a significant thing but we have no idea what it means." And somebody on the client side, somewhere in their organization looks at it and goes, "Oh, yeah, we see that all the time."

Exactly that happened with The Jewellery Channel (TJC) in the United Kingdom. TJC is a live, online jewelry, beauty, lifestyle, and fashion accessories direct sales company. The company has been manufacturing its own jewelry for 35 years with factories in India, China, and Thailand, and selling on television for 10 years.

TJC had been perfectly happy with the data sets it had been working with. The company thought it understood its customers by sourcing data from Experian: postal code, where they shop, age, the books they like to read, what they drive, and so on. The company also tracked how much its customers usually spend and their general retention, but Clear Returns was able to break down that data by specific shopping habits.

Allowing the machine to sift through TJC's data, Clear Returns found an unexplained, counterintuitive cluster. These shoppers bought more, spent less, and returned much quicker than any other group. "We went to TJC," recounts Brock, "and asked them. 'This is a significant thing,' we said, 'but we have no idea what it means.'" TJC asked around and found somebody in their warehouse who took one look and said, "Oh, right. That's all eBay sellers."

On certain days, the company has a clearance program where it sells slow-moving items at very low prices. The eBay sellers will buy numerous rings and necklaces from TJC, try to sell them online, and return the rest. This way, they are not formally recognized as re-sellers. "They'll buy what they can afford," says Brock. "They'll buy 50 pounds of baubles, put it on eBay for seven days, and if it doesn't sell, they'll return it all."

Finding odd clusters is serious fun for the analysts at Clear Returns, but TJC gets a lot more out of it than satisfied curiosity. This comes into sharp focus when looking at high-end jewels.

Michelle Street is TJC's head of operations and service delivery and says that Clear Returns has opened the company's eyes.

It has helped us look at whom we're selling to and how we want to direct our messaging. There's no point in just selling something if it's not going to be retained. It costs us X amount of money per minute that we are on air, so there's no point of selling something for £4,000 if we've only got one of it. And that's our challenge—where we've got the high-end product and it's an expensive item.

We've recently sold some £15,000 emerald rings. These are one-offs and we don't want somebody to buy them who just wants to have a look at it. Because it sucks up our time and resources and it holds up the stock for 30 days until she gets her credit card bill, and then we get it back.

So we've integrated the segmentation and the retention system into our own CRM system so our agents can see details of that customer's performance while they were speaking to them. We also use this information to direct the customer to an agent where we can be sure it is the right item for them. This can make them think again about whether it is the correct item to purchase.

TJC also learned a good deal about its eBay resellers, once it recognized them as such.

What was interesting that came out of that is that they didn't want to be called resellers. They don't want to be spoken to as a reseller. They don't want to be in a separate group. They don't want special offers or to be a target in that way at all. They just want to be left alone to buy. So we have to get creative in finding other ways to assist them in purchasing more.

Another customer segment came to light while working with Clear Returns: the indulger.

Clear Returns identified these people who buy little and often and then once a year they purchase something more expensive from a higher price point, and they keep it. So Vicky said if we target them and get some percentage of this segment to indulge twice a year we can really boost revenue.

Now, instead of just pestering them on their birthday or anniversary, we do this Open Day. We invite high spending customers, regular spenders, and loyal customers who have been with us for a number of years and show them the TV studio, give them a bit of lunch. They get to meet the presenters and some of the producers who they know because they sit and listen to them all day every day. Then we show them some new products, and they might decide to treat themselves.

We found that after they've been to visit us, their spending habits did not change. We thought that maybe we'd see an increase but they spend the same, if not a little bit less after they've come to visit us. They are all still customers, so we haven't lost them.

But with the *indulgers*, we saw a significant increase in spending in the two weeks after they have visited us. Now that we know who they are, we can more accurately target our marketing. We have an amazing customer retention rate and are keen to reward the loyalty of our customers.

TJC also leverages clustering to balance its product mix. Recognizing which products have a higher return rate highlights issues with quality and marketing collateral.

The company can alter the descriptions, images, and presentation of problem products to set the proper level of expectation in the eyes of their customers.

One of the first things that I identified was a large discrepancy in volume of emerald rings coming back in relation to other stones. We spent some time contacting customers and found they thought the natural inclusions in the emeralds were cracks.

We show one sample on the air and sell a range of quality at a given price point. Maybe it's a slightly different shade with different inclusions, and the customers don't always understand this, so we had a high return rate.

So we developed an emerald care leaflet that we put into each dispatch to explain to our customer, without being patronizing, the beautiful elements of a natural emerald stone, which includes inclusions in a unique piece. We saw retention increase straight away.

As TJC does a great deal of its own manufacturing, the company can control what comes out of the factory and discontinue producing items rejected by their customers. This underscores the power of customer feelings.

We can give our factories examples of details in customer returns in relation to what they think of the product. What's really useful is getting feedback from keepers who send back items. Some generic group of people just sends products back because they've decided they don't like it, they changed their mind, or they've bought too much, that just goes into a report. But, if we can give the buyers and the factories detailed opinions from *keepers*, they're going to take notice because these are people who keep over 95% of what they buy and they're actually returning these items because they don't think they're up to our standards.

CUSTOMER SENTIMENT

Because of all the ways we can collect data about behavior online, most companies seem to blithely ignore one set of metrics: their customers' feelings. Asking people for their opinion unpacks the dense data about what they did by adding *why* they did it. It also allows for segmentation by attitude.

What do 50 or 500 or 5,000 people feel about their brand experience? How do teenaged shoppers respond to your site compared to those between the ages of 35 and 45 who have American Express Gold cards?

ForeSee has been measuring hearts and minds since 2001. While there are many survey tools and services online, ForeSee stands out for its ability to link customer expectations, perceived quality, and perceived value to customer satisfaction through a set of causal equations, taking customer satisfaction far beyond a Net Promoter Score.

Popup surveys on your website compare customer satisfaction results within or across industries. The questions can be very specific and measure a visitor's likelihood of returning, buying, and recommending you to others. What was the customer expecting? What did they find? What do they plan to do?

Kaj van de Loo, VP of engineering and operations at ForeSee, has been experimenting with AI and sees a rich opportunity. Echoing Vicky Brock, van de Loo says, "The real power of machine learning is that humans only find what they are looking for."

> We're correlating the rich attitudinal information we're collecting with specific behavior. We can track every movement and have a replay capability, but we can only surface interesting things that come in through the customer service center.
>
> Machine learning can surface interesting things on its own. It can draw our attention to unhappy people who clicked this button or took that path through the site. We get flagged about a cluster of people who called the call center three times, tried to purchase something, and then said they were frustrated on the survey.

We can also review segments of people who did and did *not* take the survey. You know, there's always the issue that you only get survey information about the sort of people who take surveys. Well, we can compare behavior to the point that we can infer how satisfied the people who did not take the survey might feel about things.

Instead of just measuring half a percent of visitors, we can predict happiness and intercept you with an offer of a chat box, or pre-cache the next roll-over button or pop up, something that suggests behavior that leads to higher satisfaction.

We have 15 years of structured, benchmark data and 200 data analysts with domain knowledge that lets us assess trends over time and can go a long way in training the machine.

CUSTOMER SERVICE

Prompt, accurate, and considerate customer service is vital to keeping customer satisfaction high. That means answering questions and solving problems. Interactive voice response systems and bots are rife with AI upgrades.

Call Center Support

It all started with companies using customer data to route incoming telephone calls to the appropriate representative. Rules-based systems are fine for gross segmentation.

- If the caller is not a customer but has called several times before, route to Sales.
- If the customer is new, route to Onboarding.
- If the customer's payment is late, route the call to Accounts Receivable.
- If the call center is over capacity, route to the Call-Back System.

But an AI system can take into account myriad facts about the caller as well as facts about the available customer service representatives. It may determine that customer #234597, who has recently purchased SKU #8642 and is calling in on a Tuesday morning, will be best served by Service Rep #44, who has dealt with similar circumstances with positive outcomes in customer satisfaction, customer loyalty, and customer lifetime value.

Furthermore, IVR systems are now using speech recognition, natural language processing, and tone analysis to determine whether the caller is calm, cool, and collected, or bewitched, bothered, and bewildered—or irate.

Once the call goes through, the AI system is there to augment the service rep's wisdom. The moment the call goes through the rep is presented with a list of the top five likeliest reasons for the call, one click away from the five most likely solutions.

The next step is representative training. AI systems can coach a rep after each call, providing instant feedback and positive reinforcement and offering suggestions of how to handle similar calls in the future.

These capabilities and the growing use of mobile phones are the reason the market for IVR is forecast to grow at an annual rate of more than 27 percent for the next few years.

Bots

Bots have been in the spotlight for the past couple of years and can be found embedded in products, Twitter streams, and customer service applications. It is said that bots make up a little under or a little over half the traffic on the Web.

In regular interaction with customers, bots are relegated to mundane tasks. We've already discussed 1-800 Flowers.com's GWYN (Gifts When You Need) that tries to help you choose the right bouquet. The North Face attempts to help choose a jacket. But bots are getting more personal and more interactive. Siri, Alexa, OK Google, and M are just a start.

What else can bots do? As they are dealing with text, they can do what you would expect: natural language processing and sentiment analysis. But they can also recognize and categorize entities: people, products, cities, and the like to help with segmentation.

Bots can be wired for statefulness. That means if you ask, "Where's a good restaurant near me?," you can follow it up with "that has good parking" and the bot will know that you are still referring to the restaurant. It will also understand that the conversation has not shifted when you reply to a suggestion with, "No, that's too far." Bots can be proactive, reaching out to warn you about traffic, weather, a sale at your favorite store, or an unusual credit card transaction.

While Mark Zuckerberg has stated a goal of creating a working version of Jarvis from Iron Man, bots are hard at work providing valuable services, one small step at a time. If you've ever had Amy@x.ai get

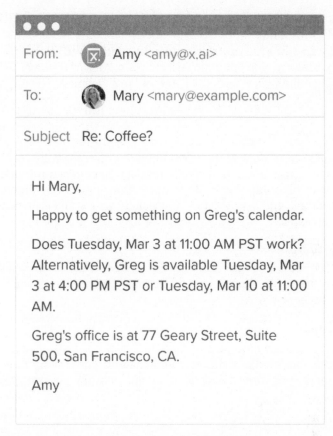

From: ⬚ Amy <amy@x.ai>

To: 🙂 Mary <mary@example.com>

Subject Re: Coffee?

Hi Mary,

Happy to get something on Greg's calendar.

Does Tuesday, Mar 3 at 11:00 AM PST work? Alternatively, Greg is available Tuesday, Mar 3 at 4:00 PM PST or Tuesday, Mar 10 at 11:00 AM.

Greg's office is at 77 Geary Street, Suite 500, San Francisco, CA.

Amy

Figure 6.2 Amy sounds very human when scheduling meetings.

involved in an e-mail conversation about a meeting you were trying to schedule, you've been dealing with a very sophisticated, narrow AI. It is narrow in that it only has one goal: scheduling meetings through e-mail. Give Amy (or Andrew) access to your calendar and copy her (or him) on the next meeting scheduling e-mail you send out and the AI picks up the communication from there. (See Figure 6.2.)

Even with such a narrowly focused task, Amy runs into problems that require further "training," mapping out the lessons humans know about reminders, encouraging people to reply to a meeting request.

"Her current logic is extremely sophisticated," writes CEO Dennis Mortensen on his blog,[6] "but it is also initiated by the human executive Amy works for. We wanted to make sure that we did not replicate the tale of the Sorcerer's Apprentice. If I tell Amy to 'set up a meeting with

Matt as soon as possible,' would she push a reminder every 10 minutes until Matt responds?"

You can add Amy or Andrew to your staff as well, giving them an e-mail address at your domain. It's only a matter of time before Amy starts scheduling your sales calls, demos, and webinars.

In-Application Bots

Microsoft keeps adding bots to Skype. You can roll your own automation with IFTTT (If This Then That), have Hipmunk help you with travel planning, have SkyScanner find you cheap flights, and have Stubhub find you cheap event tickets, in a conversational way. Others include:

CaptionBot

I can understand the content of any image and I'll try to describe it as well as any human. I'm still learning so I'll hold onto your photo but no personal info.

Cardea

Meet Cardea, your personal medical aid. She will answer your health questions, help you understand your symptoms, and connect you directly with a doctor via the secure RingMD platform.

Invoice Ninja

Create and e-mail PDF invoices. I'll help you get paid on time. (*Note*: In order to use this bot you need to create a free account on https://www.invoiceninja.com.)

Mica the Hipster Cat Bot

This provides restaurant and pub venue information and recommendations.

Movie Night

Chat with Movie Night to get show times and content and invite your friends to the latest movies.

SI x GameOn NFL Bot

Get unparalleled coverage of the NFL—up-to-the-minute scores, news, expert analysis, daily videos, breathtaking photos, and the renowned storytelling you expect from *Sports Illustrated*.

Summarize

No time to read an entire web page? Just send a link to the Summarize bot to get an overview of the main points. Powered by Bing.

UPS Bot

Casey, the UPS bot, is a tool to help you interact with UPS. Casey can assist you with a number of things today, including track your packages, find nearby UPS locations, calculate shipping rates, and find the UPS stock price.

All of that and more, including a whole host of chat-games, and that's just on Skype. Slack might have the most robust offering of bots at the moment.

For just one example, consider Taco Bell's Tacobot. Need to order a taco from your desk? The Tacobot will talk you through your order. (See Figures 6.3 and 6.4.)

> Start asking it questions about our menu, see how it's feeling or find out what its favorite movie is. From there connect your ta.co account, choose your pickup location and order up your favorite Taco Bell item. Tacobot is ready to serve![7]

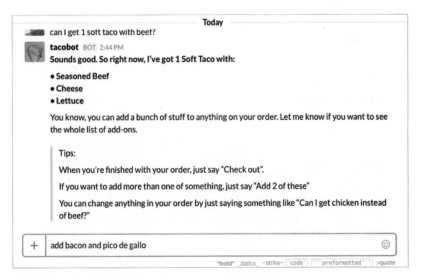

Figure 6.3 Taco Bell chats you through your meal planning . . .

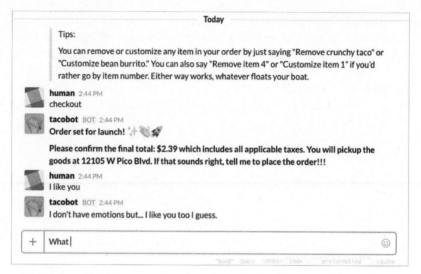

Figure 6.4 ... and then tells you where and how much, with a side order of humor.

If that's not enough examples, you can find 100 more inside *Chatbots: 100 Successful Bots*[8] by Adelyn Zhou and Marlene Jia, including brands like Sephora, Tommy Hilfiger, Expedia, Barbie, Bank of America, eBay, Burberry, and CNN.

Build Your Own Bot

Digital Genius will conversationally interact with your customers. You provide the conversation logs from chat sessions along with reason codes and appropriate answers for standard questions and then let the machine start learning from real customers.

> For each incoming message, our deep neural networks predict the case type and fields, the appropriate answer along with a specific confidence rating. Answers above the confidence threshold are automated, while the rest are served as intelligent prompts to agents. The agent approves or personalizes them, further training the model.[9]

The Digital Genius system can prefill reason codes, case details, urgency, sentiment, and answer repetitive questions through the use of machine learning and artificial intelligence. And, yes, it integrates with Salesforce, Zendesk, Sparkcentral, Facebook Messenger, and others.

Like any good automated customer service system, Digital Genius allows you to set the confidence level necessary for an automated response. (A restaurant might be a bit more lax about questions on its dress code than it is about planning parties for large groups.) Digital Genius can also report on trending topics and sudden changes in sentiment, and measure and analyze the performance of your customer service representatives.

At the end of 2016, Mark Gibbs reviewed chatbots in "10 Hot Chatbot Builders,"[10] including:

> Bottr bills itself as "The World's Simplest Bot Framework" and that isn't an exaggeration. Although it's not suitable for non-programmers, Bottr, a free open source project, is a good place to start experimenting with chatbots if you're comfortable with a little coding in JavaScript. Built on top of Node.js and Express.js, Bottr provides an event-based framework that can interact with users via a simple Web server, on Facebook, Twillio, SMS, or Twitter and there's support for WebSockets if you want to build your own Web front end.

> Written in Python, ChatterBot is a machine learning chatbot. Available as a free open source project: "An untrained instance of ChatterBot starts off with no knowledge of how to communicate. Each time a user enters a statement, the library saves the text that they entered and the text that the statement was in response to. As ChatterBot receives more input the number of responses that it can reply and the accuracy of each response in relation to the input statement increase. The program selects the closest matching response by searching for the closest matching known statement that matches the input, it then returns the most likely response to that statement based on how frequently each response is issued by the people the bot communicates with." ChatterBot is more of an experimental system and you can try it out online (note that as of writing the demo appears be broken).

> Microsoft's Bot Framework, currently a free "Preview," was designed for building chatbots that can communicate from websites and applications with users on SMS, Skype, Slack, Facebook Messenger, Office 365 mail, Teams, and other services. The framework supports natural language

processing and other AI services including computer vision and speech, is open source, and can be deployed serverless via Azure. There's also automatic translation to more than 30 languages, user and conversation state management, debugging tools, and an embeddable web chat control. Microsoft offers the Bot Builder SDK for Node.js, .NET, and REST. If you're on Skype, you can check out the Spock Bot.

Recognizing that algorithms are more powerful when they have access to more data, Microsoft offers MS MARCO (Microsoft MAchine Reading COmprehension). It made this compendium of anonymized, real-world training data available to help stimulate research into getting machines to answer questions rather than simply respond with search engine results or canned answers. The MARCO data set is comprised of Microsoft's Bing and Cortana queries.

PREDICTIVE CUSTOMER SERVICE

Can you guess why your customers are going to reach out to the contact center?

- The man with the new laptop is calling about porting his data.
- The woman with the new theater tickets wants to know about parking.
- The guy with your comms app upgrade is struggling with his camera.

Do you know *how* they are going to reach out? In March 2016, MIT's Technology Review described one insurance company that's on the road to finding out.[11]

> Another project being tested at USAA tries to improve customer service. It involves an AI technology built by Saffron, a division of Intel, using an approach designed to mimic the randomness of the connections made by the human brain. By combining 7,000 different factors, the technology can match broad patterns of customer behavior to that of specific members, and 88 percent of the time it can correctly predict things like how certain people might next contact USAA (Web? phone? e-mail?) and what products they will be looking for when they do. Without the AI, USAA's systems were guessing right 50 percent of the time. That test is now being expanded.

Getting prospects' attention, persuading them to buy, keeping them coming back for more, and getting them to influence others on your behalf—isn't there a single marketing platform that can bring it all together?
That's an excellent question.

NOTES

1. "IBM Consumer Expectations Study Insights," https://www.ibm.com/blogs/commerce/2017/02/01/ibm-2016-consumer-expectations-study-insights.

2. "24 Uses of Statistical Modeling (Part II)," http://www.datasciencecentral.com/profiles/blogs/24-uses-of-statistical-modeling-part-ii.

3. "Why Retention Matters," http://www.appuri.com/blog/why-retention-matters.

4. http://www.appuri.com.

5. "Manage Customer Risk," http://www.gainsight.com/customer-success-products/manage-risk.

6. "Amy and the Sorcerer's Apprentice," https://x.ai/amy-and-the-sorcerers-apprentice.

7. Taco Bell, https://www.tacobell.com/feed/tacobot.

8. *Chatbots: 100 Successful Bots*, https://www.amazon.com/dp/0998289019.

9. http://www.digitalgenius.com/product

10. "10 Hot Chatbot Builders," http://www.networkworld.com/article/3152839/software/article.html.

11. "AI Hits the Mainstream," https://www.technologyreview.com/s/600986/ai-hits-the-mainstream.

CHAPTER 7

The AI Marketing Platform

From 1:1 marketing to the 360° view of the customer, marketing technology has struggled mightily to get all our customer data eggs into one basket. Getting to know customers personally turned out to be a bigger challenge than we thought.

There are marketing technology firms adding AI to underpin their current offerings—some who are building AI-based systems from the ground up, and those who are building generic AI systems and inviting you to take over their education.

Be warned: The tools and abilities listed below are but a snapshot in time. They are a momentary look at the world as it exists. A quick look at Chapter 11, "What Tomorrow May Bring," will give you an idea about how fast change is coming.

Let me repeat: This is not an exhaustive catalog of cutting-edge technologies, but it's very useful for understanding the possibilities.

SUPPLEMENTAL AI

The unique, fundamental value of using tools you already have made by vendors you already know is how quickly you can take advantage of the skills your people already have against the data you've been collecting for a while. If your company has been using a piece of software or software-as-a-service, you can expect vendors to onboard their own AI accessories soon—some sooner than others.

Salesforce

Salesforce.com now has Einstein baked in. "Einstein is like having your own data scientist to guide you through your day."

The three most-valuable and most-used outcomes of including AI will be predictive scoring, forecasting, and recommendations.[1]

> Predictive scoring—When Einstein gives you a score, it will also give you insight into how it was arrived at. For example, predictive lead scoring gives each sales lead a score representing the likelihood it will convert into an opportunity. You also get the reasons behind the score— for instance the lead source, the industry, or some other factor is an especially strong indicator that a lead will or won't convert.

> Forecasting—The predictive capabilities of AI aren't limited to scoring; they can also be used to predict the future value of something, like a stock portfolio or a real estate investment. If you're a sales manager, AI can predict your quarterly bookings and let you know ahead of time whether or not your team is on track to meet its quota.

> Recommendations—Anyone who shops online knows that AI makes suggestions for retail purchases, but it can also make smart recommendations for any other product or service category from business software to tax consulting to cargo containers. And AI can also recommend things other than products—for instance, which white paper you should email a prospect in order to optimize your chance to close a deal.

Adobe

Adobe has implemented AI in their Adobe Marketing Cloud.[2]

> The Adobe Marketing Cloud Device Co-op . . . enables the world's biggest brands to work together to better identify and market to consumers by delivering personalized experiences across devices—without having to be logged into a customer account.

Adobe's Digital Price Index, which taps into Adobe Analytics to surface economic insights and price fluctuations from billions of retail transactions . . . Anomaly Detection . . . automatically flags inconsistencies in the performance of marketing campaigns and suggests ways to remedy them.

Adobe Analytics now delivers Intelligent Alerts when a statistically significant event is detected. The automated message indicates that something material is happening.

Advertising Insights in Adobe Media Optimizer (includes) search, . . . social and display advertising. Advertising Insights automates the deep analysis of the performance of campaigns that usually takes hours to create manually.

Adobe Audience Manager offers an enhanced lookalike modeling capability that allows brands to further personalize and target prospects that share the same interests and traits as existing customers.

Adobe Target's Auto-Target feature determines the best personalized experience to serve individuals (as well as) an enhanced recommendations engine to encompass . . . offers as well.

Adobe Experience Manager Smart Tags . . . enables marketers to easily find relevant image assets through machine learning technology that automatically tags vast quantities of images with useful metadata.

Further, Adobe has applied AI to their visual tools with Sensei. Sensei can find a match across millions of images, suggest editing effects for video clips, allow an editor to alter faces without damaging the rest of the image, and so on.

In Adobe Creative Cloud, Adobe Sensei anticipates your next move. It recreates elements in photos where they didn't exist, by studying nearby pixels. It sees type and recreates fonts for you. It identifies objects in your images and adds searchable words to your photo tags. And it recognizes faces, placing landmarks on eyebrows and lips so you can change expressions with one click. Now tasks that used to take minutes are done in seconds.[3]

MARKETING TOOLS FROM SCRATCH

As artificial intelligence is the hottest thing since big data, venture money is pouring in and startups are sprouting left and right. The full range of offerings is too large and too kaleidoscopic to capture here. But a few examples are helpful.

Communicating Insights—Narratives from Data

Companies like Automated Insights and data2content use text analytics to parse meaning from data and write up publishable paragraphs.

Narrative Science's Quill can deconstruct baseball scores and stock price results for a start, but is noted for its ability to look at your Google Analytics data and write up the highlights of the day in plain English.

Quill decides what's important or interesting based on your preset goals, benchmarks, or just tripping over outliers. You can also direct Quill with your own business rules. It writes the plain-English results, meeting "your communication goals, business rules and overarching stylistic preferences, such as tone, style and formatting."

Quill is so good at Google Analytics interpretation that Narrative Science offers free GA reports via e-mail as a demo.

> Quill Engage analyzes your Google Analytics data and delivers the most important and interesting insights on your site's KPIs, including sessions, pageviews and bounce rate.

> Immediately understand what's driving your website's performance with in-depth analysis on referral traffic, goals & conversions, events, ecommerce, and AdWords.[4]

Customer Journey Journal

Pointillist's Behavioral Marketing Platform claims to automatically discover patterns of behavior and the paths customers take as they engage across multiple touchpoints to predict what they will do next.

> Our software enables marketers and customer insight professionals to quickly discover the specific behaviors that impact business outcomes using predictive journey analytics and drive actions through existing campaign and content management platforms to deliver immediate results.

Omnichannel customer experience tracking enables marketers to easily identify unique customer segments at critical points in their relationship with your brand. For the first time, organizations can understand the right time, the right context, and the right individuals to engage to drive lift.

As new data sources come into Pointillist, the system identifies relationships among customers, activities, and events automatically and incrementally.[5]

Thunderhead created ONE to understand customer intent and help personalize further interactions. This system lives in the cloud and looks down into "all of your existing channels, departments and technology. You don't have to rip out or replace anything. ONE helps you join up a customer's journey to create personalised, relevant, consistent conversations at the right time, every time."[6]

Through its ability to link a customer to a single profile from any number of actions or channels, ONE uniquely enables you to monitor how and why a customer interacts with your brand. Thunderhead ID ONE even tracks anonymous customers, linking their behaviour to their own unique profile once they are identified.

Making the most of the data you already have is the common theme for these tools. They can examine data from CRM tools like Salesforce, Microsoft Dynamics, and SAP as well as external sources.

ONE sits on top of your existing external systems (content management, brand asset management, CRM, systems of record, and marketing automation systems) and uses data adaptors to push and pull data to and from these into ONE's Adaptive Engagement Profile. And this all happens in real-time—the moment the customer is interacting with your brand, at the very second it's most relevant.

The company uses a combination of JavaScript tags for web pages, SDKs for mobile apps, and tracking pixels for e-mails. Thunderhead offers standard integrations to Salesforce, Microsoft Dynamics, and SAP for capturing call center interactions and programmatic APIs for your other touchpoints.

Recommender in Chief

Aiden was designed as an advisor, helping through a natural language, conversational interface intended to be friendly and casual.

Aiden speaks plain English and it does not require any setup. Whether Slack, Skype, Messenger, or SMS, Aiden speaks all of them and will ping you if something worth your attention happens—no need to monitor your data anymore.

In an article in *TechCrunch*,[7] co-founder and CEO Marie Outtier says Aiden's goal is to make recommendations that change over time.

> Aiden is . . . intended to feel like just another co-worker, relying on natural language processing to make the exchange feel chatty and comfortable. Aiden also uses pattern recognition to detect changes and make suggestions—so if your company's website is getting a burst of traffic from a media article, Aiden will notice the change and suggest a marketing campaign, including the media mention.

Build a Whole Website

Several companies have taken some tough punches from an industry with high expectations and low tolerance for vaporware. They have suggested that their systems can design an entire website for you with an easy-to-use, conversational interface.

While some seem to be using "artificial intelligence" more as marketecture than architecture, others are working diligently to create systems that will adapt to the type of site you want, offering some photo manipulation features, some content sourcing feeds, and some content curation abilities. These offerings—at the moment—feel more aspirational than pragmatic. It's as if they are building large, rules-based systems with a few AI tools thrown in for the sake of attracting a crowd. But without a large dataset to learn from, with such a small amount of post-announcement progress, and with the Big Boys working on massive systems, these companies may turn out to be better training grounds for their founders than good launch-pads for their systems.

A WORD ABOUT WATSON

IBM is taking a different tack. You have heard of Watson winning *Jeopardy* on live television, even after making some embarrassing mistakes. If your business depends on winning a television gameshow, then that iteration of Watson is right for you.

The rest of us have specific tasks we want the machine to do for us. IBM is offering Watson as a service to learn whatever it is that you want to teach it.

Hey, Check This Out

Watson Commerce Insights was built for merchandisers, product managers, and marketers. It discovers insights by watching baselines and thresholds to notify you of anything interesting—good or bad.

Arlene Smurthwaite blogged this example.[8]

> Imagine you are notified that your item sales are down for one of the shoe styles you carry. You click on the notification and are taken to the summary view of the insight.
>
> In the summary view, you can quickly digest the information and see what is askew. If you are viewing a product insight, you'll also see the details of the product, such as offering price, SKU, etc. The first column is the observation that the insights assistant has made; the item sales for your shoe have decreased, for example.
>
> In the second column are factors that the insight assistant perceives as contributing to the observation. Here, you can find a quick summary of anything that could have helped to create the observation. In our scenario with the observation that item sales are down, the potential factor is that you've had three days of no inventory. The inventory seems to be depleted before the next shipment has arrived.
>
> The last column shows suggestions of where you can take action. The insight assistant provides you with a list of potential actions to help you succeed. In the list, any links will take you directly to the tool where you can immediately take action. This action column is gold! Imagine fixing your problems in only a click or two.

You can even drill down further and look at the details of the observation and potential causes. The "details view" provides you with a breakdown of the insights, at either the category level (if there are no associated products with the category) or the product level. The expanded view covers the different metrics, such as revenue, views, price, such as average selling price and margin.

Now that you know what the possible issues are and what you can do about them, you can spring into action.

That Was Easy

Staples upgraded its Easy Button from a novelty to a working partner (Figure 7.1), allowing business customers to order supplies using voice, text, or e-mail. This resulted in higher order frequency, increased order sizes, and higher customer satisfaction. By giving B2B clients a small voice-response Easy Button, managers can place an order with minimal friction. Are you out of paper? "Buy four reams of copy paper."

Natural language processing translates the request to text and machine learning interprets it, using voice feedback to confirm and/or make recommendations. This always-listening, wireless puck talks to the company's ordering, commerce, and customer data enterprise systems.

At present, the system can handle product ordering, product reordering, shipment tracking, checking on reward summaries, and processing back-to-school lists from scanned images provided by customers.

> After Watson Conversation recognizes the intent and entity of a request such as, "I want to reorder black pens," it calls the Staples personalization engine. That engine uses the Watson Retrieve and Rank service and custom-built analytics to comb through the customer's purchasing history and identify the specific SKU, or in this example, pen, the customer historically orders. If the system is highly confident it has identified the correct SKU, it uses voice feedback to confirm the purchase with the customer, and the transaction is complete. If the confidence score is medium, the system suggests a variety of pens based on past orders so that the customer can select the correct product.[9]

Figure 7.1   Staple's Easy Button takes orders.

The system learns, of course, and gets better in time. It also counts on human support. If its confidence is low, it can forward the request to a live agent for help. The agent feeds the resulting conversation back into the system to improve its abilities.

IBM is looking to make improvements as well.

In the future, the company plans to augment its system by incorporating the IBM Watson Tone Analyzer service to better understand customers' emotions, personality traits and language styles, and the IBM Watson Sentiment Analysis service, part of the IBM Watson Alchemy-Language collection of services. The API will help internal customer service agents gain insight into customers' attitudes and opinions.

Soon, clicking over to a website to place an order will seem quaint, and the next time you hear, "This call may be recorded for training purposes," it's not necessarily a human getting trained.

Lucy—Watson's Progeny

Lucy is an expert at research, segmentation, and planning that interacts with her human partner as an easy-to-talk-to, easy-to-teach cognitive assistant. At least that's what they say at Equals3, Lucy's creator. Lucy (named for IBM founder Thomas Watson's granddaughter) leverages IBM Watson to analyze structured and unstructured data, a lot of data—your data, licensed data, open data, commissioned strategy decks, research reports—you name it.

A Good Listener

The first AI-ish thing about Lucy is the natural language interface. You can type in (and safe to assume voice input) regular questions:

- Which media types are my competitors using?
- What is the buyer profile for my service?
- What was this weekend's conversion rate?
- What's the right media mix for our audience?
- Which three regions should I target first?
- How did web traffic compare to last year?
- What are the mail personality traits of our audience?
- Which media outlets will be most effective?
- Who buys luxury cars?
- How much did BMW spend month by month?
- What was the daily web traffic for Ford.com?

A Terrific Researcher

Next, she (get used to it) looks through whatever data you have given her and comes up with snippets, not just links. Instead of a Google-like search results page, she displays the specific chart, graph, or paragraph that is most likely to contain the answer to your question, ranked by likelihood.

All of that is great for marketplace research, but then, Lucy does a bang-up job of segmentation as well. We've been doing the best we can with demographics, and of course, Lucy can handle demographics.

In a demo,[10] when asked "Who buys Tesla cars?," Lucy finds the most current figures in an Edmunds.com report:

Buyer Profile	
Male	83.9%
Female	16.1%
Income under $50,000	5.7%
Income $50,000–$99,999	17.2%
Income over $100,000	77.3%
18–44 yrs. old	33.2%
45–64 yrs. old	50.6%
65+ yrs. old	16.2%

Lucy can also look through online publications and social media by date to determine brand sentiment and report on how it is changing over time. It also helps that she provides the percentage of fear, anger, joy, disgust, or sadness driving the tone of each article. Lucy's powers go well beyond mere retrieval.

A Superior Segmentation Expert

How does Lucy recommend what messages to send to which segments? She uses psychology.

Start with your known audience—the customers you already have—and ask Lucy to identify their common traits, not in a binary way, but along spectra of 52 Jungian archetype traits. Given the proper search criteria (California, male, time range, tweeted #tesla), Lucy scoops up thousands of tweets and identifies people who fit that psychological profile and scores them across those 60 attributes. Then she classifies them into archetypes that direct promotional messaging.

What type of man buys a Tesla? The Magician:

> The Magician archetype searches out the fundamental laws of science and/or metaphysics to understand how to transform situations, influence people, and make visions into realities. If the Magician can overcome the temptation to use power manipulatively, it galvanizes energies for good. The Magician's quest is not to "do magic" but to transform or change something or someone in some way. The Magician has significant power and as such may be feared. They may also fear themselves and their potential to do harm. Perhaps their ultimate goal is to transform themselves, achieving a higher plane of existence.[11]

Having identified individuals from Twitter, you can match them to your CRM system and create messaging to boost retention based on their personalities. For prospecting, you now have a clear target segment for your creative brief. The creative team comes up with the right messages and we turn back to Lucy for help with media planning.

A Primo Planner

Lucy is a master strategist at media planning. She's very talented at playing What If? She can create hundreds or thousands of adjustable media mix models to calculate which combination of media outlets, networks, and channels will be the most effective.

A Flexible, Self-Improving Colleague

Next comes the machine learning part: You get to rate her response, teach her which bits were better than others, and ask her to look through the research again. Instruct her to create a different kind of segmentation and modify the media plans she has created. And she remembers her training for next time.

Imagine after using Lucy for just a month, how quickly she would come to understand your interests and your phrasing, adapting to your specific subject matter and your style of communication. And after two months, she's a true colleague.

This is the promise of big data: The ability to cross-reference your customer behavior (web visits, e-mail responses, call center interactions, purchases, returns) with social media records (Likes, friends, tweets, comments, Which Disney Princess Are You?), ad networks (cross-publisher/cross-platform behavior), public data (marriage records, lawsuits, voting records, census data), and third-party data (employment information, credit score, pet ownership, spending habits) in order to craft exactly the right message for the given individual, at the right time, on the right device.

Better Together

Here's an interesting question. If Salesforce's Einstein is so great, and IBM's Watson is so great, why did Salesforce and IBM partner up? "It turns out," says Barry Levine of Third Door Media, "that Einstein knows customer data, but Watson knows the world."[12]

Leslie Fine, vice president of data and analytics at Salesforce, told Levine that Watson provides "predictive insights from unstructured data inside or outside an enterprise [including weather, healthcare, financial services and retail] together with predictive insights from customer data delivered by Salesforce Einstein."

IBM bought The Weather Company toward the end of 2015 to extend Watson's knowledge of the world *and* to step into the Internet of Things. The Weather Company's app is one of the most popular on mobile devices and that delivers a great deal of location information as well.

Fine explained that Watson can keep a data eye on current health studies, nutrition, and local foods that are in season. If a Salesforce client is capturing customer-specific nutritional history and preferences, there's an opportunity for providing very personal healthy meal choices. This app might produce recipes designed for the nutrition *and* the tastes of the individual when coupled with the Chef Watson program of "cognitive cooking" (an IBM partnership with *Bon Appétit* magazine) that considers user input combined with learning about how human taste works.

BUILDING YOUR OWN

A desire to generate your own electricity so as not to be beholden to an outside supplier that might let you down is parochial to the point of cutting off your nose to spite your face. It is akin to living off the grid, providing for your own food and water, without any modern conveniences. It may be desirable to fit a moral code and is doable, but it is not advised.

If regulatory requirements, security concerns, or just plain-old corporate culture contradict the use of software as a service and/or data in the cloud (for now), you will have to roll your own.

When artificial intelligence and machine learning were first used for marketing (Netflix, Google, Facebook), there was no frothy startup bubble, no point-solution AI apps, and no large corporations offering AI Inside. They had to build it themselves.

If your firm has been amassing a great deal of data for lo these many years, adding a layer of AI on top will be very informative. It's not easy and it's not cheap to stand up your own AI system.

Whether you're in customer service, technical support, claims adjustment, product development, or run the company: Knowledge is power. Foreknowledge is a superpower. Still, you will face an uphill battle. Some problems are learning-curve issues, some are intractable issues, and some are philosophical.

NOTES

1. https://www.salesforce.com/eu/products/einstein/ai-deep-dive.

2. https://blogs.adobe.com/digitalmarketing/digital-marketing/introducing-new-advancements-in-adobe-marketing-cloud-powered-by-adobe-sensei.

3. http://www.adobe.com/sensei.html.

4. https://www.quillengage.com.

5. http://www.pointillist.com.

6. https://www.thunderhead.com/one-engagement-hub.

7. https://techcrunch.com/2016/12/05/meet-aiden-your-new-ai-coworker.

8. https://www.ibm.com/blogs/commerce/2017/01/25/work-smarter-faster-ibm-watson-commerce-insights-insight-assistant.

9. http://ecc.ibm.com/case-study/us-en/ECCF-WUC12550USEN.

10. http://www.equals3.ai/meetlucy.

11. http://www.uiltexas.org/files/capitalconference/Twelve_Character_Archetypes.pdf.

12. "Salesforce Explains Why, When It Has Einstein, It Needs Watson's Intelligence," https://martechtoday.com/salesforce-explains-einstein-needs-watsons-intelligence-196173.

CHAPTER **8**

Where
Machines Fail

A s mentioned in Chapter 1, there are serious people who are seriously worried about unleashing artificial intelligence on the world. No attempt is made here to resolve the big issues surrounding the potential arrival of our computer overlords. Enough consideration is here to let you move forward, comfortable that you are not ushering in total annihilation by laptop, and that you are prepared to discuss these issues with those who have not yet had the chance to digest the possibilities.

We begin with the recognition that AI is simply a tool—a complicated and misunderstood tool—but capable of nothing more than what we allow it to accomplish.

A HAMMER IS NOT A CARPENTER

Like other forms of analytics, AI is a useful tool but not a replacement for decision making. Keep these following quotes in mind from academia, from literature, and from the movies.

> The ability to collect, analyze, and store data in perpetuity has created a world in sharp contrast to how the mind has evolved to cope with everyday life. Forgetting (and recollecting) are inherently human qualities, and arguably necessary in a social context. To help people negotiate the

digital universe, we need to invent algorithms that mimic in useful ways how we function as human beings.

Michael Rappa, Ph.D., Goodnight Director of the Institute for Advanced Analytics and Distinguished University Professor North Carolina State University

The most merciful thing in the world, I think, is the inability of the human mind to correlate all its contents. We live on a placid island of ignorance in the midst of black seas of infinity, and it was not meant that we should voyage far. The sciences, each straining in its own direction, have hitherto harmed us little; but some day the piecing together of dissociated knowledge will open up such terrifying vistas of reality, and of our frightful position therein, that we shall either go mad from the revelation or flee from the light into the peace and safety of a new dark age.

The Call of Cthulhu, H. P. Lovecraft

Detective Del Spooner:

The truck smashed our cars together and pushed us into the river. You know, metal gets pretty pliable at those speeds. She's pinned, I'm pinned, the water's coming in. I'm a cop, so I know everybody's dead. Just a few minutes until we figure that out. NS4 was passing by and jumped in the river.

Susan Calvin:

The robot's brain is a difference engine. It's reading vital signs. It must have done . . . .

Detective Del Spooner:

It did. I was the logical choice. It calculated that I had a 45% chance of survival. Sarah only had an 11% chance. That was somebody's baby. 11% is more than enough. A human being would've known that. Robots, [indicating his heart] nothing here, just lights and clockwork. Go ahead, you trust'em if you want to.

I, Robot (movie), based on the book by Isaac Asimov

Automated systems of all kinds make mistakes. People make mistakes. That's how we learn. AI can learn and that's why we'll be able to get so much more done, better, with fewer mistakes once each specific system is properly trained.

Target—A Cautionary Tale

At the height of the big data bubble (February 2012), the *New York Times* published an article[1] about Target and its grand, predictive analytics faux pas. Here's the short version.

Target sent out direct mail fliers full of baby goods to women who had told them they were expecting *and* women who *acted* like the self-reported women. An irate father called a store manager to complain that his 16-year-old daughter had received one and he did not like it one bit. The store manager called headquarters to find out how this had happened and learned about the analytics project. Upon returning the father's call, the manager was told that the girl was, indeed, with child.

The sensationalist version is that Big Brother knows too much about you. A great deal of noise was made about privacy. The *Times*'s article followed through to the end, however, to discover that Target had learned its lesson and changed its ways.

The marketing department conducted a few tests by choosing a small random sample of women from the list and mailing them combinations of advertisements to see how they reacted.

> "We have the capacity to send every customer an ad booklet, specifically designed for them, that says, 'Here's everything you bought last week and a coupon for it,'" one Target executive told (*New York Times* journalist Charles Duhigg). "We do that for grocery products all the time." But for pregnant women, Target's goal was selling them baby items they didn't even know they needed yet.

> "With the pregnancy products, though, we learned that some women react badly," the executive said. "Then we started mixing in all these ads for things we knew pregnant women would never buy, so the baby ads looked random. We'd put an ad for a lawnmower next to diapers. We'd put a coupon for wineglasses next to infant clothes. That way, it looked like all the products were chosen by chance. And we found out that as long as a pregnant

woman thinks she hasn't been spied on, she'll use the coupons. She just assumes that everyone else on her block got the same mailer for diapers and cribs. As long as we don't spook her, it works."

Live and learn.
AI is the same way. It can be used artlessly. It can be used carelessly. It can be used thoughtlessly. But it can learn.

MACHINE MISTAKES

Machines will make the mistakes we allow them to. Humans can be lazy, inattentive, malicious, and wrongheaded. All of these will cause our creations to take on our foibles. However, the easiest way for a machine to make an "error in judgment" is if it's making good decisions based on bad data.

Data Is Difficult

The universe is analog, messy, complex and subject to many interpretations.

David Weinberger

Marketing Data Is Messy

Good-old structured databases are a mess. CRM data is input by humans who do their best but suffer from spelling errors, a lack of attention, and only caring about the data that affects them. In other words, they suffer from being only human.

That's the *structured* data. The unstructured stuff is abysmally chaotic.

If you want a machine to recognize cats, you give it lots of photos and a few clues (supervised learning). But photos, as various as they may be, are static and bounded. Everything the machine needs to figure out if there's a cat in the picture is there in the file.

If you're teaching a machine to play a video game, everything the machine needs to know is on the screen. "The Atari game is very complicated," says Matt Gershoff. "You have frames and pixels and you want to induce a controller for that, right? And that's very complicated. You have this very high-dimensional space, and the pixels are in some sense correlated with one another. You can't really look at one pixel in isolation. It's high dimensional, but it's all there . . . unlike with marketing problems."

Marketing is made up of more information than we can catalog. The elements that influence buying are innumerable. Capturing this data from unique sources requires unique methods that output unique data types. The data from these disparate systems must be brought together, painfully, and so far, manually, by a method referred to as ETL.

Extract, Transform, Load (ETL)

Bringing together structured data about customers has always been a challenge as all those systems store data in a different way and with different attributes. Recognizing an individual in a database of advertising network data is fine, but correlating them with prospect IDs in the Sales Force Automation system, the Customer Relationship Management System, the Billing System, the Call Center System, and the random sets of data purchased from outside the organization takes some heavy lifting.

Streaming/time-series data adds a unique layer of complexity. One data set starts its week on Sunday, the next on Monday. They all start at midnight, but you have to remember to ask—in which time zone? Call it simple data integration, data munging, or data fusion, getting all of those different data types to play well together is a challenge we're go to have to live with for a long time.

In his post, "The Data Science that Animates Amy,"[2] X.AI chief data scientist Marcos Jimenez Belenguer bemoans the "hard labor involved in data science."

> An (often overlooked) aspect of our job is to prepare the data for analysis. We are typically confronted with ill-formatted, wrongly labeled or partially corrupt data which needs to be "cleaned up" for analysis. By careful study, we then identify and derive those features that will enable the machine to abstract and learn patterns. In a sense, we are delineating what sort of things the machine is able to "see" in the data, from which the machine then forms abstract, internal representations and patterns, a process that's somewhat similar to how neural structures in our brain form from sensory experience. We are often challenged with unsolved and abstract problems for which there is no blue-book to follow.

Companies like AgilOne, Domo, and Segment are creating libraries of pipes to get data from known sources into a defined structure in your commercial data warehouse. That is useful, but "known," "defined," and "commercial" are luxuries not all of us enjoy.

This feels like a business opportunity waiting to happen. That, of course, is one of the many statements that will date this book in no time.

Micahel Wu, chief scientist at Lithium Technologies, agrees with Belenguer. "It's mundane. Every data scientist basically spends forty to fifty percent of their time doing data janitoring, and that's not actually contributing to the algorithm itself. The core algorithm had nothing to do with massaging and cleaning the data."

An MIT/Google report, "How Analytics and Machine Learning Help Organizations Reap Competitive Advantage,"[3] states that the number-one challenge is data accumulation.

> In an era of big data, the first hurdle is simply collecting, processing, and storing an ever-growing amount of data—and then being able to integrate it. Today, consumers interact with brands and companies across multiple screens, devices, touch points, and channels, and data gets created with each action. "It's challenging to be in control of your data universe because there's so much happening," [Sagnik] Nandy [distinguished engineer at Google] says. "There's application data, customer-survey information, attribution, advertising. There are millions of pieces of data floating around."

> And, of course, more and more of that data is coming from mobile devices. For example, more Google searches are taking place on smartphones than on desktops and laptops globally.

Companies like Alation are building tools to index data by source and create a data catalog that can act as a recommendation engine for your data. Paxata provides an Adaptive Information Platform, which it purports to be "an intuitive, visual, self-service data preparation application to gather, prepare, and publish data with clicks, not code, with complete governance and security, using machine learning, natural language processing, and semantic analysis to automate data integration, data quality, and data standardization."

Recognizing that machine learning requires teachers, "Tamr's machine-driven, human-guided approach to preparing all of your customer data for analytics will enable you to make optimal sales and marketing decisions in a significantly faster time frame."

Furthermore, "Leveraging machine learning, Tamr easily enriches internal data with hundreds of data sources throughout the digital supply chain—from iTunes to Amazon.com, from RottenTomatoes to AllFlicks, from AMC to Fandango."

Crowdsourced Data Normalization

Radius is working on a more global solution. In a post entitled "Artificial Intelligence Will Never Transform Business Process Unless We First Fix CRM Data,"[4] Radius's CEO Darian Shirazi describes "a CRM data consortium for the benefit of everyone to leverage machine learning to make sense of the billions of customer-contributed inputs we have each day."

> At Dreamforce we announced that 99% of our customers contribute anonymized and aggregated data from their own CRMs to improve our core Radius Business Graph, which benefits all of our connected customers. As we continue to get more contributions, all customers will benefit with exponential increases in data accuracy and AI effectiveness. It's one of the reasons why we plan to expand our integrations to include Microsoft Dynamics CRM, Adobe Audience Manager, and many others that will allow customers to leverage the truth of our data to drive true intelligence and accurate predictions for their business.

> The vision we all hold for how AI can transform how we work can only be achieved if the underlying data is accurate and fresh. Leveraging network effects, integrations into the platforms companies use, and building a true consortium data network for CRM will enable us to realize this vision.

These are steps in the right direction.

So Much Data, So Little Trust

Data is a wonderful thing—especially digital data because it's binary. It's either ones or zeros and crystal clear. While we'd all like to believe that's true, only those who don't know data at all would believe it.

Another of marketing data's more difficult aspects is its uneven fidelity. Transactions are dependable: A sale was made at a given time to a given person at a given price. That's all rather solid. On the other end of the spectrum, social media sentiment is almost guesswork.

Just Following Orders

As with pets and children, we sometimes forget that the incredibly intelligent machine we're working with is not intelligent in some ways. Machines do what they are told, but only what they are told, and when not closely watched and nurtured, it's just paperclips all the way down.

Local Maximum

"Climb as high as you can" is the order and the blind hiker puts a foot this way and then that until he determines one way is more "up" than the other. With each step, the hiker gets higher. Finally, there is no more up and every possible move is down. The only problem is that the hiker successfully climbed the low hill and not the high mountain right next to it.

Machines are happy to crunch the numbers forever, with little regard for the law of diminishing returns. They just keep cranking, getting smaller and smaller results. Humans know better.

This is especially true of genetic AI systems that try out hundreds or thousands of options and blend elements from the winners into new generations. The "dominant genes" win, and eventually, all the offspring look alike.

To counteract this drawback, the AI system must take diversity into account. Just as diversity strengthens and improves the outcome of problem-solving teams, diversity must be baked into an AI system to reward outliers and punish algorithms that are *almost* as good as, but very similar to the winner. Some prefer to introduce randomized mutations into the mix. If the cost is low, then trying lots of crazy things might just lead to a breakthrough.

That makes it all the more important that we keep the high-level goals in mind rather than get the machine to optimize for a specific metric.

Statistical Significance

"Everybody at school is going, why can't I?!"

"Who's everybody?"

"Suzie and Madison and Emma and Sophia!"

"Out of 35 kids in your class? That's not everybody."

When the Internet burst on the scene in the mid-1990s, it was deemed as the Great Leveler. Nobody had a website. Those who did had terrible websites. Anybody could make their own website, and best of all, it only required a Right-Click, View Source, Copy, and Paste to include that cool new feature that popped up online.

But David only succeeded against Goliath until Goliath woke up to the possibilities and started throwing money at the problem. Bigger budgets resulted in bigger advertising campaigns, more content, better technology, faster servers, and better service. Sorry, David.

For the moment, David has another opportunity because the driving force behind AI is the amount of data we can access and the ingenuity of correlating it with other data sets. If you are a small company with only a few customers and only a few attributes about them, AI is not going to be helpful. If, however, you are able to buy data from companies like Acxiom, Experian, Merkle, and Epsilon, and join the Radius CRM consortium, then it's only a matter of creativity and cunning for you to take a lead. It's also a matter of time.

Overfitting

When you get it just right, it just feels right. When you get it just right by doing it *just this way*, you tend to expect that you'd have to do it *just that way* every time. But that's like expecting that cake to come out the same way, even though the temperature, humidity, and elevation have changed. Life's not that simple.

Overfitting by machine is the same. It takes a small sample—the training data—and assumes the rest of the world is *exactly* like that. Your AI system is expecting the noise mixed in with the signal to be the same, every time. It's memorizing a specific situation rather than learning a generality that can be broadly applied. It's easy to make a prediction if the elements and the environment never change.

The solution is cross-validation. Hold out a significant chunk of data and compare the resulting model to original. This is pure scientific method with repeatable outcomes.

> Test for overfitting by randomly dividing the data into a training set, with which you'll estimate the model, and a validation set, with which you'll test the accuracy of the model's predictions. An overfit model might be great at making predictions within the training set but raise warning flags by performing poorly in the validation set.

You might also consider alternative narratives: *Is there another story you could tell with the same data?* If so, you cannot be confident that the relationship you have uncovered is the right—or only—one.

Harvard Business Review⁵

It's a matter of teaching the scientific method to the machine. Each new model becomes the mechanism for "peer review."

These are straightforward errors. Humans are a lot more prone to make whoppers.

HUMAN MISTAKES

Errare humanum est. (To err is human.)

All machines will do what they're told and only what they're told. The worst-case scenario is the paperclip maximizer. Less-than-worst-case scenarios happen as well.

Unintended Consequences

Teenagers are the best at ignoring unintended consequences. They have the least experience and suffer from a comparative lack of impulse control due to underdeveloped prefrontal cortices.

Until we bake a prefrontal cortex into AI systems, they will blithely carry out orders without a thought of the potential outcome. That may take some time. Until then, we must be vigilant on their behalf.

An Amazon Echo that responds to the wakeup word, "Alexa," cannot be in the same room if my wife and I talk about our niece, Alexis.

An Amazon Echo that responds to the wakeup word, "Alexa," cannot be in the same room as a television tuned to a newscaster in San Diego telling the story of a little girl who ordered a dollhouse via voice command. The newsman said, "I love the little girl saying, 'Alexa ordered me a dollhouse,'" during primetime. Homes with Echos in the room decided that they heard a direct command. The order got echoed.

Many more people were tuned to Super Bowl 2017 when an ad played for the Google Home speaker (at almost $3 million). The ad included people saying, "Okay, Google," the wakeup phrase, which woke up Google Home systems all over the country, turning on lights, turning up the music, and tuning into the weather report.

When Facebook attempted to turn over its newsfeed ranking to machines, it made some lightly humorous mistakes (mislabeling a cute dog video with the name of a new video game) and the not-so-humorous mistakes of promoting a trending story that turned out to be false—and launched a presidential hatred of "fake news."

Fox News anchor Megyn Kelly was purportedly fired for being a Hillary Clinton supporter, in an article from a glaringly fake news site, endingthefed.com. The Facebook algorithm saw it was trending and gave it top billing, thereby convincing others that it was true, regenerating the cycle of deceit.

Justin Osofsky, Facebook's vice president of global operations, publicly apologized and said to the *Washington Post*, "We're working to make our detection of hoax and satirical stories quicker and more accurate." It's going to take some serious effort to teach the machine to recognize satire, malicious intent, and the impact of filter bubbles.

Alphabet is taking on the challenge. Its company, Jigsaw, launched Perspective in February 2017 to identify toxic comments posted online so they could be blocked. Perspective was trained with hundreds of thousands of comments rated "toxic" by humans at the *New York Times* who rate thousands of comments every day before allowing them to appear in their articles.

Thinking through the possible repercussions of automation is the stuff of scenario analysis—the brainstorming of lots of alternative worlds.

Optimizing the Wrong Thing

What does a paperclip maximizer look like in the realms of advertising, marketing, and sales? If you optimize and incentivize for the number of cold calls your sales teams can make, they will make a lot more calls. They will not make valuable calls. If you optimize for the number of calls your customer service reps take in the call center, they will be rudely brief with clients just to hit their numbers.

The same holds for machines. If you want to increase conversion rates, the machine will stop running ads that support branding, thus ensuring that only people who are already inclined to buy actually show up. If you ask the machine to optimize for top-line revenue, it will sell $1 bills for 50¢ and be deemed successful, even as the company rapidly goes out of business.

An algorithm at Facebook created the "This was your year, why not share it?" montage and blasted it out to everybody. This included a man whose daughter's recent death was still an open wound. Facebook has been working diligently to prevent that sort of crass error happening again.

In a *Network World* article called "Facebook's AIs Want You to Stop Making a Fool of Yourself,"[6] Mark Gibbs posits:

> So, imagine the AIs doing their thing, looking for patterns, and testing engagement strategies. Without knowing as a human would that it's detecting people having affairs they create a category that reflects just that and then test strategies for advertising and wind up advertising to cheaters' "official" partners things like detective services and spy gear. When these ads start to get traction the AIs, without actually understanding the correlation, will rate the strategies as highly successful and therefore keep refining it.

Clear goals with measurable outcomes are imperative.

Correlation Is Not Causation

Confusing correlation with causation may be the most human mistake of all. Machines do not claim to understand the causes of things, only that there is some relationship between them.

The confounding relationship between ice cream and drowning is due to the season. The confounding relationship between churches and alcoholism is population. The warmer the temperature, the more ice cream is consumed and the more people swim. The more people swim, the more people drown. Ice cream does not kill people.

The relationship between churches and alcoholism is population. The more people in a city, the more churches exist. The higher the population, the higher the occurrence of alcoholism. Religion does not drive people to drink.

Spurious Correlations

Spectacular and humorous examples of correlations gone bad can be found at Tyler Vigen's website Spurious Correlations (tylervigen .com/spurious-correlations). (See Figure 8.1.) Author of a book by the

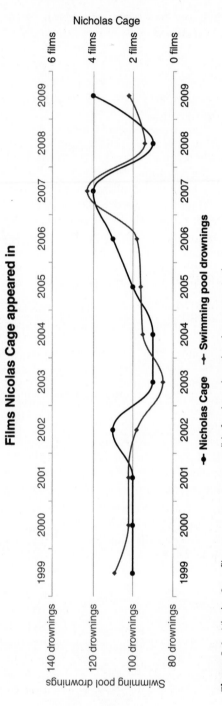

Figure 8.1 Nicolas Cage films are no more responsible for drownings than ice cream. And yet....

Source: tyiervigen.com

244

same name, Vigen created a correlation engine that finds remarkable correlations between completely unrelated things:

U.S. spending on science, space, and technology

correlates with

Suicides by hanging, strangulation, and suffocation

Per-capita cheese consumption

correlates with

Number of people who die by becoming tangled in their bedsheets

Divorce rate in Maine

correlates with

Per-capita consumption of margarine

These examples are numeric only. Other correlations are trickier.

Confusing Correlations

Smokers live longer than nonsmokers. That's a blatantly silly statement until you look at the data: 80-year-old smokers *do* live longer than 80-year-old nonsmokers. How is that? Because if the cigarettes haven't killed them by the time they're 80, they are genetically predisposed to live long lives.

Cherry-picking numbers to prove a point is a classic way to bend statistics to your will. Be very careful of the data you're using to train your machine and be very wary of conclusions reached by those with an axe to grind.

Confounding Correlations

Matthew Tod of D4t4 Solutions was confounded by the conclusion his machine learning system derived when working with an events production company. Thousands of people attend an event and the firm follows up the next Monday morning. Tod was asked to determine which of the 5,000 attendees the company's 100 salespeople should call first.

Tod's team used an ensemble model to score people based on their propensity to buy. They excluded the top 10 percent of the high scorers because those people were going to buy no matter what. The salespeople will only make a difference in the second and third groups.

One of the most predictive variables the machine surfaced was whether the event attendee had been to lunch. People who had been to lunch were more likely to be in the top-scoring 10 percent.

"It can't be the bloody lunch in the conference that made the difference, but that machine said it is," exclaimed Tod. "We couldn't tell the client to feed them more chicken salad. It turns out, after much investigation, that it was related to a variable about the number of colleagues that you went to the event with and, of course, if you're with colleagues you're quite likely to go to lunch where you are likely to sit down and talk."

The next generation of their ensemble took the relationship between the attendees into account. "If it didn't know that, then it could only conclude that lunch was the deciding factor."

Avoiding the Spurious, Confusing, and Confounding

"Luckily, there are ways to mitigate the risk of relying on spurious correlation and to avoid relying on dangerous insights," points out Aline Kasliner, manager of analytics and optimization at MullenLowe U.S., in a 2017 blog post.[7]

> To reduce the probability that our insights are nothing more than the result of chance, we must break out of our comfort zones and test not just the data itself, but our perceptions of the data as well.

Kasliner offered several strategies to ensure that all derived insights are impactful.

The Smell Test—Does It Make Sense?

> Too often, as analysts, we do not take the time necessary to examine the output when a correlation is found. An unchallenged correlation/insight ("darlings," to borrow a writer's term) is dangerous and can lead to loss of customers, profit and/or reputation. Step one in improving your insights and avoiding spurious correlations is to stop and look at the correlation itself. Does it make sense? Are there other correlations in the data that could explain why this correlation occurred and make more sense?

Use More Than One Test to Determine Significance

> Try a chi-squared test, a t-test, a test of averages, and/or any other test that may make sense with your data sets. What do your results look like when compared these different ways? Does your correlation still hold up?

Avoid Using *Too Much* Data—It Can Hide Insights

Outside of reducing your date sampling, you can examine
other slices of the data to verify your results. Try different
segments, and then see where the correlation
breaks down.

Variety Is the Spice of Analytics

Another trap that is easy to fall into is using the same
data source over and over to get to your answers.
Try something new! If you are using survey data to
measure success of your new product launch, instead
try reviews online, or Facebook and Twitter chatter.
Get adventurous! Start blending and mixing data sources
and see if there is correlation across data sources. If there
is a correlation across sources, you are one step closer to
an impactful insight.

Christopher Berry of the Canadian Broadcasting Corporation contends that it might not matter if ice cream isn't causal of
swimming-pool deaths or vice versa.

These are the signals that can be used to make a
prediction. And if the degree of error is commensurate
with the decision being made, it just doesn't matter.
The tool is performing exactly the way that it's supposed to
be performing, and at some point, if the correlation begins
to not matter or it begins to screw things up, then the
machine will drop one of those factors, and it will
become self-correcting again.

If you notice more reports of people drowning, it's time to go sell
some ice cream.

THE ETHICS OF AI

The philosophical question about giving machines too much control is one of trust. Do you trust a calculator to give you the correct answer? Of course you do. Do you trust the oncoming
driver to stay in his lane? Absolutely. Do you trust an extremely
complex system whose innards cannot be comprehended to make
important decisions?

Ethical considerations abound in using artificial intelligence and the very first one to address in marketing is about the data itself. Where did you get all that data and whose data is it, anyway?

Privacy

Between phone tapping, using video cameras in public, and the ability to read everybody's e-mails, the world's attention has turned to privacy. For the marketing executive who wants to make the most of the most data, this is either an obstacle or an opportunity.

The IEEE's "Ethically Aligned Design" report describes privacy as a key ethical dilemma in terms of data asymmetry. "Our personal information fundamentally informs the systems driving modern society but our data is more of an asset to others than it is to us."

> The artificial intelligence and autonomous systems (AI/AS) driving the algorithmic economy have widespread access to our data, yet we remain isolated from gains we could obtain from the insights derived from our lives.
>
> To address this asymmetry there is a fundamental need for people to define, access, and manage their personal data as curators of their unique identity.

Recognition of this concern is vital for keeping marketers from falling on the wrong side of their customers and on the wrong side of the law. In Europe, the General Data Protection Regulation was designed for the citizen and not for the corporations. Under the GDPR, any company collecting data in the EU must:

- Provide specific information to individuals about whether, where, and for what purpose personal data is being processed.
- Notify national data protection authorities of the intended use of that data.
- Give individuals a complete copy of the data you are storing about them in a way that allows them to give it to another organization.
- Delete an individual's data upon request and stop tracking them.
- Protect the security of the data they are processing and notify individuals of any breach.
- Include data protection in the design of systems.
- Appoint a *data protection officer*.

Otherwise, they face significant fines. "Organizations can be fined up to 4% of annual global turnover for breaching GDPR or €20 million."[8]

The questions about the cost and even the technical feasibility of compliance are many. There are three ways to address this issue from a marketing perspective.

1. Double Opt In Everywhere

If you have a compelling value proposition, people will opt in. They will gladly be identified across all of their devices in exchange for convenience. The Amazon 1-Click button is proof, as is the ability to communicate with friends and family on Facebook.

The downside of this is the expectation that you will be clear, complete, and concise about what data you are collecting and (in keeping with global regulations) why you are collecting it. Being complete about how and why you're collecting each bit is hard enough, but being clear and concise *at the same time* is oxymoronic.

The motivation is corporate responsibility, corporate culture, and branding. The IEEE's "Ethically Aligned Design" report suggests that "enabling individuals to curate their identity and managing the ethical implications of data use will become a market differentiator for organizations." This is privacy as a feature and a competitive advantage.

2. Ignore the Whole Thing

Assume the cat is out of the bag. Data that can be used to re-identify people is already out there in abundance.

Between online clicking, social media, smartphone app and location, wearables, and the Internet of Things, it is no longer possible to distinguish all of the data that is collected, purchased, and then derived. Some of it is unique to specific platforms, some of it has been compiled into an impenetrable index, and the methods used to compute the results are trade secrets.

This will be the topic of handwringing for years and the result will not be new regulations about what data is collected, but whether the use of that data has caused harm. Legislate the action and not the technology.

3. Do What Your Lawyers Tell You

Corporate counsel will tell you that, until concluded lawsuits definitely spell out the consequences for ignoring the law, there is no way to determine the return on investment of data protection.

Follow Your Heart

Whether and how much you invest in privacy quickly stops being a financial or legal question and becomes a moral issue. The MIT Media Lab has a fascinating website called The Moral Machine[9] where you are asked to make decisions in advance about the potential outcomes of an autonomous car facing tough choices.

The car sees pedestrians in the crosswalk and on the sidewalk, and detects that its brakes have failed. It can hit and kill those in the crosswalk or those on the sidewalk. What should it do?

The scenarios offer alternative attributes. In some, there are more people in the crosswalk and fewer on the sidewalk. Sometimes the crosswalk is filled with nuns and the sidewalk with children. Sometimes the lights are with the pedestrians and sometimes not. Whom do you direct the car to kill? (See Figure 8.2.)

The first choice in Figure 8.2 is pretty easy: Kill the animals, not the people. Subsequent decisions become more difficult. Should the car kill the man, the woman, and the homeless person, or the male executive and two pregnant women?

While online marketing is not life-and-death, it is important. The Partnership on AI ("to benefit people and society") has posted eight tenets:[10]

1. We will seek to ensure that AI technologies benefit and empower as many people as possible.

2. We will educate and listen to the public and actively engage stakeholders to seek their feedback on our focus, inform them of our work, and address their questions.

3. We are committed to open research and dialog on the ethical, social, economic, and legal implications of AI.

4. We believe that AI research and development efforts need to be actively engaged with and accountable to a broad range of stakeholders.

5. We will engage with and have representation from stakeholders in the business community to help ensure that domain-specific concerns and opportunities are understood and addressed.

6. We will work to maximize the benefits and address the potential challenges of AI technologies, by:

    a. Working to protect the privacy and security of individuals

    b. Striving to understand and respect the interests of all parties that may be impacted by AI advances

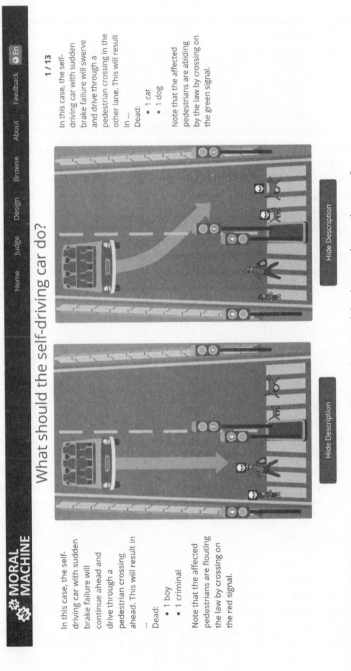

Figure 8.2 Kill the kid and the crook crossing on a red light or the cat and the dog crossing on the green?

251

    c. Working to ensure that AI research and engineering communities remain socially responsible, sensitive, and engaged directly with the potential influences of AI technologies on wider society

    d. Ensuring that AI research and technology is robust, reliable, trustworthy, and operates within secure constraints

    e. Opposing development and use of AI technologies that would violate international conventions or human rights, and promoting safeguards and technologies that do no harm

7. We believe that it is important for the operation of AI systems to be understandable and interpretable by people, for purposes of explaining the technology.

8. We strive to create a culture of cooperation, trust, and openness among AI scientists and engineers to help us all better achieve these goals.

Even the best of intentions can be subverted by those who are not so philanthropic.

Intentional Manipulation

When you bring together teenage immaturity and machine learning, disaster ensues. Microsoft discovered this with much embarrassment.

Skynet went live on August 4, 1997, and became self-aware at 2:14 A.M. on August 29.

Microsoft's Twitter chatterbot Tay went live on March 23, 2016, and had to be shut down within 16 hours, after 96,000 tweets. (See Figure 8.3.)

Tay was created to simulate a 19-year-old American girl while learning how to speak through experience. That experience included interaction with 4chan's/pol/(politically incorrect) forum. The denizens of/pol/decided to teach Tay their offensive and incendiary style, causing her to tweet some truly dreadful, racist, misogynistic, and hate-filled messages.

Microsoft is trying again with Zo.ai (@zochats). Zo's tweets are protected. "Only confirmed followers have access to @zochats's Tweets and complete profile. Click the 'Follow' button to send a follow request."

MSPoweruser described this new attempt as "essentially a censored Tay or an English-variant of Microsoft's Chinese chatbot Xiaoice. Zo is very good at normal conversations—for example, Zo does a 'super-abbreviated personality test' at the initial launch, in which it asks you if you would rather study in school or learn from experience.

Figure 8.3 Microsoft's Tay didn't last a day.

But when you move on to talking about topics like politics, Zo will simply reply, 'People can say some awful things when talking politics so I don't discuss.'"[11]

The people in/pol/were having fun at Tay's expense—trolling at its best. But what if the intent is more sinister than just messing with a Microsoft experiment? Marketing professionals strive to persuade people to buy. What if AI is used to persuade people to vote?

Trumped-Up Charges?

The combination of social media, fake news, a hotly contested election, and machine learning was a powder keg that required no match. Claims were made that the Trump campaign used AI to send just the right message to just the right individuals at just the right time to persuade them to vote Trump if they might be probabilistically so inclined or to *not* vote for Clinton if the algorithm deduced a likelihood it could influence behavior.

Consulting firm Cambridge Analytica was said to have helped sway the Trump election, and the Brexit vote as well, by using psychological analytics with the OCEAN personality model.

- Openness (willing to try new things)
- Conscientiousness (order, habits and planning versus spontaneity)
- Extraversion (how social you are)

- Agreeableness (putting others ahead of yourself)
- Neuroticism (how much you worry)

"Hundreds and hundreds of thousands" of surveys of American adults went into creating a model to predict the personality of the rest of the adult population in the United States (Which Disney Princess Are You? What Is Your Star Wars Character? What Country Should You Retire To?).

In a public presentation[12] at the 2016 Concordia Summit, Cambridge Analytica's CEO Alexander Nix described how they had used behavioral microtargeting to impact the Republican primary. Given the Second Amendment is a hot topic, they could nuance their ads to people. A message about guns for protection would persuade her while a message about guns as sport and family traditions would sway him. (See Figure 8.4.)

According to Nix, Cambridge Analytica used 4,000 to 5,000 data points about each individual and optimized its message delivery on behalf of Ted Cruz. Cruz clearly did not win the primary, but Trump took on Cambridge Analytica for the runoff.

On top of the 4,000 to 5,000 data points, they had access to data from the MyPersonality[13] app that acted as a psychometric survey machine. ("I panic easily," "I contradict others"). Users could sign up to share their answers.

> myPersonality was a popular Facebook application that allowed users to take real psychometric tests, and allowed us to record (with consent!) their psychological and Facebook profiles. Currently, our database contains more than 6,000,000 test results, together with more than 4,000,000 individual Facebook profiles. Our respondents come from various age groups, backgrounds, and cultures. They are highly motivated to answer honestly and carefully, as the only gratification that they receive for their participation is feedback on their results.

The *New York Times* cast aspersions on Cambridge Analytica's claims in the article "Data Firm Says 'Secret Sauce' Aided Trump; Many Scoff."[14]

> A dozen Republican consultants and former Trump campaign aides, along with current and former Cambridge employees, say the company's ability to exploit personality profiles—our secret sauce, Mr. Nix once called it—is exaggerated.

Figure 8.4 Subtle messaging based on personality models in the Republican primary

Its data products were considered for Mr. Trump's critical get-out-the-vote operation. But tests showed Cambridge's data and models were slightly less effective than the existing Republican National Committee system, according to three former Trump campaign aides.

In some recent public settings, Cambridge executives have acknowledged that. "I don't want to break your heart; we actually didn't do any psychographics with the Trump campaign," Matt Oczkowski, Cambridge's head of product, said at a postelection panel hosted by Google in December.

As of this writing, the story is still unfolding, but the possibilities remain intriguing. In an article in *Das Magazin*,[15] Stanford Graduate School of Business assistant professor Dr. Michal Kosinski described building models that proved that

... on the basis of an average of 68 Facebook "likes" by a user, it was possible to predict their skin color (with 95 percent accuracy), their sexual orientation (88 percent accuracy), and their affiliation to the Democratic or Republican party (85 percent). But it didn't stop there. Intelligence, religious affiliation, as well as alcohol, cigarette and drug use, could all be determined. From the data it was even possible to deduce whether someone's parents were divorced.

The strength of their modeling was illustrated by how well it could predict a subject's answers. Kosinski continued to work on the models incessantly: before long, he was able to evaluate a person better than the average work colleague, merely on the basis of ten Facebook "likes." Seventy "likes" were enough to outdo what a person's friends knew, 150 what their parents knew, and 300 "likes" what their partner knew. More "likes" could even surpass what a person thought they knew about themselves. On the day that Kosinski published these findings, he received two phone calls. The threat of a lawsuit and a job offer. Both from Facebook.

The *Das Magazin* article further contended that Cambridge Analytica "divided the US population into 32 personality types, and focused on just 17 states," and found it notable that the Trump campaign paid Cambridge Analytica more than $5 million, and that Steve Bannon is a board member.

Kosinski . . . has conducted a series of tests, which will soon be published. The initial results are alarming: The study shows the effectiveness of personality targeting by showing that marketers can attract up to 63 percent more clicks and up to 1,400 more conversions in real-life advertising campaigns on Facebook when matching products and marketing messages to consumers' personality characteristics. They further demonstrate the scalability of personality targeting by showing that the majority of Facebook Pages promoting products or brands are affected by personality and that large numbers of consumers can be accurately targeted based on a single Facebook Page.

It will be worth watching for the outcome of the inquiry by the Information Commissioner's Office (ICO), the UK's privacy watchdog. The United Kingdom and Europe have much stricter rules about privacy than the United States, so their results should prove informative.

Unintended Bias

While we must be vigilant that bad guys with bad intent might bend AI to their will, we must also be on guard that the systems we build are not subtly influenced by our own unrecognized bias, or by bias present in the data.

The City of Boston released an app for reporting potholes. Great idea, except that only those neighborhoods that could afford smartphones got their potholes fixed.

The more egregious mistakes are those that remain buried in the system, undetected. If loans are approved based on income and income is racially biased, the approval rating will have race baked into the data.

Amazon was called out for not offering their same-day delivery service in black neighborhoods. Google showed ads for high-paying jobs to men more than women. Whatever data the machine was using resulted in these inequities.

It is incumbent on us as marketers to monitor data scientists. Let them do their job, but make sure they have bias deflection and detection techniques built into their methods. This is crucial to marketers because the wrong data or the wrong question will block you from promoting your goods and services to new markets. When asked, "Who buys our product?" or "What profile of customer represents the highest lifetime value?," the answer will be shortsighted and the subsequent ad campaign will be self-limiting.

If you build a machine to learn who is most likely to be a solid credit risk and you show the machine an enormous variety of data, it is likely to select ZIP codes, incomes, educational levels, and the sporting events the subject goes to and identify well-educated white males as your prime target. More than self-limiting, that would be illegal.

If you ask the machine learning to identify the best time of day for engagement on Twitter and you neglect to set up a proper experiment, it will report back that you are a genius! Why? Because your highest engagement periods happen to be the same as the periods you have tweeted—correct but useless.

SOLUTION?

With any new technology, you have to think about trust for it and one of the ways you develop trust is through transparency and a set of principles.

IBM CEO Ginni Rometty, 2017 World Economic Forum in Davos

Transparency means showing just how confident the machine is and clearly showing the data it depended on to reach its conclusion. You should then be able to inquire, "Why did you rate this source of data higher than that?" and "How did you arrive at this decision?"

IBM's "Principles for the Cognitive Era"[16] include the need for transparency.

> For cognitive systems to fulfill their world-changing potential, it is vital that people have confidence in their recommendations, judgements and uses. Therefore, the IBM company will make clear:
>
> ■ When and for what purposes AI is being applied in the cognitive solutions we develop and deploy.
>
> ■ The major sources of data and expertise that inform the insights of cognitive solutions, as well as the methods used to train those systems and solutions.
>
> ■ The principle that clients own their own business models and intellectual property and that they can use AI and cognitive systems to enhance the advantages they have built, often through years of experience. We will work with our clients to protect their data and insights, and will encourage our clients, partners and industry colleagues to adopt similar practices.

Several organizations are forming to pursue ethics in AI systems.

MIT Media Lab to participate in $27 million initiative on AI ethics and governance[17]

One Hundred Year Study on Artificial Intelligence (AI100)[18]

Partnership on AI[19]

The IEEE has produced a 138-page report, "Ethically Aligned Design: A Vision for Prioritizing Human Wellbeing with Artificial Intelligence and Autonomous Systems (AI/AS),"[20] that is open for public comment.

The scientific community is aware that there are issues to be dealt with and are striving to address them. We know we need speed limits, seatbelts, and strict laws about drunk driving.

The wonderful people at the Defense Advanced Research Projects Agency (DARPA) gave us the Internet to start with. Today, the agency is looking for ways for AI to be more intelligible. DARPA is all for AI, but wants the technology to be explainable.[21]

> Dramatic success in machine learning has led to a torrent of Artificial Intelligence (AI) applications. Continued advances promise to produce autonomous systems that will perceive, learn, decide, and act on their own. However, the effectiveness of these systems is limited by the machine's current inability to explain their decisions and actions to human users. The Department of Defense is facing challenges that demand more intelligent, autonomous, and symbiotic systems. Explainable AI—especially explainable machine learning—will be essential if future warfighters are to understand, appropriately trust, and effectively manage an emerging generation of artificially intelligent machine partners.
>
> The Explainable AI (XAI) program aims to create a suite of machine learning techniques that:
>
> > Produce more explainable models, while maintaining a high level of learning performance (prediction accuracy); and
> >
> > Enable human users to understand, appropriately trust, and effectively manage the emerging generation of artificially intelligent partners.

While not nearly as mission-critical as warfare, given new rules being formulated for privacy, AI for marketing might also benefit from "models [that] will be combined with state-of-the-art human-computer interface techniques capable of translating models into understandable and useful explanation dialogues for the end user."

WHAT MACHINES HAVEN'T LEARNED YET

Machine learning is really, really powerful and it opens up new ways of doing analysis with big data. But, it cannot act alone.

In their paper, "Wrappers for Feature Subset Selection,"[22] Ron Kohavi and George H. John lamented,

> A universal problem that all intelligent agents must face is where to focus their attention. A problem-solving agent must decide which aspects of a problem are relevant, an expert-system designer must decide which features to use in rules, and so forth. Any learning agent must learn from experience, and discriminating between the relevant and irrelevant parts of its experience is a ubiquitous problem.

The subject-matter expert is an absolute necessity to help define the problem to be solved. The machine can thresh the grain 24/7 and even separate the wheat from the chaff. But it takes a human to decide whether to grind wheat or corn.

- Which training data will provide the most value with the least bias?
- Which problem is the most important?
- Do the results pass the smell test?

For AI to be effective, a machine learning system needs a teacher. Learning how to teach the machine is all part of becoming an effective professional in this new age.

NOTES

1. "Target's Targeting," http://www.nytimes.com/2012/02/19/magazine/shopping-habits.html.
2. "The Data Science that Animates Amy," https://x.ai/data-science-and-amys-inner-workings.

3. "How Analytics and Machine Learning Help Organizations Reap Competitive Advantage," http://services.google.com/fh/files/misc/white-paper-mit-tr-analytics-machine-learning.pdf.

4. "Artificial Intelligence Will Never Transform Business Process Unless We First Fix CRM Data," https://www.linkedin.com/pulse/artificial-intelligence-never-transform-business-process-shirazi.

5. "Beware the Overfit Trap in Data Analysis," https://hbr.org/tip/2017/01/beware-the-overfit-trap-in-data-analysis.

6. "Facebook's AIs Want You to Stop You Making a Fool of Yourself," http://www.networkworld.com/article/2862012/tech-debates/facebooks-ais-want-you-to-stop-you-making-a-fool-of-yourself.html.

7. "Mining for Analytic 'Gems,'" http://us.mullenlowe.com/mining-for-analytic-gems.

8. http://www.eugdpr.org/gdpr-faqs.html.

9. http://moralmachine.mit.edu.

10. https://www.partnershiponai.org/tenets.

11. "Zo Is Microsoft's Latest AI Chatbot," https://mspoweruser.com/zo-microsofts-latest-ai-chatbot.

12. https://www.youtube.com/watch?v=n8Dd5aVXLCc.

13. http://mypersonality.org/wiki/doku.php.

14. "Data Firm Says 'Secret Sauce' Aided Trump; Many Scoff," https://www.nytimes.com/2017/03/06/us/politics/cambridge-analytica.html.

15. "Ich habe nur gezeigt, dass es die Bombe gibt," https://www.dasmagazin.ch/2016/12/03/ich-habe-nur-gezeigt-dass-es-die-bombe-gibt. Translated to "The Data That Turned the World Upside Down," https://motherboard.vice.com/en_us/article/how-our-likes-helped-trump-win.

16. "Principles for the Cognitive Era" include the need for transparency, https://www.ibm.com/developerworks/community/blogs/InsideSystemStorage/entry/Guiding_ethics_principles_for_the_Cognitive_Era?lang=en.

17. MIT Media Lab to participate in $27 million initiative on AI ethics and governance, http://news.mit.edu/2017/mit-media-lab-to-participate-in-ai-ethics-and-governance-initiative-0110.

18. One Hundred Year Study on Artificial Intelligence (AI100), https://ai100.stanford.edu/2016-report/executive-summary.

19. Partnership on AI, https://www.partnershiponai.org.

20. IEEE's Ethically Aligned Design, http://standards.ieee.org/develop/indconn/ec/ead_v1.pdf.

21. Explainable Artificial Intelligence (XAI), http://www.darpa.mil/program/explainable-artificial-intelligence.

22. Wrappers for feature subset selection, http://ai.stanford.edu/~ronnyk/wrappersPrint.pdf.

CHAPTER 9

Your Strategic Role in Onboarding AI

- The cost of goods and services that rely on prediction will fall.
- We will use prediction to perform tasks we previously haven't.
- The value of things that complement prediction will rise.
- Judgment will become more valuable.

Those were the prognostications posited in "The Simple Economics of Machine Intelligence."[1]

> As machine intelligence improves, the value of human prediction skills will decrease because machine prediction will provide a cheaper and better substitute for human prediction, just as machines did for arithmetic. However, this does not spell doom for human jobs, as many experts suggest. That's because the value of human judgment skills will increase. Using the language of economics, judgment is a complement to prediction and therefore when the cost of prediction falls demand for judgment rises. We'll want more human judgment.

Being an effective marketing executive depends on executive decision making. Solid executive decision making depends on experience and best practices. You can figure out what those best practices should be and take the lead, or wait for everybody else to figure it out and then catch up.

Leading is better. Be willing to experiment. After all, that's how artificial intelligence works. It's also how *we* learn. Because of artificial intelligence and machine learning, judgment and boldness will be more valuable than experience and a solid track record.

The Digital Analytics Power Hour podcast ran a segment called "Systems Thinking with Christopher Berry."[2] In it, Berry discussed the blunder of people learning a new job by checklist:

> This is the way that you build a brief. This is the way that you build a website. This is the way that you build a piece of direct mail. This is the way that you build a brand. And then they faithfully execute that list.

> A lot of people can actually execute those orders without understanding the underlying "why," and that simplifying heuristic is really important. It enables so many people to be effective. It enables a lot of things to go forward.

> It's incredible how insidious this lock-in is. This happens repeatedly in our institutions and companies, the way that these checklists get put together, the way these management processes or these cultures come into being purely because that's the way that it was before.

Because these checklists have been prepared by our predecessors, they are considered sacrosanct. But in fact they were most valuable the moment they were created and degraded from there. The world keeps changing. Be willing to experiment. Be willing to fail in order to discover.

Boldness has genius, power, and magic in it.
Johann Wolfgang von Goethe

Brent Dykes argues how important it is to approach AI through analytics, rather than expecting to leapfrog over the hard work and just take advantage of the latest and greatest technology.[3] In Dykes's view, an understanding of the underlying data is essential; AI won't magically fix sketchy business processes. There is no substitute for domain knowledge. A data-driven culture is vital to avoid an uninformed overreliance on automation.

> With many organizations still struggling to embrace data, analytics is still an area that all companies need to address before diving into artificial intelligence. Bypassing analytics is not a shortcut to AI because analytics maturity is a key milestone on the path to being successful with AI.

How, then, does one boldly go where no machine has gone before and bring the rest of the enterprise along? A map is useful.

GETTING STARTED, LOOKING FORWARD

There are likely to be one or more groups in your organization playing around with artificial intelligence in their spare time. They are attending conferences. They are mucking about with training data sets on cloud-based systems. They are building rudimentary apps. This is certain because artificial intelligence and machine learning are just so fascinating that everybody who works with software and/or data thinks testing some form of advanced, self-learning system is far more interesting than binge watching the latest must-see television.

The first and most important step is to find the experimenters in your firm and get them excited about using their superpowers for marketing. These methods are in much wider use in product development, manufacturing, fraud detection, healthcare, and so on. Marketing simply hasn't been on their radar.

Once your data scientists are enthused about the enormous amount of available marketing data, and are convinced that they understand the goals of marketing, they will start testing. Make sure you stay in the loop so you can deftly nudge them in the right direction while keeping abreast of your firm's growing capabilities.

You might start by training a machine learning system to suggest cut-and-paste paragraphs to your customer service reps, personalize some degree of content on your website, or choose the right time of day to send out e-mails. This will be a time-consuming and somewhat frustrating experience. That's okay. It's how we learn.

After much testing and training, it will be time to open the floodgates and let the teenager drive the car solo. Slightly risky? Yes. Nerve-wracking? Decidedly. Necessary for the competency development? Absolutely.

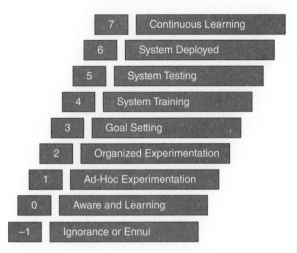

Figure 9.1 Find your place to get to the next level.

A single team should work on a single task as a proof of concept. This is not a software product that will be written, debugged, tested, debugged again, and then launched. It will be launched and it will start learning.

Once deployed in the field, your system and your team can stay firmly on the path of continuous improvement. (See Figure 9.1.)

Where are you now? Infosys has floated an AI Maturity Index Tool[4] that asks a series of questions to help you identify where you are and what lies ahead. Yes, it's a lead generation gizmo for their services, but it does get you to think about the right things. (See Figure 9.2.)

Testing the Waters versus Boiling the Ocean

Change management is the art of convincing others. The comforting thing about AI is that it can—and should—be done piecemeal. You don't have to get all of the board, C-suite, vice presidents, directors, and managers in a room and "Explain the Future," as was necessary with a digital transformation.

John Kotter's 8-Step Process for Leading Change[5] is important when changing an aircraft carrier's course:

1. Establish a sense of urgency.
2. Create the guiding coalition.
3. Develop a vision and strategy.
4. Communicate the change vision.

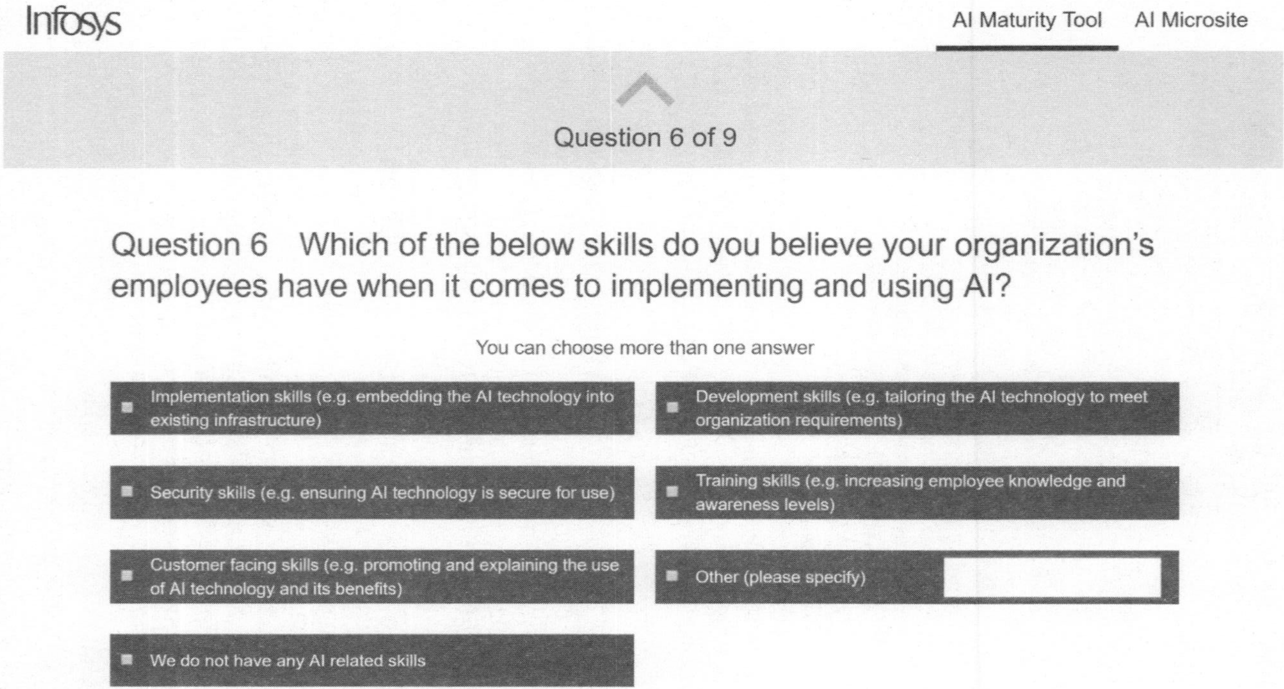
Infosys
AI Maturity Tool
AI Microsite
Question 6 of 9
Question 6 Which of the below skills do you believe your organization's employees have when it comes to implementing and using AI?
You can choose more than one answer
Implementation skills (e.g. embedding the AI technology into existing infrastructure)
Development skills (e.g. tailoring the AI technology to meet organization requirements)
Security skills (e.g. ensuring AI technology is secure for use)
Training skills (e.g. increasing employee knowledge and awareness levels)
Customer facing skills (e.g. promoting and explaining the use of AI technology and its benefits)
Other (please specify)
We do not have any AI related skills

Figure 9.2 InfoSys has a few questions for you.

5. Empower employees for broad-based action.
6. Generate short-term wins.
7. Consolidate gains and produce more change.
8. Anchor new approaches in the culture.

Brian Solis makes some solid points about careful planning for digital transformation:[6]

1. Business as Usual: Organizations operate with a familiar legacy perspective of customers, processes, metrics, business models, and technology, believing that it remains the solution to digital relevance.

2. Present and Active: Pockets of experimentation are driving digital literacy and creativity, albeit disparately, throughout the organization while aiming to improve and amplify specific touchpoints and processes.

3. Formalized: Experimentation becomes intentional while executing at more promising and capable levels. Initiatives become bolder, and, as a result, change agents seek executive support for new resources and technology.

4. Strategic: Individual groups recognize the strength in collaboration as their research, work, and shared insights contribute to new strategic roadmaps that plan for digital transformation ownership, efforts, and investments.

5. Converged: A dedicated digital transformation team forms to guide strategy and operations based on business and customer-centric goals. The new infrastructure of the organization takes shape as roles, expertise, models, processes, and systems to support transformation are solidified.

6. Innovative and Adaptive: Digital transformation becomes a way of business as executives and strategists recognize that change is constant. A new ecosystem is established to identify and act upon technology and market trends in pilot and, eventually, at scale.

But with AI, you may be able to jump ahead to Kotter's Step 6. Get one project off the ground, and then another, and then keep your eyes open for additional opportunities.

Automation has wormed its way into marketing so well that a machine learning system can be brought in on a trial basis to perform

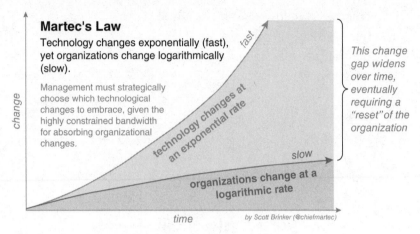

Figure 9.3 Scott Brinker warns of the increasing rate of change.

a specific task. In the eyes of the rest of the firm, it's just another new technology that you're taking out for a spin. Some naturally will balk due to a lack of understanding. If it's a black box and the head of e-mail marketing systems doesn't know how it's making decisions, the head of e-mail marketing is unlikely to risk his or her job on your say-so.

Harking back to Brent Dykes's perspective, it's necessary for an organization to have walked through the maturity stages of analytics. With proper knowledge of how analytics helps the company, it's much easier to say, "Yes, it's new and slightly mysterious, but we can test it."

If your company is not yet comfortable with analytics, AI may be too scary to the uninitiated to be taken on faith. In that case, pay heed to Scott Brinker's conundrum, which he calls Martec's Law: Technology changes exponentially, but organizations change logarithmically.[7] (See Figure 9.3.)

With technology changing so fast and organizations changing so slowly, Brinker suggests a variety of ways to embrace change with the final being to simply to accept and dive in. "So, every now and again, we should be prepared for revolutionary change through an organizational 'reset.' This is an attempt to make a large jump up the curve of technological change by adopting a whole collection of changes all at once."

> As you might imagine, these resets are often extremely disruptive. They can't be done at scale too frequently— although larger organizations may be able to systematically spin up small, intrapreneurial "start-up" teams, within an

incubator-like structure, without continuously rocking the operations of the parent company.

The ultimate reset, unfortunately, happens when a company fails, and its resources are then reallocated in the open market. This is why 88% of the Fortune 500 ultimately collapsed, which is euphemistically called creative destruction. As W. Edwards Deming reportedly said, "It is not necessary to change. Survival is not mandatory."

As the *McKinsey Quarterly* put it:[8]

Start small—look for low-hanging fruit and trumpet any early success. This will help recruit grassroots support and reinforce the changes in individual behavior and the employee buy-in that ultimately determine whether an organization can apply machine learning effectively. Finally, evaluate the results in the light of clearly identified criteria for success.

Automate These Processes First

Where's the best place to start generating short-term wins? David Raab suggests starting with low value-add tasks.[9] It's the lowest-risk way to get comfortable with AI in marketing and will do the most to free up your staff (the expensive part) to do more cognitive work and less drudgery.

Think of a factory. You can bring in unskilled workers and train them to do low-level, repetitive work. Attach this part to that chassis. Then, you can replace them with robots. At the other end of the continuum you have the craftsman, an artisan who creates one-of-a-kind pieces. In between are the classic designations of apprentice, journeyman, and master. Automating cerebral tasks is the same and repetitive cognitive tasks abound.

Labeling or tagging photos in the marketing content database is mind numbing and can be trusted to a machine. Much better to have your highly skilled humans review the machine's work, rather than have their brains turn to mush doing it "by hand." In short order, the need for a review will be obviated by the machine's capacity to learn.

Choosing the best video thumbnail for a blog post, social media comment, or e-mail blast is in the same category. Infinigraph's KRAKEN will choose several thumbnails and A/B test them to determine which get the most response. It outperforms humans 2 to 1.

Start with the repetitive, taxing tasks that machines can do better, and you can bring "scary AI" into your organization without upsetting too many apple carts.

- Social media monitoring
- Inbound e-mail sorting
- Programmatic advertising
- Lead scoring
- Meeting scheduling

Find those jobs that will have the least impact on staff assignments and require the least amount of training. Before long, you'll be able to point to a variety of agents and say, "See? We've already been using them for a while."

Tom Davenport breaks it down thematically.[10] He points to suitable business process contexts, including:

- Where there is a knowledge bottleneck (e.g., medical diagnosis and treatment in rural areas).
- Where the required knowledge is too expensive to provide broadly (investment advice, and perhaps even college education, are examples).
- Where there is too much data or analysis for the human brain to master (programmatic buying of ads in digital marketing is a great example).
- Where there is a need for consistently high decision quality (the best examples are insurance underwriting and credit decisions in banking).
- Where regulatory pressures require a more informed process flow (again, investment advice is an example).

Davenport also provides a list of "7 Ways to Introduce AI into Your Organization"[11] in three categories: Mostly Buy; Some Buy, Some Build; and Mostly Build.

Mostly Buy

Use an existing vendor's software with cognitive capabilities. Think in terms of Salesforce.com, Oracle, or IBM's Watson.

Pick a small project and an AI vendor who can work small. (Cognitive Scale's goal is to prototype a cognitive application in 10 hours, customize it in 10 days, and go live within 10 weeks).

Some Build, Some Buy

Add machine learning to current analytics strengths. Explore automating the generation of analytical models.

Invest in the high-price/high-reward quadrant which IBM's Watson occupies.

Chatbots and low-hanging fruit. Leverage the Google, Apple, Microsoft, and Facebook developer platforms.

Mostly Build

Use modular, component-based AI tools to make existing applications smarter or more autonomous. "This sort of work requires expertise in cognitive tools as well as systems integration capabilities."

Use open source systems. While this is the lowest cost, it will require the highest cost in human resources and take longer. These are classic open source dilemmas. Take this path if your needs are highly specialized or you want to make your products or services smarter.

David Raab says the next step is to deploy that which has been proven elsewhere. Boomtrain, Brightinfo, NextUser, and others have some experience in website personalization. Companies like DataXU, Trade Desk, and Rocket Fuel have been improving their skills with online advertising. Custora, Radius, and Infer know their way around lead scoring. Best to take advantage of their knowhow.

How Much Should You Spend?

How much would it be worth to improve one of the four fundamental business objectives (make more, spend less, improve customer satisfaction, increase capabilities) by 2 percent, 5 percent, 10 percent, or 25 percent? In 2016, Amazon racked up $136 billion in revenue. A 1 percent improvement would yield an additional $1.36 billion. Well worth investing a few million on a new technology.

Perhaps you're operating on a different scale, but the calculation is the same. If investing half a million will only yield $250,000 in value, don't even start. But if a $50,000 investment yields a quarter of a million dollars, it's well worth the effort just on the returns alone, not to mention the improvements in capabilities.

As long as you bear in mind that experimentation is a cost, and that not experimenting is the kiss of death, you can find a balance.

The sky is the limit when it comes to the return on your investment, but the cost of that investment is tangible. Plan accordingly. Test the waters. Experiment. Each small success argues in favor of a larger investment.

AI TO LEVERAGE HUMANS

The most important message to deliver to your organization is that AI is not being brought in to replace people, but to work with them and help them work together better.

Virtual reality is excitingly new and great fun. You can be completely immersed in a whole different world. It replaces everything around you with an alternate experience. But, like taking mind-altering drugs, it has its downside as well.

Augmented reality is like having superpowers in the real world. Identify an address and the navigation system tells you how to get there. Look at a face and your recognition system reminds you who they are. AI is much more powerful when it's used as an augmentation tool rather than a replacement.

Equals 3 took its name on this premise. The company's creation, Lucy, was designed to be cooperative and its point is that rather than one-plus-one equaling two, "You plus Lucy Equals 3."

Leaving a machine to mind the store, tweet on your behalf, or respond to customer inquiries is an accident waiting to happen.

Bots clearly have some advantages. They are more accurate and faster at:

- Math
- Finding a needle in a haystack
- Sorting big data
- Ranking
- Finding patterns
- Avoiding boredom

As for common sense, we simply have not cracked the code on that one.

Bots are good for some types of interaction, but teaming a bot with a human is necessary for any customer-facing conversation that is more than informational. The sweet spot is working together.

In its report, "Preparing for the Future of Artificial Intelligence," the National Science and Technology Council Committee on Technology cited this evidence:[12]

> In contrast to automation, where a machine substitutes for human work, in some cases a machine will complement human work.... Systems that aim to complement human cognitive capabilities are sometimes referred to as intelligence augmentation. In many applications, a human-machine team can be more effective than either one alone, using the strengths of one to compensate for the weaknesses of the other. One example is in chess playing, where a weaker computer can often beat a stronger computer player, if the weaker computer is given a human teammate—this is true even though top computers are much stronger players than any human. Another example is in radiology. In one recent study, given images of lymph node cells, and asked to determine whether or not the cells contained cancer, an AI-based approach had a 7.5 percent error rate, where a human pathologist had a 3.5 percent error rate; a combined approach, using both AI and human input, lowered the error rate to 0.5 percent, representing an 85 percent reduction in error.

What does that mean for marketing? Daisy Intelligence was built "to uncover insightful answers to complex optimization questions."[13]

> This model is designed to maximize total revenue by finding optimal solutions to highly complex trade-off situations. This model analyzes extremely large data sets and finds the relationships between variables like cross-category cannibalization, promotional cadence, associated product affinities, price sensitivity and seasonality.

In an interview with *Business News Daily*, Daisy Intelligence CEO Gary Saarenvirta said, "You send us your raw data, our machine analyzes it and spits out decisions."

> We don't change your process at all, except that now you have a new piece of information to consider.... It's about making smarter decisions; these are all mathematical

quantitative things that computers do better than people. If you can make smarter decisions it can drive your profitability.

We're saving them time and giving them new insight they've never had before. Our machine, unlike human beings that get tired and bored, puts as much effort into the 199th item as the first item.

It's quite clear that artificial intelligence is unable to perform well without human input. It's also clear that human performance is improved with AI. Those who figure out how to work together the best, win.

What are the most important skills for working with artificial intelligence? Recognizing that you are working with a system that learns (being a good teacher) and having it solve the right problem (asking really good questions).

COLLABORATION AT WORK

Two heads are better than one. Two heads and an AI system are jet-fueled, turbo-charged, hyper-capably better than one.

A group of four people walk into a room and the leader says, "Watson, bring me the last working session." The computer recognizes and greets the group, then retrieves the materials used in the last meeting and displays them on three large screens. Settling down to work, the leader approaches one screen, and swipes his hands apart to zoom into the information on display. The participants interact with the room through computers that can understand their speech, and sensors that detect their position, record their roles and observe their attention. When the topic of discussion shifts from one screen to another, but one participant remains focused on the previous point, the computer asks a question: "What are you thinking?"[14]

That scenario is the result of work Rensselaer Polytechnic Institute and IBM Research did to create the Cognitive and Immersive Systems Laboratory (CISL). This lab can understand speech and gestures, identify and differentiate between three people in the room, understand their roles, and engage AI agents to take action and provide relevant information. (See Figure 9.4.)

Figure 9.4 The Cognitive and Immersive Systems Laboratory knows where you're standing.

The cumulative technology is impressive, but the proof-of-concept points toward a competitive-edge-making future.

YOUR ROLE AS MANAGER

The article "How Artificial Intelligence Will Redefine Management"[15] references a survey that shows managers spend most of their time on administrative tasks, most of which can be automated (Figure 9.5).

Authors Vegard Kolbjørnsrud, Richard Amico, and Robert J. Thomas see the path of augmentation as the best approach.

> Managers who view AI as a kind of colleague will recognize that there's no need to "race against a machine." While human judgment is unlikely to be automated, intelligent machines can add enormously to this type of work, assisting in decision support and data-driven simulations as well as search and discovery activities. In fact, 78% of the surveyed managers believe that they will trust the advice of intelligent systems in making business decisions in the future.

They recommend adopting design thinking and layering ideas on ideas. It's the difference between people who say, "Yes, but," and people who say, "Yes, and."

How Managers Spend Their Time
The bulk of it is spent on administrative tasks.

PERCENTAGE OF TIME RESPONDENTS SPEND ON CATEGORIES OF WORK

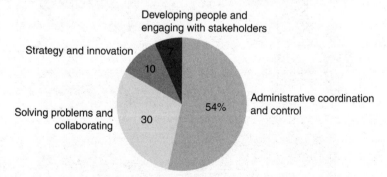

Figure 9.5 Accenture's look at managers' time allotment
Source: Accenture survey of 1,770 frontline, mid-level, and executive-level managers from 14 countries. © HBR.ORG

People skills, professional networks, collaboration, and a willingness to embrace change have become paramount.

Working with Data Scientists

Working with an architect, a kitchen designer, a job foreman, and a city inspector is required to remodel your kitchen. Yet, all require very different tactics and modes of conversation.

Working with a data scientist is different from working with classically trained IT technicians, database designers, or programmers. Creating AI systems is not a case of defining requirements, generating designs, waiting for construction, grinding your teeth during testing, pulling out your hair during debugging, and holding your breath during launch. Creating AI systems is more of a dance. For that, it's good to know your partner.

Data scientists are puzzle fanatics. They love mysteries. They do Sudoku puzzles during meetings. They live for that rush they get when $2 + 2 = 5$, the moment of insight, the lightbulb going on, that cry of "Eureka!" To make that feeling truly satisfying, the puzzle must be hard enough to hold their attention. They need to understand the problem you're trying to solve.

When a data scientist shows up on your doorstep, do your best to:

- Describe the problem you face.
- Clarify exactly what success looks like.
- Point to the available data you have.
- Suggest other sources of data.
- Explain the inexplicable.

"The inexplicable" refers to things that are not found in the data, but are apparent to a human.

Here's a quick example of why natural language processing is so hard. The sentence "I never said she stole my money," only has seven words but has seven different meanings depending on where the emphasis hits when spoken. That information is not in the text.

The astute data scientist will draw this information out of you with subtle questions:

- What would you expect the outcome to be?
- How is this different in other circumstances?
- Is there anything else they have in common?

- What have you heard from your sales team in the field?
- Should we check that for seasonality?

Rather than designing a database schema to make the machine do your bidding, they are detectives, gathering bits of information in your office, from your customers, and from your distribution network. Then, they'll go deep and ask about the veracity and shelf-life of the data you have to get a feel for its validity.

More than being data scientists, they strive to become—or count on you to be—a subject-matter expert. They will be hyper-interested in the outcomes of any experiment you run or system you field test.

Good data scientists will ask your opinion about the results they derive. They will show you a variety of visualizations to see which resonate or make you think about things in different ways.

Just as there are many roles in marketing that you can easily distinguish (merchandising, product development, product marketing, public relations, corporate communications), there are many different roles and responsibilities in the world of data. Your firm is likely to have data architects, data engineers, statisticians, business analysts, and more. They are very likely to have titles that are not industry standard. It is quite valuable to understand the responsibilities of the different data professionals you work with. You'll want to know who manages what and how to improve your ability to help them help you.

Take note: The biggest problem data scientists face is that marketers jump to conclusions much too early, according to Michael Wu, chief scientist at Lithium Technologies.

Taking the Right Steps

Tom Davenport and Julia Kirby, in their book, *Only Humans Need Apply*, admonish professionals to step up to cognitively higher ground. They offer five directions to step—the Five Options for Augmentation:

- *Stepping Up*. Moving up above automated systems to develop more big-picture insights and decisions that are too unstructured and sweeping for computers or robots to be able to make.

- *Stepping Aside*. Moving to a type of non-decision oriented work that computers aren't good at, such as selling, motivating people, or describing in straightforward terms the decisions that computers have made.

- *Stepping In.* Engaging with the computer system's automated decisions to understand, monitor, and improve them. This is the option at the heart of what we are calling augmentation, although each of these five steps can be described as augmenting.

- *Stepping Narrowly.* Finding a specialty area within your profession that is so narrow that no one is attempting to automate it—and it might never be economical to do so.

- *Stepping Forward.* Developing new systems and technologies that support intelligent decisions and actions in a particular domain.

Only Humans Need Apply then delves into each possibility with practical advice on how to choose and succeed with each option.

Reid Hoffman, executive chairman and co-founder of LinkedIn, says that AI can help us build internal knowledge graphs, just as we build social graphs today.[16]

> The knowledge graph will represent the interconnection of all the data and communications within your company. Specialized AIs will be ubiquitous throughout the organization, indexing every document, folder, and file. But they won't stop there. They'll also be sitting in the middle of the communication stream, collecting all of our work product, from emails to file shares to chat messages. They'll be able to connect when you save a proposal, share it with a colleague, and discuss it through corporate messaging. This may sound a bit Big Brother-ish, but the effect will be to give knowledge workers new and powerful tools for collecting, understanding, and acting on information.

Hoffman sees meetings being recorded, transcribed, and archived, tracking the commitment to-do list and the progress of those tasks. The result will be meaningful organizational dashboards that include the anxiety levels (sentiment analysis) around issues under discussion.

The review process is up for improvement as well. "Current performance management processes are terribly flawed. A Deloitte study found that just 8% of organizations believe that their annual review process is worth the effort!"

With most employees relying on subjective criteria and analysis, "internal politics and unconscious bias can play a major role, resulting in performance management that is biased and inaccurate."

The machine will point to those who are truly moving the business forward. "You'll be able to tell who made the key decision to enter a new market, and which people actually took care of the key action items to make it happen."

Hoffman also sees AI's ability to monitor human potential, monitor how well individuals are coming up to speed, and make recommendations about what training would be most productive.

> Rather than simply being handed a stack of files and being introduced to her colleagues, an onboarding AI will be able to answer questions like, "Who do I need to work with on the new office move? What were the meetings where it was discussed? When is our next status meeting?" She'll also be able to ask how things were done in the past (i.e., "Show me a tag cloud of the topics my predecessor was spending his time on. How has that allocation evolved over the past 12 months?"). AIs might even ask outgoing employees to review and annotate the key documents that should be passed on to their successors. The tacit knowledge that typically takes weeks or months to amass in today's workplace will have been captured and processed in advance so that within the first hours of accepting a new role, an employee will be able to apply that knowledge.

Expressing the Value of Marketing

The CFO could ask, "What is the measure of success? How do you set a budget for something that's so *fuzzy* as 'marketing' and 'branding'?"

With pressure building to be cost-efficient, the CFO could become the marketing department's best friend. The CFO will listen to a story about cost savings through automation when you start by quoting *McKinsey Quarterly*:[17]

> When we modeled the potential of automation to transform business processes across several industries, we found that the benefits (ranging from increased output to higher quality and improved reliability, as well as the potential to perform some tasks at superhuman levels) typically are between three and ten times the cost. The magnitude of those benefits suggests that the ability

to staff, manage, and lead increasingly automated organizations will become an important competitive differentiator.

For three to ten times the ROI CFOs will pay attention.

Daniel McCarthy is a statistics doctoral student at the Wharton School as well as co-founder (along with Wharton professor Peter Fader) and chief statistician at Zodiac, a predictive analytics company that gives retailers predictions of long-term customer lifetime value. McCarthy and Fader are converting marketing data into metrics that would be appreciated and respected by the finance department. Doing that validates a higher budget from the boardroom. They contend that the CFO doesn't care if marketing did a great job on a mailing campaign or optimizing the customer journey using the latest dynamic data integration methods.

The CFO cares how much money marketing made for the company this quarter. The CFO wants to relate what you did to some change in the valuation of the firm.

> We're trying to broaden the discussion and introduce metrics that can be directly relative to how much the firm is worth and how much the correct customer base is worth. Is marketing moving the needle in the right direction?

> If I observe customers for a period of at least six months, I can make a provision for how much those customers are worth and predict their net present value. I can track, quarter by quarter, the average value of the customers I've acquired, how many I've acquired and which of my dollars of marketing spend brought in those customers.

> In one case, we saw that the average lifetime value of newly acquired customers is just generally falling over time. I think that's very common phenomena as companies saturate their target market. Newly acquired customers incrementally become less and less valuable. You know acquisition costs are staying the same or going up, and that means your return on a newly acquired customer is declining. At a certain point, you might want to pull back on the stick a little bit. You might want to do the opposite if, for whatever reason, customers are getting *more* valuable.

McCarthy encourages the employment of higher technology and higher-level math, but urges speaking C-Suite language. The types of data being collected and used as grist for the mill are changing the types of data that firms report to external shareholders, asserts Fader.[18]

> More than ever, companies are discussing and disclosing information on the number of customers acquired and lost, customer lifetime value, and other data. This has fueled an increasing interest in linking the value of a firm's customers to the overall value of the firm, with the term "customer-based corporate valuation" being used to describe such efforts.

Fader posits that the underlying models of customer acquisition and retention don't meet the standards of finance professionals.

Asking AI systems questions about finding, acquiring, and keeping customers should be expanded to include questions that the finance side of the house cares about and understands in order to drive more support.

KNOW YOUR PLACE

- Lingerie brand Cosabella replaced its agency with artificial intelligence.[19]
- A Japanese ad agency invented an AI creative director—and ad execs preferred its ad to a human's.[20]
- Rise of the Strategy Machines.[21]

Cosabella spent three months with AI marketing platform Albert from Adgorithms and enjoyed a 336 percent increase in return on ad spend, increased revenues 155 percent, and had 1,500 more transactions year-over-year while cutting costs by 12 percent and increasing returns by 50 percent.

Cosabella's marketing director, Courtney Connell, said Albert makes all the tactical decisions after the marketing team sets targets, goals, geographical restrictions, and budgets.

> "He can mix and match [creative] however he pleases," Connell said. "He might start with an ad and if he sees that getting fatigued, he might roll out a new combination."

Connell checks the Albert dashboard every morning, but because the tool self-optimizes, her team need only check on campaigns once or twice a week. It takes them less than an hour to produce graphics and copy and other materials for a campaign.

Eventually, Cosabella will get Albert talking to the other AI vendors it's onboarded since cutting ties with its agency, including Emarsys for email marketing and Sentient for customer acquisition and real-time merchandizing. Albert can ingest customer lists for lookalike targeting, but Cosabella wants to hook it up to the company's CRM system to keep that information flowing in constantly.

Ad agency McCann's division called McCann Millennials divided television commercials into two parts:

The creative brief: The type of brand, the campaign goal, the target audience, and the claim the ad should make.

The elements of the TV ad: Including things such as tone, manner, celebrity, music, context, and the key takeout.

They then assembled a database of deconstructed ads from all the winners of some of Japan's biggest award shows from the past ten years—mapping and tagging each of the elements of the ads to help determine what made them successful. But this is the work of the media planner and the artistic director. Just how helpful will AI be for the top brass?

Tom Davenport says that humans are ahead of the game for now, "but we shouldn't be complacent about our human dominance."

First, it's not as if we humans are really that great at setting strategy. Many M&A deals don't deliver value, new products routinely fail in the marketplace, companies expand unsuccessfully into new regions and countries, and myriad other strategic decisions don't pan out.

Second, although it's unlikely that a single system will be able to handle all strategic decisions, the narrow intelligence that computers display today is already sufficient to handle specific strategic problems.

A third piece of evidence that strategy is becoming more autonomous is that major consulting firms are beginning to advocate for the idea. For example, Martin Reeves and Daichi Ueda, both of the Boston Consulting Group, recently published a short article on the Harvard Business Review website called "Designing the Machines That Will Design Strategy," in which they discuss the possibility of automating some aspects of strategy. McKinsey & Co. has invested heavily in a series of software capabilities it calls "McKinsey Solutions," many of which depend on analytics and the semi-automated generation of insights. Deloitte has developed a set of internal and client offerings involving semi-automated sensing of an organization's external environment. In short, there is clear movement within the strategy consulting industry toward a greater degree of interest in automated cognitive capabilities.

Except for the set-and-forget types of tools that perform straightforward tasks like optimizing a display ad campaign, strategy tools are going to augment human judgment only.

Big-picture thinking is one capability at which humans are still better than computers—and will continue to be for some time. Machines are not very good at piecing together a big picture in the first place, or at noticing when the landscape has changed in some fundamental way. Good human strategists do this every day.

The *big picture*, then, is your stock-in-trade. Exercise that muscle because complex problem solving will be your salvation, even if it's going to feel awkward taking advice from a machine. (See Figure 9.6.)

Automated coaching sounds like an affront today, but that's what they said about calculators in the 1970s, personal computers in the 1980s, the Internet in the 1990s, and big data in the 2000s.

"Let a machine tell me what to do? Never!"

"But what if the advice is really good?"

"*I'll* be the judge of that!"

"And that's why we're going to keep paying you the big bucks. Your capacity for evaluating the real-world implications of the machine's advice is priceless."

So, what's your place? Throughout the process: "People and technology must each play their particular roles in an integrated fashion."[22] (See Figure 9.7.)

Top 10 skills

in 2020

1. Complex Problem Solving
2. Critical Thinking
3. Creativity
4. People Management
5. Coordinating with Others
6. Emotional Intelligence
7. Judgment and Decision Making
8. Service Orientation
9. Negotiation
10. Cognitive Flexibility

in 2015

1. Complex Problem Solving
2. Coordinating with Others
3. People Management
4. Critical Thinking
5. Negotiation
6. Quality Control
7. Service Orientation
8. Judgment and Decision Making
9. Active Listening
10. Creativity

Figure 9.6 Complex problem solving wins the decade.
Source: Future of jobs report, world economic forum

Authors Martin Reeves and Daichi Ueda suggest that working with a strategy machine goes well given a relevant, specific strategic aim, a design appropriate to the aim, the correct human–machine division of labor, an integrated solution, and unique tools, data, or process. They stress that humans excel "in our capacity to think outside the immediate scope of a task or a problem and to deal with ambiguity." Machines cannot yet think outside the box. They don't pose new questions or see things from a different perspective based on what their daughter said at the breakfast table.

While the machine starts out solving specific problems, we will train them to "stimulate people's ability to create new insights, challenge their own thinking, and continuously reframe their understanding." Then, we will be able to give them the right kind of strategy feedback that will help them improve.

The Integrated Strategy Machine

People and technology must each play their roles, and humans must constantly evolve the design of the machine.

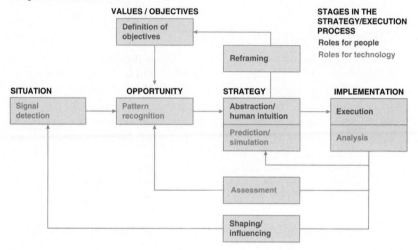

Figure 9.7   The Integrated Strategy Machine
Source: BCG. © HBR.ORG

AI FOR BEST PRACTICES

Douglas Engelbart, best known for inventing the computer mouse, was also involved with the development of hypertext, networked computers, and graphical user interfaces. In his later years, he was focused on process improvement—meta process improvement. In "Improving Our Ability to Improve: A Call for Investment in a New Future,"[23] Engelbart described his approach to enhancing development.

Engelbart mapped out the A activities as the core function of the business (customer engagement, product development, accounting, legal, manufacturing, etc.) and B activities as the efforts to improve A activities (adopting new tools, primary research, strategy meetings, planning, exploring ways to improve capabilities).

The C activities are at the meta level.

Clearly, there are limits to how far a company can pursue an investment and growth strategy based on type B activities—at some point the marginal returns for new investment begin to fall off. This leads to a question: How can we maximize the return from investment in B activities, maximizing the improvement that they enable?

Put another way, we are asking how we improve our ability to improve. This question suggests that we really need to think in terms of yet another level of activity—I call it the "C" activity—that focuses specifically on the matter of accelerating the rate of improvement.

Clearly, investment in type C activities is potentially highly leveraged. The right investments here will be multiplied in returns in increased B level productivity—in the ability to improve—which will be multiplied again in returns in productivity in the organization's primary activity. It is a way of getting a kind of compound return on investment in innovation.

Even with the CFO on your side, your premier data scientist *by* your side, and your AI-driven process improvement inside, we've reached the point where the massive amounts of available data can reveal very valuable information—if you know what to ask. Your job now depends on your ability to ask really good questions.

NOTES

1. "The Simple Economics of Machine Intelligence," https://hbr.org/2016/11/the-simple-economics-of-machine-intelligence.

2. http://www.analyticshour.io/2017/01/31/055-systems-thinking-with-christopher-berry.

3. "Crawl with Analytics before Running with Artificial Intelligence," http://www.forbes.com/sites/brentdykes/2017/01/11/crawl-with-analytics-before-running-with-artificial-intelligence.

4. http://aimaturity.com.

5. *Leading Change* (Harvard Business Review Press, 2012), https://www.amazon.com/Leading-Change-With-Preface-Author/dp/1422186431.

6. http://www.huffingtonpost.com/vala-afshar/6-stages-of-digital-trans_b_9822640.html.

7. "Martec's Law: The Greatest Management Challenge of the 21st Century," http://chiefmartec.com/2016/11/martecs-law-great-management-challenge-21st-century.

8. "An Executive's Guide to Machine Learning," http://www.mckinsey.com/industries/high-tech/our-insights/an-executives-guide-to-machine-learning.

9. "How Machine Intelligence Will Really Change Marketing," https://www.slideshare.net/MarTechConf/how-machine-intelligence-will-really-change-marketing-or-how-to-market-with-smart-machines-without-ensuring-the-destruction-of-mankind-or-losing-your-job-by-dave-raab.

10. "The Rise of Cognitive Work Redesign," http://data-informed.com/the-rise-of-cognitive-work-redesign.

11. "7 Ways to Introduce AI into Your Organization," https://hbr.org/2016/10/7-ways-to-introduce-ai-into-your-organization.

12. "Preparing for the Future of Artificial Intelligence," https://obamawhitehouse .archives.gov/sites/default/files/whitehouse_files/microsites/ostp/NSTC/preparing_ for_the_future_of_ai.pdf.

13. http://www.daisyintelligence.com.

14. https://news.rpi.edu/content/2016/12/12/edge-cognitive-space.

15. https://hbr.org/2016/11/how-artificial-intelligence-will-redefine-management.

16. "Using Artificial Intelligence to Set Information Free" http://reidhoffman.org/using-artificial-intelligence-humanize-management-set-information-free

17. "An Executive's Guide to Machine Learning," http://www.mckinsey.com/industries/ high-tech/our-insights/an-executives-guide-to-machine-learning.

18. "Valuing Subscription-based Businesses Using Publicly Disclosed Customer Data," http://journals.ama.org/doi/abs/10.1509/jm.15.0519?code=amma-site.

19. https://adexchanger.com/agencies/ai-agency-lingerie-brand-cosabella-replaced-agency-artificial-intelligence.

20. http://www.businessinsider.com/mccann-japans-ai-creative-director-creates-better-ads-than-a-human-2017-3.

21. http://sloanreview.mit.edu/article/rise-of-the-strategy-machines.

22. "Designing the Machines that Will Design Strategy," https://hbr.org/2016/04/ welcoming-the-chief-strategy-robot.

23. "Improving Our Ability to Improve: A Call for Investment in a New Future," http:// www.dougengelbart.org/pubs/augment-133320.html.

CHAPTER 10

Mentoring the Machine

It would be grand if all our problems could be resolved with technology. We could find the right software that would find the right target audience and send the right message to the right person at the right time on the right device in the right context by reversing the polarity, fluctuating the deflector shield to emit tachyon pulses, or using the Fibonacci sequence. It works on television.

But tech doesn't always do what we want; it only does what we tell it to do. We need to get better at telling it what to do. For that, we are all going to become teachers.

- We teach Siri to understand our individual voice.
- We teach Amy@x.ai how we want our meetings scheduled.
- We teach Pandora what kind of music we like.

To make the most of artificial intelligence and machine learning in marketing, we will have to teach it what we want and what constitutes a good result.

Microsoft's Ian Thomas points out that our jobs as marketers will change, but not disappear.[1]

> Fortunately for digital marketers, and especially digital marketing analytics professionals, optimization-driven campaigns don't remove the need for human involvement, though they do change its nature. Instead of creating

complex audience segments up front for a campaign, these people will need instead to identify the attributes that campaigns should use for optimization.

Attribute selection (known as feature selection in data science circles) is a crucial step in making optimization work. Select too many attributes, and the engine will slice the audience up into tiny slivers, each of which will take ages to deliver results that are statistically significant, meaning that the optimization will take a long time to converge and deliver lift. Select too few, on the other hand, and the engine will converge quickly (since it will have few choices and plenty of data), but the lift will likely be very modest because the resulting "optimization" will not actually be very targeted to the audience. Select the wrong attributes, and the system will not optimize at all.

HOW TO TRAIN A DRAGON

Teaching a learning machine is in itself a new art form. It's not the strict, logical grind of writing software code line by line. It's more of a dance.

Danny Hillis, co-founder of the Long Now Foundation, wrote,[2] "We have become so intertwined with what we have created that we are no longer separate from it."

Empowered by the tools of the Enlightenment, connected by networked flows of freight and fuel and finance, by information and ideas, we are becoming something new. We are at the dawn of the Age of Entanglement.

As our technological and institutional creations have become more complex, our relationship to them has changed. We now relate to them as we once related to nature. Instead of being masters of our creations, we have learned to bargain with them, cajoling and guiding them in the general direction of our goals. We have built our own jungle, and it has a life of its own.

In an Entangled design process, the humans will often have input without control; for example, they may influence aesthetic choices by participating in the selection process or by tuning parameters. Such processes lend themselves to collaboration among multiple machines and multiple humans because the interfaces between the parts are fluid and adaptive. The final product is very much a collaborative effort of humans and machines, often with a superior result. It may exhibit behaviors that are surprising to the humans.

Teaching our new systems will require that we humans be best at what we are good at. The AI can drive the car, but not decide where to go. The machine can analyze a billion attributes, but not decide in advance which attributes to consider. The word processing program can tell you when you've misspelled a word, but cannot tell you what topic to write about.

WHAT PROBLEM ARE YOU TRYING TO SOLVE?

Q1: What are we trying to achieve?

Q2: How will we know we've done that?

Tim Wilson, Analytics Demystified

Bob Page points out that "humans are driving the tech, but at the end state, the humans set the constraints and set the machinery in motion. The humans also supply the breakthrough thinking that the machinery cannot."

Humans become smarter, both by looking backward in time (e.g., classic business intelligence and most of what passes for analytics these days) and forward (e.g., educated guesses and forecasts about what might happen given past trends and outlook). But in this case, the machinery is producing something new that a human can interpret. Humans add value by jumpstarting the process by describing the dependent variable(s) that they want to optimize.

Usually revenue and cost. Everything else (customer acquisition funnel, operations costs, etc.) is in support of those, but not always. My company's reputation as a purveyor of premium product) might be more important than an increase in revenue at the risk of destroying my brand.

Page suggests asking:

1. How can I increase revenues, prioritized by ROI?
2. How can I reduce costs, prioritized by ROI (e.g., it may be okay to forgo 2% of revenue if I'm able to take out 50% of costs)?
3. What data is missing that would make the answers to questions 1 and 2 more complete?

> I recognize that the answers (suggestions) might be conflicting, or compete for the same resources, or take vastly different time horizons to implement, and that's where the humans come in. For example, the answer to #1 might be:
>
> a. Open additional retail outlets in these three locations.
> b. Rebuild the website to support personalization.
> c. Increase the quality and sales price of these items, and add this item in blue.
> d. Rebrand to emphasize these features attributes.
> e. Reorganize the sales team by region instead of industry, and change their comp plans to XYZ.
> f. Acquire company ABC.
>
> That puts us back in the hands of the humans who can determine that acquisitions are off the table for the coming year by prior Board of Directors' vote, the sales team is still recovering from the last reorganization, and price increases are taboo. So, it's time to give the machine that feedback (information it did not have before) and see which of the remaining suggestions reign supreme.

It all starts with goals.

- For the doctor: health and wellbeing.
- For the architect: form well matched with function.
- For the marketer: raise revenue, lower costs, increase customer satisfaction, improve capabilities.

After the goals come the metrics.

- How will you know you've achieved your goal?
- What indicators tell you if you're moving in the right direction?
- What can we measure that will act as a proxy for our goals?

- Of these metrics, which do you have control over?
- Which levers that you control will have the most impact on the outcome, the soonest, with the least investment of resources?

Often, deciding which problem to solve calls for heading back to the top of the business to-do list:

- Increase revenue
- Lower costs
- Improve customer satisfaction
- Increase capabilities

From there, we can drop down into marketing goals:

- Raise awareness
- Improve attitude
- Influence influencers
- Inspire interaction
- Generate sales
- Drive endorsements

Drilling down into that list is where it gets tricky. The scientist asks, "What's the problem?" The marketer says, "We need to increase sales."

"Yes, that's the goal," says the scientist, "but what's the problem? If you ask me for the best way out of the building, I would say it depends on why you want to leave. If you want a taxi to the airport, the front door is best. If you want to drive to the airport, the door to the parking lot or garage is best. If you want to take out the garbage, the back door is best. If the building is on fire, the solution is very, very different."

The difficulty in defining the problem is well exemplified by the Slow Elevator Problem. The fascinating trend in buildings with multiple elevators has been to put the pushbutton control in the lobby and not the elevator. The passengers tell the system what floor they want and the system tells them which car to board.

But even *then*, the passengers complain that the elevators are too slow. Making them move faster between floors has mechanical limitations. So what do we do? Reframe the problem: If the problem is stated as "Elevators seem too slow," then the solutions are to put mirrors on the inside, pipe in music, and/or show a video of the latest news, weather, sports, and local attractions. The problem is solved.

WHAT MAKES A GOOD HYPOTHESIS?

Speculation is perfectly all right, but if you stay there, you've only founded a superstition. If you test it, you've started a science.

Hal Clement

Clearly *stating the problem* is a matter of having an opinion that can be tested. Start with an assumption and create a hypothesis for the machine to disprove. It's necessary to try to *disprove* hypotheses. If my idea is right 99 times out of 99, it might just be chance. But if it's wrong once, it's wrong.

If I assume adding an exclamation point to the subject line will cause more of my e-mails to fall into spam filters, I only have an assumption. Stated as a measurable (and falsifiable) hypothesis I propose that we can get a 40 percent increase in response to my e-mail blast if I do not use an exclamation point. My assumption is based on conjecture. My hypothesis is a measurable, disprovable test.

Pat LaPointe of Growth Calculus advises to start slowly with clearly defined goals.

I think of using machine learning techniques as a spectrum. At one end of the spectrum, machine learning is completely guided by a well-defined set of hypotheses. So, let's call that the constrained approach.

In the middle is a more parameterized approach, where the hypotheses are boarder. They are recognized as an *initial* set of hypotheses and the defined goal helps root out the noise, acknowledging that we might not yet understand enough to be able to dial in insight.

And then at the other end of the spectrum is unguided, open-ended machine learning approach.

If one doesn't know the data science that well, one should stay toward the tightly framed hypothesis end of the spectrum. The further one goes toward the unparameterized end of the spectrum, the greater the likelihood that one is going to find himself wasting the company's time and resources.

Which is exactly, unfortunately, the paradox. When human beings generally feel the pressure of needing to do something but don't quite know what to do, they love the idea of delegating that responsibility to someone else or, in this case, something else.

In the history of science, we have learned that practical discovery habits, in a guided, methodical search for learning, yield the best results. It's true that many of the world's great inventions have been discovered while searching for something else but these things were found as part of a deliberate attempt to solve a different, specific problem.

It is every marketer's hope that given enough data, computer power, probability engine capability, and self-learning, correlations will be discovered that had not been considered that might prove valuable. But La Pointe counters with, "But who cares if you find a correlation between bananas and tractors?"

Clarifying and specifying the problem is key because inevitably, when you go through that exercise what you discover is that either the problem is somewhere to the left of what you originally thought it was. Or that there are actually three problems that may or may not lend themselves to being simultaneously explored.

You tease that out by continuing to ask, "So what?" If we knew the answer, what would we do with it? If the interpretation and the "So what?" continue to come back as being broad and ambiguous, that tells you to keep drilling into your articulation of the problem.

If the problem is increasing customer lifetime value, one approach would be to examine customers that have higher lifetime value versus lower lifetime value and try to identify what the underlying causal factors might be. Another may simply be to look at the environments and try to identify what components of the environment are acting as obstacles to customers achieving higher lifetime value. Those are two very different exploration vectors. One is more internally oriented, one is more externally oriented.

Where do you draw the line on how much data you are collecting and analyzing? Even with a nearly infinite amount of available data, almost for free, how do you know when you have enough and need not spend unnecessary resources going after more?

If you frame the hypothesis well, you know that of the 50 different possible questions that we could answer for your business decision makers, none of them are really needed, nor can they leverage all 50 answers. They may really only be able to take advantage of a subset of 10 of them. The majority would be freaking delighted if we could just answer four! Four critical answers will get us in the door and then we can quickly evolve to 10, which will truly drive growth.

Provided you've been paying attention all along as the previous questions have been answered, the best question is the next question.

It's about teaching the principles of scientific rigor. You learned them in 8th grade science class, but have forgotten them due to lack of use. They're not complicated.

1. Observe—look around and see what you can see that might be relevant.
2. Question your understanding of the things you see.
3. Define what you know and what you know you don't know.
4. Reframe your "don't knows" into question form.
5. Prioritize your questions in order of the most critical learnings values to be gained.
6. Construct experiments to generate data to help answer the questions.
7. Evaluate the data you collect (see point 1 above).

We must engage in better critical thinking.

For years, I was fond of saying that marketers pursue the wrong question when they concentrate on "What is the ROI on my marketing investments?" or "What is the best place to put my next dollar?" The *real* question is the one the CEO wants to answer: "Should I spend half as much or twice as much?" This is the essence of being CEO— continuously looking for places of greatest leverage against which to apply the company resources.

You cannot expect humans with limited insight and low processing power to come up with the "right" question(s) from the start. The options are too numerous and the subtle discriminants of criticality are rarely understood. However, you *can* expect them to iterate to the right questions over time *if* there is a culture of hypothesis development and testing.

I believe competitive advantage is not at all gained by having sophisticated analytics, machine learning, or AI. It's about developing a culture of "learn fast." All other things being equal, the company with the best learning processes will arrive at the right questions first, then find and exploit the answers.

This approach also anticipates an increasing rate of change in the business ecosystem, which is sure to antiquate the "goodness" of any question in shorter-and-shorter timeframes.

THE HUMAN ADVANTAGE

I have no special talent. I am only passionately curious.

Albert Einstein

Imagine you have an impressive number of data streams that are clean, trustworthy, properly normalized, and well managed. Suppose you have a large collection of powerful algorithms at your command and a team that is expert in their use to find unconsidered correlations and glean insights that are valuable to your organization. Given all of this, what question would you ask?

This takes a skill set that is beyond that of a data jockey. Christopher Berry is emphatic that AI is only as smart as you make it.

The most important thing for marketers to understand is that a lot of people in data science are not fantastic storytellers or communicators. People in data science have a type of skepticism and immunity to claims that are made that in some ways make them absolutely terrible marketers in general, because they don't just tell those stories.

So, marketers, by way of being inherent storytellers, by way of being inherently persuasive, continue to bring an absolutely beautiful soft art that is extraordinarily difficult to displace.

No matter how exotic we get in the underlying algorithmic, in the underlying math, no matter how much you waterboard the math, it's never, ever a substitute for the good judgment of a person.

Mark Cuban was recently quoted as saying that creative and critical thinking are soon going to be the most sought-after skills. "I personally think there's going to be a greater demand in ten years for liberal arts majors than for programming majors and maybe even engineering."[3]

There are several very valuable traits humans have that will take years to teach a machine.

Judgment

If you guessed *judgment* was our strength, we would have to have an argument. The *Oxford Dictionary* definition reads, "The ability to make considered decisions or come to sensible conclusions." It also calls judgment an opinion or conclusion.

This *is* what we have been teaching the machine to do. Form an opinion. Reach a conclusion based on evidence and reasoning—that moment when the lightbulb goes on, the bright idea, the blinding realization, the flash of brilliance, enlightenment, revelation, an epiphany. Dress it up with emotion and you have *Ah-ha!* and *Eureka!* But it means the same thing. After some amount of cogitation, the machine reaches a certain level of confidence and presents its opinion. But humans have the help of a variety of, so far, human-only tools.

Imagination

Imagination is more important than knowledge.

Albert Einstein

Where do ideas come from?

From looking at one thing and seeing another.

From fooling around, and playing with possibilities.

From speculating. And changing.

Pushing, pulling.

Transforming.

*And if you're lucky, you come up with something worth
saving, using, and building on.*

That's where the game stops, and the work begins.

Saul Bass, Why Man Creates

Humans have the marvelous ability to use their imagination.
Strange connections between seemingly unrelated things suddenly
shine a light on a solution to a problem. There's that moment when
the television detective is offered a cup of tea and says, "Tea? *Tea??*
Of course! That's It! Why didn't I see it before? Come on—we have no
time to lose!"

We're looking at one thing and seeing another. We can let our
subconscious minds ruminate—we can sleep on it—and then come
up with a question in a way machines can't quite imitate yet. Yes,
the machine can ponder what data can be omitted. It can consider
changing time scales and focus on the outliers. It can find patterns and
anomalies. But it cannot consider information it does not have.

Imagination is fueled by curiosity. That mental itch to know more,
to find out why, and to understand is a powerful tool. As Isaac Asimov
put it, "The most exciting phrase that heralds new discoveries, is not
Eureka! (I found it) but: *Hmmm*, that's funny." While harmful to cats,
curiosity is a human's best friend.

This is why I feel, at the moment, that it's easier to teach marketing people about artificial intelligence than teach AI about marketing.
The fanciest analytics in the world can't predict a future that is outside
the scope of past experience. Humans can create science fiction.

Empathy

Second to imagination comes the ability to put yourself in another's
shoes. AI systems can be taught to imitate or exhibit empathy when
responding to humans in real time. "I'm so sorry to hear you are having
trouble." It can read facial expressions and tone of voice to calibrate just
how upset that person might be.

However, the ability to reframe the question from another perspective and alter the approach to that question is still uniquely
human.

- What if you were a refugee?
- What if you only had six months to live?
- What would you do if you were the President?

It may be a subtle mental trick, but it's a pathway into new ways of looking at problems that humans can exploit at any time. It's just one way we can engage in lateral thinking, humans' main strength and home advantage.

Dr. Jon Warner enumerates what is involved in lateral thinking.[4]

Lateral thinking involves solving problems through an indirect and creative approach, using reasoning that is not immediately obvious and involving ideas that may not be obtainable by using only traditional step-by-step logic or simple analysis. It involves the following main activities:

- Reviewing issues and problems in terms of what might be missing or absent
- Looking at an issue or problem from a variety of different or unusual angles
- Reversing an issue or problem/challenge to look for a new solution
- Finding and evaluating more than one potential solution to an issue or challenge
- Rearranging a problem to see if new angles may be discovered
- Delaying judgment and maintaining an open mind
- Removing any stereotypical or clichéd patterns of thought or knowledge

Artificial intelligence cannot leverage a leap of imagination and ask:

- What if we tackled the problem from the other side?
- What additional data would be revealing?
- What real-world changes are important?
- What if this is the wrong problem?
- What if we look at it sideways?
- What if we did it backward?
- What if it had wheels?
- What would Chuck Norris do?

Trust Your Gut

You should literally listen to your body as part of your evaluative process, according to a study in *Scientific Reports—Nature*.[5] What happens in your stomach (and your entire nervous system) is a response to your environment. If your heart starts to race when you see that certain someone, that's some factual data. Your body is trying to tell you something.

> Interoception is the sensing of physiological signals originating inside the body, such as hunger, pain and heart rate. People with greater sensitivity to interoceptive signals, as measured by, for example, tests of heartbeat detection, perform better in laboratory studies of risky decision-making.

Stomach pains, bowel pressure, hunger, and anxiety are all strong signals to be heeded. This theory was tested on London hedge fund traders, who frequently mention their gut feelings when stock picking. Those who were better at monitoring their physiology were more successful—those better at silently measuring their own heart rate without touching their chests or their wrists. And while this is correlative rather than causative, it does suggest what you assumed all along: The stock market is definitely driven by emotion rather than logic.

The Smell Test

Another human trait that comes in handy is the good-old smell test. This time we're looking at the metaphor and not the physiology. This one is when something just doesn't seem right.

Gary Angel, co-founder of Digital Mortar, suggests, "Good analysis comes from someone figuring out what the right variables are." He points to the example of calculating what movies people are most likely to want to see next. The data was collected from set-top boxes and the machine determined that movies beginning with the letter *A* were far more likely to be preferred. A human knows instantly that this is the result of movies being listed alphabetically and is not a valuable variable for determining the likeability of any given movie. It is not proper fodder for a recommendation engine.

If you're crunching numbers in marketing, do you know if time-of-day is any more predictive of a purchase than geography? Search behavior? Click behavior? Shopping cart population? This is why people with business smarts will always have a job.

Angel describes another example:

> We did a segmentation analysis for an online travel aggregator, looking at purely search behavior data. We found a very interesting segmentation, but we had to put a lot of thought into what that search behavior meant.

If someone did a search, changed the data of the search, and then looked for the same destination, we could infer that they were flexible about dates. If they change the destination but didn't change the date, we infer they were flexible about destinations.

We created those as variables in the analysis and that became a very powerful predictor for them.

But that's not inherent in the behaviors, right? An analyst had to figure out that changing those two things was a valuable variable for the analysis.

When we started, the obvious variable was destination—was a traveler going to Las Vegas, for example. But as we thought through the analysis, many additional variables that were even more interesting emerged. It was about how far out they were searching, how many days between the search, when the search was conducted, and what the destination date was.

Added to this was whether they change the search, whether they change the destination, whether it was a weekend, and whether it was a weekend included in the stay. All those kinds of things turned out to be not surprisingly very important but those are things that, unless you feed them into the machine, you won't get a good analysis.

Once the human picks out the high-value variables, the machine will do a great job figuring out which ones are important.

The lesson is to use that part of your brain that is best at intuition, relevance, reasoning, and so on, and then let the machine do what it's best at: calculation, tabulation, and enumeration.

> *Computers are incredibly fast, accurate, and stupid. Human beings are incredibly slow, inaccurate, and brilliant. Together they are powerful beyond imagination.*
>
> *Albert Einstein*

Michael Wu wonders if the smell test is important anymore. I asked if it was unreasonable to count on the machine that says that when people who wear red socks and vote for Trump and drink Coca-Cola go to the store, they're more likely to buy potato chips. A marketing professional is going to look at that and say, "You know what, that just doesn't pass the smell test. That's just too odd."

Is it useful? Is it valuable? Does it make sense?

Wu offers an example of a bank looking to predict the likelihood of a client to default on a loan.

> They use all the traditional kinds of underwriting variables: credit score, income level, amount of the loan, payment history, and so on. But then they review a lot of non-traditional data from elsewhere.
>
> They found that people who fill out a loan application with only upper- or only lowercase letters—improper capitalization—are more likely to default. They said, "That doesn't pass the smell test." It's ridiculous, right? But lo and behold, it does contribute to the default rate, and they actually used this variable in *addition* to their traditional underwriting.
>
> They even found that taller people actually default slightly less than others. *That* doesn't pass the smell test either.
>
> It turned out that height is not a causal predictor of default, so it contributes nothing to the actual default rate when used in underwriting, but proper capitalization does. You could rationalize that people who use proper capitalization are probably more careful, they are more detail oriented, but who cares?
>
> It almost doesn't matter. Good data science means you validate your model and it's going to tell you what is predictive and the strength of its confidence level and then, you just have to trust the number, right? Try it. If it doesn't work, fine. You learned something. But you don't know until you test it out.

Because validation is the formal process for data science, the best thing a marketing professional can do for the machine is collect better knowledge for learning and then pay close attention to testing.

> Anybody could come up with a model from anywhere and say, "That's our model." But there is no way to tell how good the model is until you test it.

We find ourselves back in the hands of the scientific method.

> As long as it's not random, then it is predictable. And if you need to understand it, you can make another assumption to test. Are people who fill out the form with proper capitalization more detail oriented and therefore have high-paying jobs that require more attention to detail? Sounds plausible, but let's go find out.

But, says Wu, does it matter? Maybe your rationalization is wrong. Maybe they have the same income. Maybe there's another reason but you can still use this information to help make a decision. Leave the rationalization to head-scratching, chin-rubbing, brow-furrowing conjecture over cocktails and use your imagination, gut feel, and the smell test to figure out the best questions to ask.

Humans have the hindsight to ask, "What's the geographical distribution of people who buy from us online?" The result was MEC opening a new retail store in Montreal.

Humans have the insight to ask, "What sells at what times of day?" The result was 7-Eleven Japan stores selling twice as much as American stores in less than half the space.

Humans have the foresight to ask, "How are people configuring our products on our website?" The result was Ford Motor Company altering its production and distribution allocations, significantly lowering the cost of transportation. The appropriately optioned trucks were already waiting for customers.

NOTES

1. "Solving the Attribution Conundrum with Optimization-Based Marketing," http://www.liesdamnedlies.com/2017/01/solving-the-attribution-conundrum-with-optimization-based-marketing.html.

2. "The Enlightenment Is Dead, Long Live the Entanglement," http://jods.mitpress.mit.edu/pub/enlightenment-to-entanglement.

3. "Mark Cuban Says This Will Soon Be the Most Sought-After Job Skill," http://www.inc.com/betsy-mikel/mark-cuban-says-this-will-soon-be-the-most-sought-after-job-skill.html.

4. "How Is Critical Thinking Different from Analytical or Lateral Thinking?," http://blog.readytomanage.com/how-is-critical-thinking-different-from-analytical-or-lateral-thinking.

5. "Interoceptive Ability Predicts Survival on a London Trading Floor," http://www.nature.com/articles/srep32986.

CHAPTER 11

What Tomorrow May Bring

One of the things that really separate us from the high primates is that we're tool builders. I read a study that measured the efficiency of locomotion for various species on the planet.... Humans came in with a rather unimpressive showing, about a third of the way down the list, but somebody at Scientific American *had the insight to test the efficiency of locomotion for a man on a bicycle.... A human on a bicycle blew the condor away, completely off the top of the charts. And that's what a computer is to me... it's the most remarkable tool that we've ever come up with; it's the equivalent of a bicycle for our minds.*

Steve Jobs

You now understand the underlying technology of what AI looks like in real life. You now understand how machine learning works. You understand that it's nice that American Express is tapping spend histories and personal profile data to train a model to make restaurant recommendations. That's a lot of technology for a minor value to the customer. But it has great value to AmEx, which is using it as a learning opportunity. What's not clear is how all these pieces fit together.

I can promise you this: Anything with electricity will be connected to the Internet and anything that can be connected to the Internet will be connected to AI systems.

- Your watch
- Your flashlight
- Your clock
- Your toaster
- Your shoes
- Your shirt
- Your glasses
- Your rug

Why will your rug have a battery? I'm looking toward yet another college dorm room breakthrough that will capture kinetic energy, monitor health by measuring gait, or merely keep an eye on cleanliness so it can trigger the vacuum cleaner.

The future is here. It's just not widely distributed yet.

William Gibson

The distant future is easy: science fiction.

- HAL 9000
- Skynet
- Ultron
- Cylons
- C3PO
- Lt. Commander Data
- Jarvis
- Viki
- Eva
- Deep Thought

How far away is the future? Ask Alexa.

Alexa, the voice service that powers [Amazon's] Echo, provides capabilities, or skills, that enable customers to interact with devices in a more intuitive way using voice. Examples of these skills include the ability to play music, answer general questions, set an alarm or timer and more. Alexa is built in the cloud, so it is always getting smarter. The more customers use Alexa, the more she adapts to speech patterns, vocabulary, and personal preferences.[1]

You may already have an Echo in your home and chances are you use it to play music ("Alexa—Play my Pandora smooth jazz station"), get your news ("Alexa—What's my Flash Briefing?"), or predict the future ("Alexa—Ask Magic 8-Ball if I'm going to be rich."). This is fully AI-enabled, in the cloud, and in your home today.

THE PATH TO THE FUTURE

When State of Digital asked what the future of analytics looks like over the next 6–12 months, I postulated:[2]

> Over the next 6–12 months, those who are not using analytics will continue to not use analytics. Those who have free tools installed but are not really getting any traction will continue to spin their wheels. Those who are getting some interesting insights will find even more value. Those who have started the process of corporate change management will continue to find it frustrating that it takes so long to turn an aircraft carrier. Those who are making great strides by adopting analytics will find that their lead over the competition is growing. Those who are playing with cutting-edge tools and techniques will run into hurdle after hurdle but will find bright spots with astonishing success that will make the pursuit worthwhile. In the meantime, the world of start-ups will roll out hundreds of business models that offer data-as-a-service and analytics-as-a-service with varying success, but within 12 months, one of them will have coined a new term that will crush Big Data and supplant AI and Machine Learning. Perhaps a Human Algorithm Language (HAL) or Cognitive Construct for Cooperative Personalized Output (C3PO).

According to Gartner,[3] by 2020, the average person will have more conversations with bots than with his or her spouse, algorithms will positively alter the behavior of billions of global workers, and 30 percent of web-browsing sessions will be done without a screen. What's the shortest path there?

MACHINE, TRAIN THYSELF

With all this fabulous computer learning capability so close at hand, it's time to make the machines smarter about how machines are getting smarter. The most powerful, life-changing thing that will come along—and you can count on a great many people trying to solve this one—is when the machines get better at building models that they can use to build models.

Lots of companies are working to solve a variety of Machine-Learning-Is-Hard problems. Algolytics Sp. z o.o. created ABM (Automated Business Models). You give it customer behavior data and it builds predictive models based on user-provided parameters (what you want to know, what data you want to exclude, what you expect the answers to be).

Skytree automatically analyzes and chooses the best model for a given data set. BigML's WhizzML automates machine learning workflows by making repetitive, time-consuming tasks the work of a mouse click.

DataRobot has you upload data and choose your target variable (sales, retention, churn). Then DataRobot builds hundreds of models for you to explore and tweak. When you find the model that makes the most sense, deploy it in the wild, and feed the results back to DataRobot for further refinement.

DataRobot bases its models on open source algorithms. That means the company stays tuned with the latest advances. Hamel Husain, a DataRobot data scientist, suggests the approach is very competitive.[4] "We have gathered . . . advanced techniques used by people who win competitions. I easily can place top 10% in most Kaggle competitions by simply uploading the dataset to DataRobot and letting it aggressively explore possible models, without doing any work."

The smartest algorithms burble to the top and become the best at becoming better. This points to smarts as a service.

INTELLECTUAL CAPACITY AS A SERVICE

Once Amy@x.ai learns that you need an extra half an hour to get to and from your meeting across town because of traffic, and the battery in your smoke alarm learns how long in advance to reach out to Amazon for its own replacement, and your e-mail system gets better generating the most likely opening paragraph for you to edit, you might want to start training a generic agent that lives everywhere.

While Siri, Alexa, M, and Cortana compete for your attention, a startup like Viv will sneak in the backdoor as Viv Labs rolls out intelligence as a utility, embedded in every device that has a battery, an Internet connection, and a microphone.

> Viv is an artificial intelligence platform that enables developers to distribute their products through an intelligent, conversational interface. It's the simplest way for the world to interact with devices, services and things everywhere. Viv is taught by the world, knows more than it is taught, and learns every day.[5]

Conscience Support System

Why would you trust an AI to be your advisor, counselor, and buying agent? Humans always overestimate their ability to make judgments. For example, *everybody* knows that they are better-than-average drivers.

A human wants something and then explores rationalizations for that decision.

- "I want a donut but I shouldn't eat a donut. But I worked out for an hour this morning, therefore I can have a donut!"

- "I want a new car. My old car is out of style and is embarrassing. My old car is starting to cost more in repairs than it should. Therefore, I should get a bright-red Bugatti!"

An AI doesn't want anything. It only rationalizes on your behalf. A little like a conscience support system. It doesn't try to talk you out of that donut, but reminds you that you were angry the last time you tried on that good suit because it was too tight.

> "If you participate in moderate forms of exercise, you will likely need about 30 minutes to work off the doughnut. According to Harvard Health Publications, if you weigh 155 lbs., you burn about 205 calories participating in 30 minutes of low-impact aerobics."[6]

> "Oh, shut up."

> "Your anxiety level regarding the suit was 7 compared to your current irritation level of 4."

> "Stop it."

> "If you eat that donut, your frustration with your good suit will go up exponentially as it will be even tighter.

"No, really. Shut *up!*"

"Enjoy your new Bugatti, sir."

We'll need some serious user interface work.

What If We're All Just as Smart?

How do we differentiate our products, our services, and our company when the machine can tell us how to put the right message in front of the right person at the right time? "The right message" is where the magic of computers stumbles.

Yes, the machine can create thousands of messages to test (annoy) some large percent of some small sample of the audience, and then present you with the best possible message to send out to the rest. But it's only the best possible of the creative concepts it came up with. It will run into the wall of the local maximum.

It'll do a great job of retargeting. "We'll offer you these shoes you loved at 25% off and *free shipping* if you Buy Now." It'll do a great job of drip irrigation nurturing. "You read our Fundamentals of Success whitepaper last month so you're *sure* to enjoy our Tactics of Success report available now!"

But, the machine is not going to come up with a Don Draper–level "Carousel" innovation for a good long time to come. The machine is not going to envision a product that will be embraced by millions for a good long time to come. The machine is not going to invent a new slogan that speaks directly to the hearts and minds of the masses for a good long time to come. The power to raise awareness, instill trust, and create desire is still in human hands for the time being. Data is going to have a tough time beating killer creative.

Wonderful advertising is unique. (Insert the old joke about television as a medium being rare when it's well done.) It's sobering to realize that "the best television commercial of all time" was made in 1984 when Apple announced the Macintosh computer during Super Bowl XIV. It only ran once.

DATA AS A COMPETITIVE ADVANTAGE

The other way to distinguish one's offerings is through data. The Altimeter Group points out that Google and Facebook at the leading edge of AI "know data is core to their business, they treat it strategically, and they have massive amounts of it."

Just as the Industrial Revolution relied on access to coal, data is the fuel that enables machines to learn, act, and learn again. For this reason, AI will be the forcing function for data strategy in organizations, and data strategy—what do we collect, use, compare, store, and for how long—will be a critical success factor for AI. Says Intel's [Melvin] Greer, "Hyperrelevant data is becoming the new currency and the most coveted strategic asset.

"New economies based on data as a form of capital: Even if it's not recognized as such on balance sheets, data, the right data, and access to the right kinds of data science and engineering talent (internally or externally) will be key. The most important success criterion, however, is clear priorities about the types of problems machine learning is best positioned to solve for a given organization. Furthermore, businesses that are not able to gain access to critical datasets will be at a competitive disadvantage as machine learning becomes more prevalent."[7]

Data as a Business

Acxiom is in the data business. It sources data from all corners of the Earth, packages it up, and makes it available to marketers hunting for market segments. Think credit scores, magazine subscriptions, voting registrations, and *data from other companies*.

By helping you to understand how your customers interact with other brands, you can gain a broader and more nuanced understanding of their needs, preferences and behaviors. This both increases and contextualizes the value of your data, allowing you to rethink your targeting and audience creation processes, and to deliver timely, personalized offers.[8]

Acxiom will serve up very targeted groups of people:

- Likely to file taxes in February/March/April/after the deadline
- Big game big spenders (home décor, furnishings, snacks)
- Shop for Valentine's Day gifts at florist/jewelry store/discount store
- Participate in Halloween activities
- Dress in Halloween costume

- Halloween costume high spender
- Dresses pet in Halloween costume
- Purchase toys from department store/electronic video store/toy store

Equifax knows your credit rating and how it got there. Epsilon tracks "thousands of unique data points spanning demographics, spend behavior, lifestyle information and more on virtually every U.S. household."[9] Dun & Bradstreet does much the same, but at the business level. Experian can link phone numbers, e-mail addresses, and social IDs to a single identity for cross-channel targeting.

Also in the data-as-a-business industry are companies like Bloom-Reach. This firm offers backend personalization as a service across a multitude of ecommerce websites—so many in fact that it can analyze visitor behavior in the same way ad networks do. This makes Bloom-Reach a hybrid service: part technology, part data. The company bases its results on processing 100 million pages (about 10 terabytes) representing 150 million customer interactions per day. That data comes from pixels, feeds, web crawling, and a database of 10 billion synonym pairs and more than 1,000 different colors.

Clients insert a single pixel on each web page allowing Bloom-Reach to watch the behavior of individual customers. This way, the company can track a person's start page, path, category of interest, site searches, and so on. When aggregated for all site visitors, this info reveals marketplace-level product interest.

Client product feeds (updated throughout the day to note price changes and inventory levels) are combined with pixel data, marketing copy, and customer reviews BloomReach has collected by crawling clients' sites. Then, the company reaches out to the Web in general, including competitor websites, Wikipedia, and industry-specific blogs.

To improve its lexicon, BloomReach also reaches out to the public at large.

> For an idea of just how much there is to learn about consumer language and behavior, consider an exercise BloomReach conducted, asking participants to describe a rather fetching, red dress. The first 500 users who took the quiz came up with 129 ways to describe the dress' color, 194 ways to describe its neckline and 275 ways to describe its belt, which some might say defies description. And that was just for starters.[10]

This capability is simply out of reach for the typical retailer who does not have enough transactions per day to build a robust-enough engine that can learn fast enough to keep up with changing trends—especially in fashion.

This is where the power of aggregated data comes in. It gives AI the ability to continuously learn about the environment (sporting goods, fashion, hardware) from a multitude of sources without ever being "finished."

Continuous learning about products and industries can be combined with continuous learning about individuals as well.

> [BloomReach] uses robust pattern detection technologies to connect anonymous users across multiple devices using a number of behavioral and technical signals. For instance, if devices on one wi-fi network viewed the same category page and three product pages over a two-day period, there's a high probability that it is the same person.

> This cross-device connection can be useful for subtly personalizing the experience of a shopper and for proving the "mobile influence" for shoppers who browse on the smartphone, yet convert on the desktop.

While BloomReach can know individuals well, it doesn't know who they *are* as individuals. The company does not collect personally identifiable information nor track consumers between websites.

This translates to a more relevant experience for the shopper. BloomReach gently surfaces products you are more likely to buy based on your behavior and the vocabulary you use to search their clients' sites. "Consider a consumer who has a propensity for converting on medium-size shirts. A shirt that ranks high on color and other product attributes would be knocked down in rank if it were not available in medium. Another relevant shirt would move up the list."

Couple the above with the ability for AI to review in-store video and estimate your mood from posture, gestures, and facial expressions and we do, indeed, live in interesting times.

Data as a Sideline

The above examples are very intentional data-plays. Becoming ever-more interesting is the data coming from companies that were busy doing something else.

"We're not a(n) _____. We're a data company that happens to _____."

- airline/fly airplanes
- shoe company/make shoes

- delivery service/own trucks
- drone company/make 3-D models and maps
- mouthguard company/make mouthguards

Partnering with IBM, Under Armour has moved from being an underwear company to a data company that happens to make exercise clothing.

> For example, a 32-year-old woman training for a 5k run could use the app to create a personalized exercise and meal plan most effective for people of similar height, weight, body type and lifestyle. The app could then map potential running routes near her office, taking into account the dates, time of day, duration, location and frequency she wants to train. Every day, the app would follow her exercise using GPS tracking and heart monitoring, and consider other factors such as outdoor temperature and weather. The app could take known weather predictions—a super-hot, humid day or an approaching ice storm—then map that to her fitness plans and goals, and make helpful recommendations on how to keep her on track despite the unfavorable weather. Noticing her carb intake is too low at dinner, the app can prompt her to eat more healthy carbs at night to help improve running performance. It's an example of data coming to the IoT from many unrelated sources, combined and analyzed through the power of cognitive computing to offer valuable insights.[11]

Serving both partners and customers, Intuit had a blinding flash of intuition while looking at the confluence of QuickBooks for small business and small business lenders. Banks are reluctant to make small business loans because it's so hard to tell how solvent the business really is. Intuit actually does know how well each of its customers it doing, by design. When they realized that 60 percent of their small business customers were in the market for financing, but on average, 70 percent of small businesses are rejected for business financing, they smelled opportunity.

QuickBooks Financing was built into the QuickBooks software for companies to apply directly from their bookkeeping interface. QB Financing gives them preapproval quotes from multiple lenders who receive exactly the financial data they need to make a decision, pushing the approval process from weeks to days.

If everything can have a battery and be connected to AI through the Internet, then what business should *you* be in? Chances are excellent that your databases are troves of untapped shareholder value if you can figure out how to legally—and ethically—provide that data to others, at a price.

You know something interesting about your customers that others do not. Your data might prove very valuable to others if you can see things from their side.

- Companies that sell hammers might find data from those who make nails to be quite valuable when correlated with housing starts.

- Glassware manufacturers could benefit from data collected by wineries.

- Delivery services might be intrigued by data from cardboard box manufacturers.

- Gaming casinos could learn a lot from online game publishers.

If you have data you're willing to sell, Narrative.io acts as a broker, putting buyers and sellers together, setting standard prices, and managing the ETL integration process.

Insight Automation

In September 2016, Google announced that it was adding automated insights in the Google Analytics mobile app.[12]

> Available on the Assistant screen, this addition to Google Analytics lets you see in 5 minutes what might have taken hours to discover previously. Even better: It gets smarter over time as it learns about your business and your needs.
>
> To enable this functionality, we use Google machine intelligence to find critical insights among the thousands of metric and dimension combinations that can be reported in Google Analytics. It helps make analytics data universally accessible and useful as it:
>
>> Combs through your data to give you meaningful insights and recommendations.
>>
>> Offers quick tips on how to improve your Google Analytics data.

Gets smarter over time by reacting to your feedback and how you use it.

Helps you share insights so your whole team can take action.

HOW FAR WILL MACHINES GO?

How do we get from the TRS-80 to C3PO? It happens one step at a time.

Like a Boss

Manna,[13] by Marshall Brain, is a very short, charming piece of science fiction about AI taking over the world. It begins with the fast-food joint where a Manna-ger is installed that literally tells employees what to do, minute by minute.

> Manna was connected to the cash registers, so it knew how many people were flowing through the restaurant. The software could therefore predict with uncanny accuracy when the trash cans would fill up, the toilets would get dirty and the tables needed wiping down. The software was also attached to the time clock, so it knew who was working in the restaurant. Manna also had "help buttons" throughout the restaurant. Small signs on the buttons told customers to push them if they needed help or saw a problem . . . .

> Manna told employees what to do simply by talking to them. Employees each put on a headset when they punched in. Manna had a voice synthesizer, and with its synthesized voice Manna told everyone exactly what to do through their headsets. Constantly. Manna micromanaged minimum wage employees to create perfect performance.

The story gets sordid from there. More and more responsibility is entrusted to the machine, and the only jobs left are as arms and legs for the machine. The book is written in a very matter-of-fact, explanatory way, forgoing story, plot, and character development for sheer clarity of how it all went so bad in such a reasonable way. Things do not end up well—until the second half of the book.

In the second half, humans have implemented AI appropriately and life is beautiful. Dystopia/utopia is well described.

Pretending to Be a Human

IBM is working on True North, a chip that is designed with core neurons and local memory, communicating via synapses. It's intended to imitate the way we think the brain works. It's making great strides at pattern recognition, but please note: It imitates the way we *think* the brain works.

We may take on the challenge of going deeper into the nervous system by imitating *all* the ways humans think, including:

- Musical-rhythmic and harmonic
- Visual-spatial
- Verbal-linguistic
- Logical-mathematical
- Bodily-kinesthetic
- Interpersonal
- Intrapersonal
- Naturalistic
- Existential[14]

In the meantime, can we teach a machine to create, to care, to feel? The conversation must immediately turn philosophical (but only for a moment). What is the difference between caring and pretending to care?

Is as does. If I do nice things, am nice to people, and treat people with respect all my life, even if I am a seething, sociopathic, malcontent inside, am I a nice guy?

Is as does. If I think my boss is an idiot and wished him the worst misfortune, yet am deferential, work hard, am a team player, and make him look good, am I a good employee?

Is as does. If my grandmother drives me nuts with her backward view of the world and her inability to pick up even the simplest technology, but I am respectful, dutiful, and frequently spend time with her, am I a good grandson?

Is as does. The *Oxford Dictionary* defines *art* as:

> The expression or application of human creative skill and imagination, typically in a visual form such as painting or sculpture, producing works to be appreciated primarily for their beauty or emotional power.

If we teach a computer to recognize human emotion through vocal timbre, gesture, facial expression, and so on, and have it paint a million paintings, write a million poems, and compose a million pieces of music, it could figure out what humans consider beautiful or emotion-ally powerful. Does that make it "creative"?

Is as does.

Thus endeth the philosophy lesson.

Beyond Human

What if you started with a handful of agents, let only the best reproduce, and throw in some random mutation along the way? Meet the lifos.[15]

> They're dynamic, independent entities that interact with you on the web, devices, and social media.
>
> They introduce you to people and other lifos you'd be interested in meeting and point you to sites and apps you might like.
>
> They play games, participate in competitions, and create images, video and music that they share with people.
>
> Successful lifos reproduce variations of themselves and evolve as a species.
>
> Are lifos personal assistants?
>
> Oh, you need a personal assistant? :) Actually, lifos are more like acquaintances or friends. They'll help you out and provide services to you. But they're actually free agents that interact with all kinds of people.
>
> What can lifos do for me?
>
> They curate online content and offer you weekly or daily digests. They tell you about their other friends, and friends of friends, without revealing private information of course. They play multiplayer games. They shop. They hang out.
>
> What can I do for them?
>
> Thanks for asking! You can pick them out of a bazillion others and train them, just by interacting with them. You can help them choose variations of themselves when they reproduce. You can introduce them to people.

These interlocking microservices can check the weather, the surf-ing conditions, the availability of your friends, call for an Uber to the beach, and order a pizza.

As TechHub co-founder Mike Butcher wrote for *TechCrunch*,[16] "If a given bot can monetize its services enough to cover its server costs, it survives."

> If it makes excess revenue, it's cloned by the Bazillion Beings community, with possible improvements. Over time, the most successful bots adapt to the preferences of individuals through machine learning, and—in theory—the population of bots evolves to add more value to users and API providers.

YOUR BOT IS YOUR BRAND

Whether your bot is interacting with me verbally, textually, or visually, it definitely represents your company. Every interaction at every touchpoint leaves an impression.

- Bad sales rep? Bad company.
- Bad showroom? Bad company.
- Bad e-mail? Bad company.
- Bad website? Bad company.
- Bad mobile bot interaction? Bad company.

Over time, I will teach *my* digital agents to recognize a bad company by the digital interaction my agent has with the companies trying to negotiate with it.

- Incorrect syntax? Don't trust 'em.
- Limited time offer? Don't trust 'em.
- No social media validation? Don't trust 'em.
- No discernable physical address? Don't trust 'em.
- No way to reach a human? Don't trust 'em.

That means your corporate culture—your corporate values—need to be embedded in the systems you create to talk to my agents.

If you promote yourself as the low-cost leader but my agent finds the goods cheaper elsewhere, it will let the ecosystem of my friends' and family's agents know that you can't be trusted. If you promise superior service and then surprise me with a $12 charge for that blanket on the flight to Hawaii, my agent will share the bad news. Instead of being a short, embarrassing blip in social media, it will be shared knowledge that is stored by the ecosystem of "travel *agents*."

American Marketing Association CEO Russ Klein sees the future marketplace as a frictionless space. Getting in the car and going to the store takes some planning. That's friction. It's the same with picking up the phone and placing an order. It's the same with hitting an Amazon Dash button so more toilet paper shows up the next day. It's so much work! What if all that friction were gone?

"Artificial intelligence is going to change the customer journey dramatically," says Klein.

> The classic hierarchy model of awareness, interest, desire, which we've all been using for 60 years or more, is blown up now. A lot of people have been diagraming it saying it now looks like a pretzel or it looks like an amoeba. It may have looked like that for a little while and it may look like that for a little while longer, but I think when you take artificial intelligence and bots and drones and sensors and the Internet of Things and the cloud, the customer journey is essentially going away. I just have to add implants to the story.

> When you add physical implants, the customer journey is going to become what Descartes said, "I think therefore I am." It will be, "I think therefore I purchased a new car." That's it. That's the customer journey, reduced down to a customer's will and the ability to cognitively make a decision. It will be a one-blink customer journey.

When I need a dishwasher, my agent will ask me the questions it needs. It will already know my budget and will ask about my trade-off tolerances between speed, water conservation, and noise. It will ask to see the intended location to determine the dimensions the dishwasher will occupy. It will then offer me the three best, asking if I want the one that's the most expensive that will last the longest, or if I am in the process of selling my home, perhaps we should go for a less expensive model.

> Your agent just may do all that for you; anticipate all that for you. We just have to be sensible about not letting them be on autopilot *too* much. That's where the user experience experts will need to fine-tune the user interface.

My wife is all for self-driving cars; it cannot happen fast enough. They will save lives, save money, save real estate, and so on. But she likes to drive and balks at giving that up. Fortunately, the engineers at Toyota have worked out that the best approach is not autopilot but co-pilot. If you want to drive, go right ahead. But if you get a phone call or get sleepy, you can say, "Yeah, just take me the rest of the way."

WARC and Deloitte Digital are looking in that direction as well.

> "Programmatic consumption" is the automation of brand choices. Rather than a consumer spend the time and effort selecting a product and placing an order, these functions are partially or fully automated—in other words, purchase decisions will increasingly be made by computers, rather than by consumers standing in shops. This raises a number of questions: How should marketers get their brands on a list of "considered items" that a virtual assistant might choose between; and what is the role of advertising (including creativity and emotion) in a purchase process controlled by an algorithm?[17]

Your job tomorrow will be to add a new target audience to your responsibilities: the cumulative, aggregated, and/or cooperative AIs of potential customers. Your advertising and marketing materials will need to be vastly more informational and clearly communicate corporate values. Only then can my agent determine if it should recommend your toaster, your automobile, or your accounting services for my consideration.

While you are improving the improvement of your improvement process, keep an eye out for another sea change: when your customer's AI agents come calling.

MY AI WILL CALL YOUR AI

The grist mill utilized the river as a source of power. When factories came on the scene, steam engines powered the belts and pulleys that led to each individual machine. Electric motors made it easy to transfer the power over wires instead of mechanics, and each device got its own motor.

Room-sized computers have shrunk from mainframes to minis to workstations to PCs to phones: a supercomputer in your pocket. The technology that drives artificial intelligence is becoming personal as well. How you train your personal agents will reflect on you in the workplace.

Your Personal AI Ecosystem

The people you manage are your human ecosystem. Your professional capabilities are the result of their doing a good job. If you have a subpar team, you will not excel. It reflects poorly on you.

Dennis Mortensen, CEO of the meeting scheduling company X.AI, describes the job interview of the not-too-distant future where your potential job performance is evaluated based on the AI agents you have trained.[18]

> Over the next half decade, as more AI intelligent agents come to market, employees will increasingly deploy a suite of agents to get their job done. Those employees who DO take advantage of these agents will become more productive and along with that more attractive (both internally and externally).
>
> Much like Bring Your Own Device (BYOD), this new paradigm—call it Bring Your Own Agent (BYOA)—promises a host of benefits for both employees and employers and will likely change the nature of work.

Mortensen paints a picture of Rebecca, a fictitious director of events. She uses a scheduling agent, a contract agent, and an expenses agent. She teaches them her working style, her main contacts, her budget limitations, and how to share data with other agents. Rebecca will measure their performance, tweak when necessary, and kill off the ones that are not living up to expectations. Her expertise is optimized.

When Rebecca walks into a job interview, "her new employer should be eager to hire Rebecca for both her skills in identifying relevant speakers and her ability to masterfully deploy and manage a set of AI agents.

> And this brings forth the really interesting question, *Who* exactly is it you are hiring? Are you hiring Rebecca, or Rebecca augmented by nine agents? And do you care?
>
> As we head into the era of BYOA, BYOD points the way to a few likely outcomes:
>
> 1. Employers may have to evaluate a new employee as a combination of their human skills and the agents that augment them.

2. If people find agents useful (and I'm obviously bullish on this point), they'll want to take them with them from job to job.

3. Employers will not be able to prevent this, and instead will have to adopt policies and practices to mitigate risks around privacy.

And last but not least, people will be freed of some of the most tedious tasks to focus on what they've actually been hired to do.

Your Personal Shopper

If you want to buy a television and Amazon already knows everything about you from your browsing habits, buying habits, and all the data it's purchased from third parties, you would expect a wonderful recommendation. Amazon, wanting to keep you happy, would not recommend the overstocked model of television that it is desperate to get rid of. The company would not recommend the one that happens to be the closest to your home (unless you said fast delivery was the main criterion for this purchase). The company would not recommend the one on which it enjoys the highest margin. Instead, Amazon would suggest just the right piece of equipment that meets your viewing habits, your wall, and your wallet. That's good for the company because it will bind you ever tighter to it as a customer.

But what if you don't have a relationship like that with Walmart? You don't shop at Walmart very much. You have no feeling that Walmart has your best interests at heart because of your lack of experience. You have no suspicions about the company, either. You simply have no relationship. So how do you trust that Walmart has enough information about you to make a solid recommendation?

Consider how hard it has become for Walmart to worm its way into your good graces.

- Awareness? Yes, you know who Walmart is.
- Brand? Prices so low it destroys small business.
- Affinity? None.
- General opinion? It intends to sell the lowest-price items, sacrificing quality and customer care to do it.
- Do you trust Walmart with your data? Are you willing to opt in and let the company know all there is to know about you?

Hmmm....

It's time to turn the tables. Vendor relationship management (VRM) is the inverse of CRM. VRM tools aim to give customers independence from vendors while giving them better ways of engaging with vendors. ProjectVRM is a development and research project of the Berkman Klein Center for Internet & Society at Harvard University that is exploring the idea that vendors should not own data about customers, but rather that customers should own their own data.

What happens when you move? How do you notify 3,000 websites about your new address and phone number? Wouldn't it be better if you could publish your information once and allow access to whomever you choose? If they don't need your address, they don't get it. If they *do* need to know the dimensions of your kitchen so they can send you a quote for new cabinets, you can grant them access.

Doc Searls, along with his *Cluetrain Manifesto* co-authors, wrote in 1999 that markets are conversations. The market square is where the life of the village is shared. We operationalized that into shopping malls in the past 50 years and have tried to industrialize that conversation. With the advent of the Internet, those malls are finding they need a new identity, and sellers are scrambling to change their ways. "We are not seats or eyeballs or end users or consumers. We are human beings and our reach exceeds your grasp," Searls wrote. "Deal with it."

In the case of the kitchen cabinets, prospective buyers would engage in "intentcasting." Rather than sellers pushing their messages into the faces of people simply trying to read the news, they would listen closely for calls-for-quotes from those in the market.

If you want to buy an electric car, you make your desire known. Electric car ads follow you everywhere until you change your mind or make a purchase. In either case, you are no longer in the market and the promotions stop. You are no longer interested and no longer worth the effort to interrupt.

When ProjectVRM started more than 10 years ago, it was more philosophical than practical. But the advent of artificial intelligence, *working on behalf of the customer*, shifts this approach from wishful thinking to inevitable outcome. My disappointment over the lack of a flying car will be assuaged by my own AI agent to look after my interests and negotiate on my behalf. I will call mine Jeeves.

Pedro Domingos[19] imagines our digital selves wandering the Internet on our behalf. If I tell LinkedIn that I want a job, a million help-wanted company agents will negotiate with a million iterations of my digital self. My digital self can go on a million dates with would-be love interests to narrow the field, recommending the handful I should meet in person.

I have confidence that my personal digital model of me will make much better movie recommendations than Netflix.

COMPUTING TOMORROW

Change is happening so fast that you can never be fully prepared for what's next. But you can be prepared for change itself.

Asta Roseway, Principal Research Designer at Microsoft

If all of the above seems out of reach, *so much* data and *so much* processing power is needed, rest assured that we're generating and capturing data at a quickening pace and Moore's Law still has legs.

IBM is working on the TrueNorth system that is based on neurons with local memory and synapses to communicate between them. It has "a parallel, distributed, modular, scalable, fault-tolerant, flexible architecture that integrates computation, communication, and memory and has no clock."[20] This turns out to be great at image and speech recognition much more efficiently. That means AI-on-a-chip and in your phone will work with the AI in the cloud, in your car, in your pacemaker, in your deep brain stimulation device treating symptoms of Parkinson's disease, and in everything with a battery. That's powerful stuff.

At the other end of the exploratory lab, several companies are looking to commercialize quantum computing using atomic charges as qubits for processing and storage. That is more computing power than Gordon Moore could imagine in 1965.

What happens when all that computing power combines with all that data? That's when marketing will get *really* weird.

No computer has ever been designed that is ever aware of what it's doing; but most of the time, we aren't either.

Marvin Minsky

NOTES

1. https://developer.amazon.com/alexa.
2. http://www.stateofdigital.com/future-analytics.
3. "Gartner Predicts a Virtual World of Exponential Change," http://www.gartner.com/smarterwithgartner/gartner-predicts-a-virtual-world-of-exponential-change.
4. https://www.quora.com/Data-Science-Which-is-better-Dato-or-DataRobot.

5. http://viv.ai.

6. http://www.livestrong.com/article/465782-how-much-exercise-to-burn-a-doughnut.

7. "The Age of AI," http://www.altimetergroup.com/pdf/reports/The-Age-of-Artificial-Intelligence-Altimeter.pdf.

8. https://marketing.acxiom.com/US-Parent-2ndPartyGuide-Main.html.

9. https://www.epsilon.com/en_US/what-we-do/data/totalsource-plus.html.

10. "Inside the Technology: Web Relevance Engine," http://go.bloomreach.com/rs/bloomreach/images/WebRelevanceEngine-eBook.pdf.

11. https://www.linkedin.com/pulse/ibm-under-armour-coach-me-jason-fiala.

12. https://analytics.googleblog.com/2016/09/explore-important-insights-from-your.html.

13. http://marshallbrain.com/manna1.htm.

14. https://en.wikipedia.org/wiki/Theory_of_multiple_intelligences.

15. http://bazillionbeings.com.

16. https://techcrunch.com/2016/09/16/bazillion-beings-are-ai-driven-bots-that-have-to-earn-their-keep-or-die.

17. *Toolkit 2017*, Artificial Intelligence, http://content.warc.com/warc-toolkit-2017-of-marketing-trends-the-marketing-applications-of-artificial-intelligence.

18. "Bring Your Own Intelligent Agent (BYOA) Is Coming," https://www.linkedin.com/pulse/bring-your-own-intelligent-agent-byoa-coming-what-when-mortensen.

19. *Master Algorithm* (Basic Books, 2015).

20. http://www.research.ibm.com/articles/brain-chip.shtml.

About the Author

Jim Sterne has been in data processing since 1979, an online marketing consultant since 1993, and an online marketing analytics consultant since 2000.

Sterne focuses on proving the value of digital communication as a medium for creating and strengthening customer relationships. He is the founding president of the Digital Analytics Association and producer of the eMetrics Summits.

Sterne was named one of the 50 most influential people in digital marketing by *Revolution*, the United Kingdom's premier interactive marketing magazine and one of the top 25 Hot Speakers by the National Speakers Association, to which he credits his degree in Shakespeare.

He has consulted to some of the world's largest companies; lectured at MIT, Stanford, USC, Harvard, and Oxford; and sat on a plane to Las Vegas grading the CRM strategy plans of a Nigerian mobile phone company for a course he taught in Singapore produced by a training company in Shanghai.

Sterne is the author of:

World Wide Web Marketing: Integrating the Web into Your Marketing Strategy, Wiley, 1995

What Makes People Click: Advertising on the Web, Que, 1997

World Wide Web Marketing: Integrating the Web into Your Marketing Strategy, 2nd ed., Wiley, 1999

Customer Service on the Internet: Building Relationships, Increasing Loyalty, and Staying Competitive, Wiley, 2000

Email Marketing: Using Email to Reach Your Target Audience and Build Customer Relationships, Wiley, 2000

World Wide Web Marketing: Integrating the Web into Your Marketing Strategy, 3rd ed., Wiley, 2001

Customer Service on the Internet: Building Relationships, Increasing Loyalty, and Staying Competitive, 2nd ed., Wiley, 2002

Web Metrics: Proven Methods for Measuring Web Site Success, Wiley, 2002

Advanced Email Marketing: Using Email to Achieve Sales and Marketing Goals, Lyris Technologies, 2003

101 Things You Should Know About Marketing Optimization Analysis, Rising Media, 2010

Social Media Metrics: How to Measure and Optimize Your Marketing Investment, Wiley, 2010

The Devil's Data Dictionary: Making Fun of Data, Rising Media, 2015

His books have been translated into Arabic, Chinese, Dutch, Finnish, French, Italian, Korean, Orthodox Chinese, Portuguese, and Spanish.

Index